SADNESS CORRECTED

NEW POEMS AND DIALOGUES

MARVIN COHEN

© 2019 by Marvin Cohen

All Rights Reserved.

Set in Adobe Garamond with LaTeX.

ISBN: 978-1-944697-78-5 (paperback)
Library of Congress Control Number: 2019934764

Sagging Meniscus Press
saggingmeniscus.com

Contents

EXPECTING TOO MUCH	1
THE LANDLORD'S DOMINANCE	1
LIFE INTO ART	2
THE TRUE FABRIC OF LIFE ITSELF	2
NOT THE REAL THING. (MEMORY'S LIMITATIONS)	3
OLD AGE SEXUAL DISGRACE	4
A LAW CASE IN THE GUISE OF A PLAY, WITH ECHOES OF A ZOO	4
ANTI-SNOBBERY EVALUATIONS	5
AN ANTI-SUICIDE SERMON	6
SADNESS CORRECTED BY REALISM	6
A CULTURAL MAINSTAY	6
OUR SPECIALLY BRAINY RACE	7
ODE TO WORDS	8
THE DIRT-FREE LAWNMOWER	8
VULTURES OR DOVES	9
LOVE'S ROUND	10
THE INSIDE WORKINGS OF THE ART WORLD	10
NOT SISTER AND BROTHER	11
IDEALLY, HOW A COUPLE SHOULD BEHAVE	11
THE DIVIDING LINE	12
A BUSY DAY AT THE OFFICE	12
GENITALIA AND ITS DISCONTENTS	13
"HOW ARE YOU?" 'S AUTOMATIC REPLY	14
HOW TO CULTIVATE FRIENDSHIP	15
WHAT EVOLUTION HAS DONE FOR ME	16
THE ADULT STREET WAIF	17
A PLACE OF LAST RESORT	18
REPAIRING	19
AVOID LONELINESS	19
STATUS RAISING	20

MILD CONFESSIONS OF A SEX WRITER WRITING TO WEARY ADULTS	20
ODE TO GENITALIA'S MECHANICALLY REPETITIVE CYCLES	21
A BRIEF EXPLANATION OF EVOLUTION	22
A CLOSE RECOVERY? IT BETTER BE QUICK.	23
PUTTING INSOMNIA TO SLEEP	24
MEMORY'S DISCONTINUITY WITH "NOW": TWO DISTINCT SEPARATENESSES	24
AN IMPOSSIBLY IDEAL FAMILY	25
BORNOGRAPHY	26
THE LAWNMOWER ANALOGY	26
ANALYZING COMPETING VALUES	27
KING ME	28
AN OBSESSION TO IMPROVE MY SOCIAL LIFE BY BECOMING EXTREMELY POPULAR	29
AN OLD MAN'S DEATH-ATTITUDE, OR, LIVING FOREVER IS NOT POSSIBLE	30
WARNING TO ATHLETES AND OTHERS	31
TIED ON TO THE TIDE	31
A VERY COMMON THEME	32
ANOTHER MAN	32
A WELL-EARNED EXCUSE	33
PROVING YOUR INNOCENCE ON YOUR OWN TERMS	34
DIVERSE WAYS TO COMBAT BOREDOM WITH AN ASSORTMENT OF ATTEMPTS	34
A DOOMED REBELLION DUE TO UNFAIR ODDS	36
ADVICE FOR THE RECENTLY BORN, ONLY SO LATELY FROM THEIR MOTHER TORN	37
A FAMILY GROWS FROM TWO PEOPLE	37
HOW TO BREAK YOUR STUPID SKULL	38
ABSTRACTIONS IN FRUITLESS SEARCH OF CONCRETE EXAMPLES	38
TURNING IT AROUND (NOT ALWAYS EASY)	39
WHAT'S LIFE? A HOPE THAT OTHER PEOPLE WILL LIKE YOU	40
FORGING AN IDENTITY OF SORTS	40
AN ACADEMIC TEACHES SPRING	41
SPRING'S APOLITICAL INNOCENCE	41
ANY RATINGS DOWNFALL IN YOUR SOCIAL LIFE?	42
PORTRAIT OF A WISEGUY	43

GET OUT THERE, YOU FOOL!	44
AN OVERVIEW	44
ARRIVING IN PARIS	45
YOUR TRUE SELF	46
MY GENERATION'S TURN	46
MY LIFE, MY WIFE	47
A CONSTANT TRIBUTE	47
BEING A CONVERSATIONAL ITEM	48
WHAT DEATH DOESN'T MANAGE TO EXPRESS BY ITSELF	48
CURING TWO DIVIDINGS IN ONE VOW	49
AN UPSHOT NOT AVAILABLE	50
OPENLY EXPOSING GENITALIA	50
THE CON MAN COMPETITION, WON BY A LANDSLIDE (TRUMP VERSUS JESUS)	51
THE GREATER THE LOVE, THE MORE DEATHLY THE REJECTION	52
A COST WORTH TAKING?	52
THE EVOLUTION EXPRESS	53
ASSUMING THE WORST	54
DON'T CONFUSE ME	54
AN EMBARRASSMENT	55
TO LIVE FOREVER IS TO BE TIME'S THIEF. TRUE?	56
COMPENSATING A MISTRESS	56
THE MERCURIAL NATURE OF THE "NOW"	58
A PAINLESS INQUIRY INTO THE HORRIBLE THEME OF PAIN	59
WHAT REJECTION DID TO ME	59
GENERALITIES ABOUT—WHAT ELSE?—LIFE ITSELF (MIXED IN WITH ADVICE)	60
AN ABRUPT TERMINATION OF FRIENDSHIP	60
PROBING WHAT KIND OF LIFE A STONE LEADS IN HIS AUTHENTIC REPUTATION	61
ENOUGH OF THE INNER LIFE	62
A NON-REVELATION	62
PROBLEMS SEMI-SOLVED	63
CALLING THINGS BY NAMES	64
WHAT ENVY DID	65
SPECULATIONS IN THE REALM OF THE UNMISTAKABLY DEFINITE	66
THE MOTHER	66

FATHER VERSUS DAUGHTER, ARGUING OVER HER RECENT TATTOOS	68
A REVELATION BETTER NOT SPREAD	69
THE PRIDEFUL WARNER; THE HONEST DIE-ER	70
A GIFT CONVERSATION	70
OBSESSED WITH DEATH? JOIN THE CROWD	71
QUIBBLING OVER WORDS	72
LIVING IN THE COZY SUBURBS	72
IT WAS FUN	73
AN ANTHROPOMORPHIZING CONVERSATION	73
TIME SOLVES THE PROBLEM OF WHEN DEATHS ARRIVE	74
THE FUTURE FEARFULLY FRETTED ON	74
WHAT LIFE COMES DOWN TO OR EVEN DOESN'T	75
METAPHORS AS A DISTRACTION FROM TACKLING WHAT'S TOO DREADED TO ADDRESS IT TOO DIRECTLY	76
NATIONALISM (Dialogue between two Americans)	76
DIALOGUE, BASED ON A FAMOUS QUOTE	77
BESET UPON BY MY CURSED MALEFACTOR	78
WHAT TO PUT BEHIND YOURSELF TO KEEP AHEAD	79
HUMILITY BELATEDLY REALIZED	79
A MAN'S DEMAND, WHICH "REALITY" DENIES	80
A DIFFICULT GENDER PREDICAMENT	80
DIALOGUE BETWEEN TWO FRIENDS AND THE UNPAID DEBT BETWEEN THEM	81
DIALOGUE, BUT ONE SOON LEAVES AND THE REMAINING ONE MAKES DO, ETC.	82
TAMPERING WITH HUMOR	82
AN INTERCHANGEABILITY DIALOGUE	83
GIVING THE WRITER A BREAK IN A FEW MERCIFUL CASES	84
ARE YOU WITHIN MY IDENTITY, OR A STRANGER?	84
A GROUP OF OLD MEN DISCUSSING CELEBRITIES' RECENT SPATE OF SUICIDES	85
SUBJECT: LIFE ITSELF	86
TO MY LIFELONG FRIEND	86
DON'T FEAR, LITTLE BOY	87
THE TRIO	87

OUR FRIENDSHIP ON THE ROAD	*88*
DISREGARD THIS RUBBISH	*88*
HOW LIFE BEGINS	*89*
THE SELF-CONTRADICTORY HISTORY OF A CATHEDRAL	*89*
DUTIES AS DO-DEEDS	*89*
LISTEN TO ME. HERE'S WHAT YOU MAKE OF IT	*90*
INDUCING JEALOUSY: THE WINNING FORMULA	*91*
NO PLEA, NOW YOU'RE FREE	*92*
THE IDEA I LOST	*92*
THE LANGUAGES OF WORLD LITERATURE	*93*
THE HARD LIFE OF A STONE	*93*
THAT WICKED POISON, ENVY, OR, DOES THE CAMEL BLAME DARWIN FOR ITS HUNCHBACK?	*94*
YOU CAN'T REJOIN THEM	*94*
DEFINITION: TO THE LIFE	*95*
TO A FORMER LOVE	*95*
CONFUSING HOW TO FORGET. (INSOMNIA PLAYING A REDUNDANT ROLE TO DEMENTIA'S PRIMARY DOMINANCE)	*96*
A BIT MORE	*96*
MASOCHISM RELISHING IN ITS HOPE, BEING LAUGHINGLY DENIED BY THE CRUEL LOVED ONE IN WHOM HE WALLOWS HELPLESSLY	*96*
DIALOGUE ON THE FLY	*98*
HEADING DOWNWARD	*99*
LIFE—DEATH, IN A HEADLONG DICHOTOMY	*100*
LIFE VERSUS DEATH, TO THE FINISH	*100*
HOW LOVE TURNED OUT	*101*
A POLITICALLY METAPHYSICAL PROTEST	*102*
BIDDEN? OR SMITTEN?	*102*
PEOPLE, SELF, AND WORLD	*102*
WHERE I "GO," IF PHILOSOPHY WERE GIVEN A VOICE	*103*
HOT AND PLENTY	*104*
MARRIAGE, AND ITS ARBITRARY INEVITABILITY	*105*
A FRANK ADMITTANCE	*105*
REGAINING DIGNITY	*106*
A DEPRESSING EVENT	*106*

DOWNGRADING THE SOCIAL RANKING IN TERMS OF UTMOST HYPE	106
THE REPLACING GENERATIONS	107
SOCIAL LIFE	108
PEOPLE AND THE PERSON	108
THE SOCIAL NECESSITY FOR REALITY (SECRETLY DISGUISED AS A LOVE PLEA)	109
BOYHOOD MOVIES	110
A SPECIAL ENTITLEMENT	111
A LIBATION TO THE PAST	111
AN ETERNAL TRADE	112
THE CHILDREN'S REVENGE. THEN PARENTS WILL AVENGE	112
TO AL LEHMAN	113
THE LIMIT OF BEING WITH HIM AGAIN	114
A SLICE OF MUSIC	114
THIS TIME MAKE IT WORK!	114
TWO FORMS OF INEQUALITY	115
BAD TIMING	116
A DISTANCE BOAST	116
RESTORING VIRTUE AND EQUALITY	117
MAKING FRIENDS: A FINE ART	117
CONTRAST, AT YOUR EXPENSE	118
GUIDE TO IMPROVING YOUR MOOD	118
TO AL LEHMAN, FOREVER	119
THAT VITAL ELEMENT WE CALL LIFE	119
MY MOOD PLUNGE, AND HOW I GREW OUT OF IT	120
CASTING BLAME	121
WHOSE IDENTITY?	121
SOCIAL LIFE'S COMPILING OF FRIENDSHIP RATINGS	122
HOW GOOD GOVERNMENT WOULD WORK	123
DOES THE EARTH FAVOR US, AND THE WORLD CO-OPERATE? LET'S FIND OUT, WON'T WE?	124
A BIG REGRET FOR A CHEAP CAUSE	125
THE PROPER WAY TO KEEP TIME WITHIN ETERNITY'S RULE AND NOT SIMULTANEOUSLY MAKE YOURSELF A FOOL	126
KEEP THE GENERATIONAL FLOW. IT'S INSPIRATIONALLY NECESSARY, YOU KNOW.	127

COUPLE-ATING	128
THE BODY OF MY THANKS	128
LIFE'S PURPOSE INVESTIGATED	129
BASIC ANTI-WAR REASONS FOR ALL WAR-LIKE SEASONS	130
THE VALUE OF POST-ACTION TALK	130
FOOLS, TAKE HEED. (ADDRESSED TO THOSE OF YOUR BREED.)	131
WHO DO YOU ROOT FOR?	132
WHAT'S STEWING?	132
POSTING A PUBLIC WARNING	132
EXUBERANT ABUNDANCE PROSPECTIVELY GIVEN TO US IRRESPECTIVELY	133
WATCH WHAT YOU SAY? NO.	134
TEMPTED TO LET GO?	134
WATCH OUT	135
IF THE BLADDER'S TOO FREQUENT IT'S SOMEHOW DELINQUENT. THE BATHROOM I FREQUENT.	135
SELF-CONSCIOUSNESS IS OVER WHEN YOU'RE NO LONGER A ROVER.	136
WHAT MEMORY ENDEAVORED WHEN WE WERE SEVERED	136
RECOMMENDED READING	137
MAKING THE IDEAL REALISTICALLY PRACTICAL, AND GETTING CREDIT FOR IT	138
ELEGY FOR JIMMY	138
MY OLD SCHOOL BUDDIES	139
THE UNINTERFERING SNAKES IN THE BOTANICAL GARDENS ON A GORGEOUS DAY IN THE JOLLY MONTH OF MAY	139
SOME DRAWBACKS TO LIFE	140
HOW ARE THINGS GOING?	140
ME, MY WIFE, AND OUR BABY BOY CLAIM EACH OUR PART OF LIFE'S AVAILABLE JOY. WE HOPE THE WORLD'S END IS NOT "DESTROY."	141
A WALK IN THE OLD HAUNTS AFTER JIMMY STAGNO DIED	142
A VOTE FOR LIFE. LET DEATH TAKE A BACK SEAT. UNADULTERATED, I'LL TAKE MY LIFE NEAT.	142
ADVICE TO MALE BABIES BORN TO WIDE-HIPPED MOTHERS	143
WATCH OUT	144
TO JIMMY STAGNO, AS IF HE WERE STILL ALIVE	144
COMPARING LIFE WITH ITS OWN MEANING WITHOUT TO EITHER BEING DEMEANING	145

AN ENDORSEMENT	*145*
MY LAST PLAN	*146*
TITLE IN REVERSE FOLLOWS TEXT, SO NOW YOU KNOW WHAT'S COMING NEXT	*146*
THE "CONSTRUCTION" UNION	*146*
SHOULD WE MAKE A FILM ABOUT IT?	*148*
BAD SELF-NEWS WITH PESSIMISTIC VIEWS OF MISERABLE MISFORTUNE OVERWHELMING YOUR FUTILE CAUTION. OF BAD LUCK, YOU EXCEED YOUR PORTION TO AN ALMOST COMICAL DISTORTION	*149*
THE DYNAMIC LIFE CYCLE ENDING ON DEATH'S STALLED BICYCLE COLD AS A BURNED-OUT ICICLE	*150*
EVERYTHING AND NOTHING TOGETHER IN OUR MIXED METAPHYSICAL WEATHER	*150*
THE COMPOSER'S EXPLANATION	*151*
PRAISING A WIFE STILL YOUNG ENOUGH TO OUTSHINE A REALISTIC PORTRAIT	*152*
THE RUINED PICNIC, INCLUDING ITS PARTLY REDEEMING AFTERMATH	*152*
WHAT'S MISSING AND WHO BY	*153*
THE WEATHER PULLED A DAMPER FROM THE FOOD READY IN THE HAMPER FOR A GLORIOUS INTENDED PICNIC BUT UNWELCOME RAIN CREATED CONFLICT	*154*
A NEW SLANT TO JUSTIFY SELFISHNESS. IT TOOK A LONG TIME TO GET THERE. ALSO, A DENIAL OF THE GENTLE MYTH OF "SURVIVOR'S GUILT."	*155*
TWO LEGITIMATE WORDS AND ONE NOT, IN DESCRIBING THE HUMAN MENTAL APPARATUS. BUT RELIGIOUS CLERGY WILL GET AT US, AND IF WE WERE A BALL, THEY'D BAT US.	*155*
SAFELY LIVING LIFE SO IT DOESN'T GO AWAY AND GET OUT OF HAND	*156*
LET IT BE A FILM, NOT REAL, THAT YOU FLASH A WEAPON OF DEADLY STEEL	*156*
HEARING A YOUTH'S VOWS, OPEN YOUR MOUTH FOR SOME SURPRISED "WOWS" ON PARDONS HE LATER PROFESSIONALLY ALLOWS	*157*
THE COMBINATION OF MONEY AND LOVE KEEPS THE WORLD SWIRLING ABOVE. THE COMBINATION OF LOVE AND MONEY KEEPS ME SNUGGLING WITH MY HONEY. THAT MAKES SENSE, IT'S NOT FUNNY.	*158*
BALANCING DEFT POLAR EXTREMES	*158*
REVENGE ON PARENTS FOR MAKING US STRONG ENOUGH TO AVENGE THEIR EARLY PARENTAL WRONGS	*159*

CONVERSATION'S OCCASIONAL GIFT TO IDEA FORMATION, TILL YOU GET IN THE SOUP	159
AVOIDING PESKY CARS ALONG THE WAY, THAT'S CITY LIFE IN WORK OR PLAY APPLIED TO YOUR OWN NEIGHBORHOOD WHERE ROUTINELY YOUR CONCERNS HAVE STOOD.	160
IF ONLY. THEN YOU WOULDN'T BE SO LONELY.	161
THE AGE OF DECISIVE CHOICES. RAISE OR LOWER YOUR VOICES. THE DANCE HALL IS A WEIRD DEVICE TO BE MERELY FRIVOLOUS OR PRECISE.	162
RUNNING FOR OFFICE? WITH WHAT ORIFICE? YOU BARELY GRASP THE CORE OF THIS.	163
WHAT TO BE, ACCORDING TO WHAT NOT TO BE	163
FOLLOW THIS ADVICE TO THE HILT, HOPING YOUR LIFE WOULD REDUCE THE TENDENCY TO WILT.	164
EXPECT CHANGES. THIS IS WHAT LIFE ARRANGES: TO FEEL ONE WAY, THEN ANOTHER. OTHERWISE WE'RE CHOKED INTO A STERILE SMOTHER.	164
THE CRUCIAL RACE OF TWO CONTESTANTS: WE KNOW ALREADY WHICH IS BESTANT	165
A VERY WELCOME TOPIC	165
GIVING PARENTS THEIR DUE FOR GUIDING US THROUGH YOUTH'S WILD TRAVAILS LEAVING NO CRIMINAL TRAILS	166
THE SECURITY OF THE COMFORT ZONE PROTECTING PLEASURE ALL FOR YOUR OWN	166
STARTING WITH PLEASURE, BUT THEN WHERE?	167
MY SIMILARITY TO OTHERS	167
PLEASURE AND PAIN—WHAT A DICHOTOMY! OPPOSITE RESULTS OF OUR ANATOMY.	168
TRYING TO INVESTIGATE LIFE TO AN EXACT EXTENT, TRYING TO SEE JUST WHERE IT'S GONE ON A BENT FROM THE TURNING POINT OF WHERE IT HAS WENT.	168
TIME, CHANGE, PAIN, AND PLEASURE: CONTEMPLATE ALL THESE AT YOUR LEISURE.	169
YES, WHAT ABOUT LIFE? IT HARMONIZES STRIFE. YOU CAN CUT IT CLEANLY WITH A DULL KNIFE.	169

WINNING THE PARENTS-CHILDREN TUSSLE WHEN PARENTS GROW WEAKER AT THE MUSCLE AND CHILDREN ARE QUICKER TO HUSTLE TOWARD MATURE STALWART BUSTLE AND END UP WITH THE WHOLE STOLEN RUSTLE.	170
ALLOWING LIFE MY IGNORANCE	170
HOW NOT TO BE TOO FRAZZLED ABOUT LIFE	171
HOW TO SPEAK PHILOSOPHICALLY ABOUT LIFE	171
IN SUMMARY, WHAT WAS IT ALL ABOUT? I'M YET TO PUZZLE IT OUT. I RETREAT IN DREAMS, AND POUT.	171
WHERE AM I GOING IN HIS RETROSPECTIVE? BUT I'M NOT HIS INTERNAL DETECTIVE. I STUMBLE STERNLY ON SOME SORT OF PERSPECTIVE.	172
LIFE, DESCRIBED FROM ITS OWN ANGLE SO THAT DEFINITION DOESN'T HAVE TO DANGLE	172
DOES LIFE HAVE TOO MUCH MEANING?	173
SPEAKING FOR JIMMY	173
LIFE CAN CURE YOUR ILLS, WHEN YOU APPLY YOUR CO-OPERATIVE WILLS AND ASK FOR INNUMERABLE REFILLS.	174
EASE UP. DON'T TAKE THINGS HARD. LIVE A LITTLE.	174
DEATH SEEMED TO TRAIL LIFE AS ITS REVERSE MIRROR IMAGE, THE SHADOW IN WAITING	175
THE LARGER PICTURE. BUT I'M A FIXTURE?	175
WHAT'S IN STORE FOR YOU BY INNOCENTLY BEING BORN, TILL BY THE WORLD YOU'RE TORN	176
MONEY AS A FACTOR IN MARRIAGE CHOICE LOUDER IN DEGREE THAN LOVE ALONE IF YOU'RE LIVING ALREADY CLOSE TO THE BONE	176
ENERGY ON THE CHARGE AND ENERGY RECEDING BALANCE THE PURE EARTH'S BREEDING	177
WRITING'S VARIETIES	178
AVOID UGLINESS IF YOU CAN, OR IF YOU'RE STUCK WITH IT, BE DOOMED TO A MISERABLE CHOICE OF MATES DOWN IN YOUR LUCK AMONG THE UNRULY FATES.	179
GET IT RIGHT OR REVERSE THE WRONG AND SAIL ALONG ON LIFE'S UNEVEN SONG.	179
WE'RE STUCK TO OUR OWN IDENTITY. DON'T GO AFAR AFIELD. REMAINING YOU IS ALL YOU CAN YIELD. IDENTITY IS NOT PLASTIC. IT FORCES YOU TO SIMPLY STICK.	180
CONCERNING THAT MAJOR ISSUE: LIFE	181

KEEPING ABOVEBOARD	182
A BUNCH OF NEGATIVES	182
HOW SUPERSTITION GRANTS YOU UNQUESTIONABLE AFTERLIFE	183
CONVERT PLEASURE FROM PAIN FOR AN INSURMOUNTABLE GAIN	184
A BELIEVER PROCLAIMS HIS FAITH	184
MORE THAN AN ADORNMENT, THE BRAIN IS OUR PRIZED ORNAMENT THAT CHANGES THE WHOLE EQUATION WITH ITS INTELLECTUAL POWER STATION THAT CONSTITUTES A RADICAL INNOVATION FROM OUR MERE CRUDE BASIC ORIGINS BARELY ABLE TO ISSUE A PRIMITIVE GRUNT AND THE BELLIGERENCE OF A DEFENSIVE FRONT NOT TOO SUBTLE BUT CRAZILY BLUNT.	185
THE PARTY-CRASHER'S RECOVERY WITH A BANG	186
HOW TO FAIL AT CRASHING A PARTY	187
NOT BEING A PROBLEM AS AN UNCOUTH PARTY-CRASHER	188
WHAT ROMANCE CAN EVENTUALLY LEAD TO ACCORDING TO CUSTOM IN THE HUMAN ZOO THAT'S QUITE SOCIALIZED FOR ME AND YOU	188
AN OBVIOUS CHOICE IF YOU FOLLOW YOUR SANITY VOICE AND ALLOW LIFE TO REJOICE	189
WHY I PREFER NOT TO BE LIKE A MOLE	189
CONFINED TO THE BATHROOM TO DISPEL IRREGULAR GLOOM AND FEEL YOUR COMFORT SPEEDILY ZOOM	190
A PLEA FOR BEING CHOOSY EVEN IF SOMEONE HAS TO LOSE ME. THIS IS IN REFERENCE FOR THE RIGHT TO EXERCISE PREFERENCE.	190
THE WORLD GIVES ME A RIDE TILL THE "ME" PART SLIPS TO SUBSIDE AND LOSES MY MOMENTARY GRIP WHILE THE WORLD CONTINUES ITS TRIP WITH OTHERS FAR TO OUTSTRIP.	191
MY WORLDLY VENTURE: TO ME, AN ASTOUNDING ADVENTURE. BUT THE WORLD IS PREOCCUPIED IN OBSERVING ITS RATHER IMPERSONAL TIDE.	192
MY TENURE	192
HOW TO END ALL DUE DELIBERATIONS AND ACQUIRE YOUR FINAL LIBERATIONS	192
SOMETHING VERY SERIOUS: AIM AN ATOM BOMB, IT CAN'T MISS.	193
HOW TO WIN YOUR WIFE BACK AGAIN BY DOING IT MORE THAN JUST NOW AND THEN	194
AN ODE TO PEOPLE NUMERICALLY. ALL TOGETHER ACT SEMI-HEROICALLY AND THEIR VOICES ALL SOUND PHONETICALLY.	195
HURRY UP, CLOSE YOUR EYES TO AVOID AN ABRUPT SURPRISE.	195

FIRST THINGS FIRST. THEN ALL IN A BURST AND PLUNGE AHEAD, FOR BETTER OR WORST. FOR DRENCHING DEATH, WE DIE WITH THIRST.	*196*
AIMING YOUR LIFE'S APPROACH TO BE WELL OUT OF REACH OF SOCIETY'S REPROACH. TO THAT EXTENT, I'LL COACH.	*196*
HOW LIFE KEEPS GOING LIKE A LAWN UNDERGOING ITS PERIODICAL HEALTHY MOWING UNTIL IT MUST BE SLOWING DOWN FROM THE GROWING AND THE LAWNMOWER STOPS AND ITS MECHANISM POPS.	*197*
ISABEL (THE HOSTESS) VERSUS THE RAIN'S TIMING JUST AS SHE WAS PRIMING FOR A VERY PLANNED PICNIC ON WHICH THE RAIN DECIDED TO PICK. THAT DECISION WASN'T WORTH A LICK.	*198*
SOME ADVICE FROM ME TO YOU AS A PUBLIC SERVICE TO REWARD THE READERS OF WHAT I WRITE HERE DOWN / THOUGH IT MAY LACK RENOWN.	*199*
A DESCRIPTION OF WHAT YOU CAN OR CAN'T DO. HOW TO HOLD YOUR OWN IN MAYBE A VOLATILE WORLD	*200*
AN OPPORTUNE VERBAL COINCIDENCE TO FULFILL UPON THE INCIDENCE	*200*
THE WOMB-TOMB DICHOTOMY THAT GIVES POETS AN EASY RHYME THAT SPANS OUR WHOLE LIVES UNDER TIME	*201*
MEMORY, IN ITS PLUS AND MINUS, FOR OLD FOLK OR MINORS	*201*
CRUELTY TO WIFE ENDS OUR MARITAL LIFE. A VERY TERMINAL STRIFE.	*202*
LARGELY FORGOTTEN OR OVERLOOKED: THAT'S YOUR FATE FOR BEING DEAD WHICH ALREADY HAD ENOUGH DREAD.	*202*
DEATH LOSES ITS BATTLE, SUPPLANTED BY HEAVEN'S RATTLE.	*203*
GET YOURSELF DISILLUSIONED, YOU COWARD. BEING DEAD, YOU'RE NOT THE LEAST EMPOWERED.	*203*
TO A FORMER BEAUTY WHO REJECTED ME	*204*
I CRASH A MEMORIAL PARTY FOR SOME DEAD SUCKER I DON'T KNOW AND PUT A STRANGER'S DISGRACE ON IT AND CAN NEVER SHOW MY FACE THERE AGAIN FOR WHATEVER NEXT DEAD PERSON HER FAMILY PAYS TO MOURN THERE AND WASTE A LOT OF EMPTY FUNERAL AIR.	*205*
THE HEIGHT OF SQUIRREL SPITE AFTER A TREEWARD FLIGHT	*206*
EVOLUTION'S STUPENDOUS GIFT TO THE HUMAN RACE. IS THE HUMAN RACE THANKFUL? NO, IT TAKES IT FOR GRANTED. IT'S NOT EXHAUSTING ITS ENERGY BY BEING TOO PANTED.	*206*
THE PERMITTED EXCEPTION	*207*

THE TRIUMPH OF BELIEF. IT AFFORDS YOU BLESS-ED RELIEF. IF YOU DISBELIEVE, YOU'RE A THIEF LIKE A TREE TOO BARREN TO PRODUCE A LEAF.	208
THE ORIGIN OF THE FAMILY. LET THEM PROCEED ALONG AMBLY.	208
AN UNRESOLVED DISPUTE	209
A PLANETARY STATUS QUO OR MORE TO KEEP UP THE BUSY STORE	209
THE HARD JOB TO GET DONE FOR A NEW BABY TO BE WON; AND THE WIFE SIGHS, "THANK YOU, HON."	210
BETTER NOT PLAY WITH FIRE UNLESS YOU THIRST TO EXPIRE.	210
WORRYING ABOUT NOT ENOUGH FOOD TO ACCOMMODATE OUR WHOLE WORLDLY BROOD THAT KEEPS SENDING IN NEW BIRTHS: I CONTEMPLATE THE NEED FOR TWO EARTHS.	211
LIFE IS DERIVED FROM SEX IN CIRCUMSTANCES OF VARIOUS SETS FAMILIAR IN SOME CASES, AND OTHERS, PROFOUNDLY PERPLEX.	212
MY ORIGIN, BEFORE AND AFTER, IN LIFE'S MANY RIDES ALONG THE HILLS OF LAUGHTER AND OTHER THINGS, BESIDES.	212
GETTING STARTED, YOU WILL HAVE BEEN PARTED FROM ACUTE NON-EXISTENCE INTO THE ORDINARY PERSISTENCE OF THE LIFE-SPARKLE TILL THE LIGHTS TURN DARKLE.	213
THE VOYAGE FROM NON-EXISTENCE WITH MOTHER'S HELP AND A LITTLE PERSISTENCE INTO THE GREAT BEAM OF REAL LIFE TO INTRODUCE A WORLD OF BOTHER AND STRIFE.	213
DEAR EVOLUTION'S HAPPY SOLUTION TO REPLENISH POPULATION TO OUR PLANET'S ELATION BUT OUR BREEDING'S OVER-INFLATION	214
LIFE'S POLARITIES AND ALSO DISPARITIES AND TEMPORALITIES AND OTHER EXTRALITIES	214
DELAYING URINATION TO MAXIMIZE RELIEF WITH GROANING MOANS OF ECSTASY TO POUR OUT YOUR WHOLE BREAKFASTY IN DROP BY ECSTATIC DROP TILL YOUR BLADDER HEAVES TO A STOP AND YOUR MOMENTUM IS HEARD TO POP.	215
THE VALUE OF SHEER RELIEF AFTER WORRY AGONIZED TIME LIKE SADISM'S SUPER THIEF	216
GLOBE-CHASING RIVALS RECYCLING TO RE-ARRIVALS	217
DEATH AND LIFE, COMPARED. THEIR DIFFERENCE IS SOLEMNLY AIRED. CAN YOU EXPECT THEM TO BE PAIRED?	217
QUIET. WE'RE SPEAKING OF LIFE	218

MULTIPLYING YOUR LIFE SOCIALLY, INCREASING THEN THE SOUND VOCALLY	218
BELONGING TO HUMANITY IS A PROBLEM, MORE THAN ONE, SO LET'S GET TOGETHER AND SOLVE THEM.	219
PUT YOUR POLARITIES BEHIND YOU AND DON'T LET CONFUSION BLIND YOU.	220
I'M A WORLD WITHIN THE WORLD'S GALAXY. FOR GALS I THANK FOR ALL THAT ECSTASY. BUT BEING OLD, WHO HAS TO EXIT? ME.	220
THE SON ARRIVES. THE MOTHER SIGHS WITH WHISPERING CRIES.	221
OUR CURRENT STATE WHICH IMPLIES "TEMPORARILY," FROM DAY-TO-DAY STATUS TILL FATE AT LAST WILL SPIT AT US.	221
THE URINATION ACT AS A MATTER OF FACT, DROP BY DROP WITH BATHROOM PROP.	222
HOW DARE THE READER INTERRUPT OR DISRUPT THE WRITER'S CREATIVITY BY HIS AGGRESSIVE READING INSTEAD OF PASSIVELY HEEDING WHAT THE WRITER CLAIMS TO BE PLEADING.	223
HOW MY HONEY AND I OVERCAME AN AWKWARD START TO OUR WOOING. NOW WE CAN'T PART. WE TURNED ROMANCE INTO A FINE ART.	224
GOING TO A COMEDY MOVIE WITH MY HONEY. ISN'T THAT GROOVY?	224
FEEL BAD? HURRY UP AND CHANGE IT. PREFERABLY FOR THE BETTER, OF COURSE. LENIENTLY APPLY YOUR FORCE.	225
SOME PRACTICAL, COMMON-SENSE ADVICE. APPLY IT IF YOU CAN, BUT NOT OTHERWISE.	225
A FAIR WARNING: DON'T VENTURE INTO THE ALARMING. WATCH OUT. LIFE IS A TRAP. DON'T GET CAUGHT, OR YOU'RE OFF THE MAP.	226
ON LIFE'S VICISSITUDES AND OTHER PRECARIOUS INTERLUDES	226
THE VERBAL ART TO MAKE A SIGNIFICANT FRIEND BY SHARING CONVERSATIONS ALL YOUR LIVES AND NEVER RUN OUT OF WORDS BY TAKING TURNS, GOOD AND FAIR, FOR EACH TO HAVE HIS PROPER SHARE.	227
GETTING BORN IS NOT ENOUGH. THERE'S MORE AHEAD, AND IT'S ROUGH.	227
WHAT TO LOOK FOR AND WHAT TO AVOID. KEEP YOURSELF UNDESTROYED.	228
LIFE MECHANICALLY IN ACTION THROUGH AN APPARENT FREE WILL TO TAKE OFF THE MECHANICAL CHILL.	228
LIFE, AND ITS WHOLE RETINUE THAT GLADLY INCLUDES ME AND YOU. AND DON'T FORGET THE WHOLE BAMBOOZLE, TOO.	229
WHAT DEATH SEEMS TO BE LIKE, FROM A MORBID PERSPECTIVE POINT OF VIEW. I'M JUST TRYING TO BE TRUE.	230

AN EXAMPLE NOT TO FOLLOW UNLESS YOU REDUCE YOUR BODY TO SKELETAL HOLLOW AND HAVE YOUR WIDOW BELLOW.	*230*
LEARNING TO GIVE THE OTHER HIS TURN BY SHUTTING UP YOURSELF AND NOT LEAVE HIM HANGING ON THE SHELF.	*231*
THE URGE TO PURGE WITH A SURGE.	*232*
TOTALING OUR LOSS	*232*
HOW POSTHUMOUSLY TO BOAST TO YOUR MOURNING WIDOW WHAT A GREAT MASCULINE GLOW YOU SHED BEFORE YOU HAD TO GO.	*233*
DEALING IN THE WORLD WITH OTHER PEOPLE, YOU DON'T HAVE TO BE RIGID AS A METHODIST STEEPLE, NOR BE VOYEURISTIC AS A PEEP-HOLE TO SEE NUDITY AND SEE IT WHOLE.	*234*
MAN, WOMAN, AND LOVE. IS THERE ANY PROBLEM MORE ABOVE? TO WHAT EQUATION DOES THIS ADD UP? IS LOVE DRAINING OR RISING IN THE MUTUAL CUP?	*235*
A FLIRTATION IN THE TEETH OF DISMISSAL'S TIME BARRIER, WHICH IS THEORETICALLY IMPENETRABLE	*236*
A SEXUAL CONFRONTATION, WITHIN SEPARATE COMPARTMENTS	*237*
IN LIFE, YOU'VE GOT TO WIN, WHEREVER YOU ARE. LET AMBITION SET THE BAR.	*238*
HE PURSUES. SHE RESISTS. HE PERSISTS. SHE CHANGES THE RULES. HE OBEYS THE CHANGE. RECKON THE WINS AND LOSSES FOR EACH AT THE OPEN END.	*238*
DON'T LOSE YOUR HEAD, JUST FOR AN IDEA	*240*
SETTING: A YOUNG MAN AND WOMAN HAVE FRESHLY GRADUATED FROM THEIR RESPECTIVE SEMINARIES, AND MEET EACH OTHER TO GET ACQUAINTED AND TEST THE WATERS OF THE OUTSIDE WORLD.	*240*
TAKE ON THIS TONE SO YOU WON'T YELP AND MOAN. DON'T BITE YOUR OWN TELEPHONE.	*241*
YOU'RE LUCKY I'M TELLING YOU THIS	*242*
ANNA RECOLLECTS A PICNIC-SPOILING STORM FROM WHICH EVERYONE SCATTERED, ESPECIALLY HER FRIEND BERTHA WHOSE DISLOYALTY SHE FINALLY FORGIVES, SHEDDING THE SUDDEN SHOWER OF A BLESSING.	*242*
THE ONLY BIG DIFFERENCE	*243*
YOU CALL THAT A LIFE?	*244*
A MAN INNOCENTLY EVADES AN UNFAIR CASE OF BEING ARRESTED ON UNJUSTIFIABLE GROUNDS	*244*

A SWIFT ROMANCE DEFLATED BY A LESS IMMEDIATE REJECTION	246
A FRESH GRADUATE FROM PSYCHIATRIC COLLEGE IS AMBITIOUSLY LOOKING TO RECRUIT HIS VERY FIRST CLIENT ON A CUT-RATE BASIS.	247
A PRETTY "CREATIVE WRITING" STUDENT EXCITES HER OLDER INSTRUCTOR'S LUST. HE OFFERS AN IMMORAL SOP TO OFFSET HER SEXUAL REFUSAL.	248
THE CLOUD, THE CLOCK, AND OTHER CONTRARIES THAT DISCUSSION SOON BURIES BY EXHAUSTING THEM AND OTHER WORRIES	249
DON'T MAKE THIS INTO A GLOBAL CONFLICT	250
HOW EVOLUTION IS AMORAL, IT JUST WANTS US TO BE. SO HERE WE ARE, THRILLINGLY.	251
HOW EVOLUTION UTILIZES THE SEX MAGIC TO GIVE US EVERYTHING COMIC AND TRAGIC VIA THE BIOLOGICAL SPECIFIC ORGANICALLY RELATED TO OUR RACE TERRIFIC	252
TAKE CARE OF YOURSELF— IT'S YOUR OWN AND ONLY LIFE. PROTECT IT FROM HARMFUL HURT. AVOID INFECTION FROM UGLY DIRT. BE CAREFUL WITH WHOM YOU FLIRT.	252
MAKE THE RIGHT CHOICE AND WELL MAY YOU REJOICE. HEAR A HEARTENING VOICE.	253
EVOLUTION'S LIFE CYCLE WITH EARLY AND LATE CHARACTERS ALONG TIME'S RIDDLED CHAPTERS	254
TWO FRIENDS LAUNCH INTO A HUMOR-ANALYZING DIALOGUE, DEADENING HUMOR'S SPIRIT.	254
THE LOVELY INVENTION OF NOSTALGIA REVIVES THE PAST AND PREVENTS NEURALGIA.	255
SOME REFERENCES TO LIFE, ON A LOOSE BASIS, ASKING JUST WHAT THE HUMAN RACE IS	256
AN UNCELEBRATED LIFE OF ANONYMOUS POSTERITY CLOSES OUT, LACKING PUBLIC FAME AS PUNISHMENT FOR NEVER HAVING ENTERED THE RANKS OF CELEBRITY. ACHIEVEMENT: CITIZEN.	256
PROFESSOR CARLE'S SELF-FULFILLING STATEMENT ON TIME'S ESSENTIAL NATURE, WHICH BEARS REPEATING, BUT THE CONSTANT REPETITION OF WHICH COST HIM HIS JOB, BUT HE GOT ANOTHER APPOINTMENT IN A DIFFERENT UNIVERSITY, WHICH SALVAGED HIS TEACHING CAREER.	257
A FRIEND TRIES TO HELP A MAN SUFFERING FROM A NERVOUS BREAKDOWN IF DIAGNOSTICALLY THAT'S WHAT IT IS, INCLUDING HYSTERIA AND ITS URGENT PRELUDE SYMPTOMS.	258

A PRESENTABLE MAN TRIES TO "PICK UP" A PRESENTABLE WOMAN IN A MUNICIPAL ART MUSEUM, IN FRONT OF A REMBRANDT.	260
DIALOGUE-ING BIG SUBJECTS	261
A PRESENTABLE WOMAN TRIES TO "PICK UP" A PRESENTABLE MAN IN A MUNICIPAL ART MUSEUM, IN FRONT OF A VAN GOGH. SHE GETS INCREASINGLY DESPERATE.	262
PREPARING TO GO IT ON YOUR OWN, SEVERED FROM MOTHER, WHO WANTS TO OWN YOU, BUT YOU RESIST. BUT MOTHER MUST INSIST.	263
DIALOGUE ON LIFE FRIENDSHIP (STARTING OR RESUMING FROM ANYWHERE DOWN THE UN-TWINNED ROADS)	264
THE ARGUMENT THAT EVENTUALLY GOT TEMPORARILY NOWHERE, AS FAR AS IT WENT. THEN THE DISPUTANTS ROARED TO A STOP.	265
A MAN HAS A CONVERSATION WITH HIS OWN INSOMNIA, AS THEY GET TO KNOW EACH OTHER DURING THE LONG NIGHTS THEY'RE FORCED TO SPEND IN EACH OTHER'S WEARY COMPANY.	266
(TITLE FOLLOWS DIALOGUE)	267
TO MY FAVORITE COUPLE: SWEETLY SOFT AND SUPPLE.	267
TWO NEW FRIENDS TOY WITH DIALOGUE COMPLICATIONS	268
UNEQUAL LUCK DISTRIBUTION, BAD FOR HER AND GOOD FOR ME IN EQUALITY'S ASYMMETRY. WHAT MORTAL IS ACCIDENT FREE?	269
AN INFERIOR MAN CONFESSES IN ONE OF HIS SELF-ACCUSING ADDRESSES HOW HIS LIFE IS A SERIES OF MESSES.	270
OPEN TO SUPPOSITIONS, THE HARD LIFE OF A STONE CONFRONTS ME, ALONE.	270
ADVICE FOR AN AMBITIOUS CAREERIST: BUT FIRST TREMBLEY WRITE DOWN YOUR FEAR LIST.	271
AN OPEN INVITATION TO TAKE CARE THAT YOU DON'T TRIP AND UNDERGO DESPAIR IF DAMAGE MANGLES YOUR BODY FAIR WITH ACCIDENT BEYOND PHYSICAL REPAIR.	272
IF THINGS TURN WRONG, YOU'RE IN THE WRONG SONG, SO FIND THE RIGHT MELODY TO KEEP A FELLOW FREE.	272
A LOVELY EVENT BLESSING TWO ADULTS AND BABY. THEY HAD DIFFERENT TIME SLOTS BUT UNITED TO THE BEST PLOTS.	273

Sadness Corrected

EXPECTING TOO MUCH

Merely being alive is a plus,
you're ahead of the game,
what've you got to lose?
There's an abundant amount of clues
that life is right here and now.
All you have to do is look around.
Unmiraculous things will be found.
What? You expected more?
Sit down and be content, you bore.

THE LANDLORD'S DOMINANCE

When life gives you a lot of trouble,
you're still not like a house reduced to rubble
by the fierce forces of demolition
giving way to real estate ambition.
So get up and rent a new house
and conceal describing your landlord as a louse.
He holds the power like a spouse
with a superior amount of income,
who can blow a possession to kingdom come
and can survive the sneeze-inducing dust
that gathers around the destruction
and induces a necessary new construction
at higher rents of course
legally allowed to landlords by high courts
to show the feeble tenant who's the mighty Boss,
who's money-minded and his taste is coarse.
And you of course have no recourse.
Money rules, as you learn to your cost.
You think life is a cherry blossom
falling lavishly on your lady's bosom
as in enchanting romance's custom?

LIFE INTO ART

You have to grab life by the handle
and burn both ends of its candle.
The two flames will meet in middle,
and even if you're playing it, burn your fiddle
so that the tune gives way to charcoal
with which to sketch life's portrait, partially whole,
combining fine art and a musical hole,
a rich admixture of plus and minus,
hoping the police will not fine us
for dereliction of duty
by casting on the public non-beauty
and creating decadent art for the snooty.

THE TRUE FABRIC OF LIFE ITSELF

Life is so circumstantial
as well as situationality
that you're too caught up to want to cancel
your so-far ticket, no matter what your nationality,
provided your life isn't too fraught
between what it is and what ought.
Into what snare are you being caught?
The secret of life is not to want too much,
so go get yourself a lighter touch
so you'll skip away from disappointment
until of course your next appointment.
For life's ills, is there one ointment
if applied, will kill them all?
No. To life, we're all in thrall.
So go get yourself a ball
and bounce it so up high,
you're caught between should you swim or fly?
Play it by ear so by and by
solutions will bombard you
and one of them will give you your cue
of what when not to do.

Not satisfied? So go sue
and let a court of judgment solve your problem.
Either blame yourself, or else the scapegoat "them."
The structure of life is to overwhelm
your choice decisions and be at the helm
of what's too late to do or too soon.
But don't delusionally chase the awkward moon
and be the instrument to its cosmic tune
that swarms your ears up to your head
and your hunger-laden mouth to be fed
and your marital propensity to be wed.
But don't stain your silver throat with lead
or subject yourself to disease.
Seek your well-being, at your ease.
Correct mistake, if you please.
If things won't bend, then squeeze.
If you're in life, pay your fees
and gamely be the instrument of all this tease.

NOT THE REAL THING. (MEMORY'S LIMITATIONS)

Oh my dear dead friends return in memory,
but that's not as real as if they're still here.
Can memory make things any more clear?
It only goes so far
and then pales out like a star
when morning whitens and erases
those darling beings and their close faces
who go through their phantom paces
in the half mist of my editing brain
that contorts their reawakening
with the weaker measures of retrieval.
These attempts torture to the point of evil
with the dud snapshots of evasive conceival.
Death and "still living" are hardly equal.
What never comes is the dream-popping sequel.

OLD AGE SEXUAL DISGRACE

Old men whose permanent loss
of sperm-emboldened erection
become harmlessly platonic
to women who regard them as a safe tonic
and pity them for their chronic
flabbiness where once their manhood stood
in true militant neighborhood.
Men pitied as an embarrassment to the erotic:
Where can they turn to regain their pride?
"I'm gallantly protecting the women folk
from sexually transmitted disease,
thus putting women at their safety ease
and taking away their fright
at my once sperm-emboldened might.
In my new role as their protector
I'm still ashamed at being no erector.
Women see through me, as no threat,
only a meek and servile pet
without the proud production of an outlet
entitling me to romantic enchantment
and masculine ego enhancement.
I'm not even worth a passing glancement."

A LAW CASE IN THE GUISE OF A PLAY, WITH ECHOES OF A ZOO

Having accused me of insulting him, Alvin fled.
Under so unfair an accusation, my heart bled.
Then I discovered it was a scheme
to demand "guilt money," that I should atone
for imaginary hurt that I had inflicted on him
so that then in reparation I should succumb to his any whim
to pay off the scam of my assumed insult
with his intended result
that I owed him anything in the land
under the crooked trick of his immoral demand.

This was just about more than I could humanly stand.
I sued him, but the jury refused the case
under Alvin's alleged bribe. This was too much to bear.
In my outrage I just didn't care
and willingly dared to break friendship's sacred oath.
He sentimentally said, "This hurts us both,
so let's turn another page.
Friendship can tolerate even outrage.
We're friends forever. Now let us age."
Thus the play ran on, with friendship holding the stage.
But to make sure, we each had a separate cage
and roared our lines, like two lions
kept apart by the bars of irons.
Our roars were too loud, so police sirens
invaded the public stage, to put us in irons,
giving us handkerships for us to cry on
after politely first asking us to try on.
So let's turn another page.

ANTI-SNOBBERY EVALUATIONS

Despite evolution, we live in the present
whether we're obsolete royalty or a mere peasant.
Let's eliminate too much class distinction
as the status prerequisite to be linked in
to all our fellow human beings together,
whether rain or fair will forecast the weather.
Biologically, we're all hauled in tether
to our basic common race, no matter what the feather.
Let no one whip another, even wearing leather
as supremacy's fashion indicates who's better,
or who wears the most knitted together sweater.
You can fall behind, and still be a go-getter,
and the inferior can still beat their better.

AN ANTI-SUICIDE SERMON

If life seems too wretched to endure,
and even its shining moments are impure,
and medicinally there seems to be no cure,
don't kill yourself: Keep alive
rather than take an unruly dive
into the dark underworld without relief
where people perish because of grief
and other assorted ills
to give suicide a complexion that chills.
Keeping alive is the safe bet: forget what kills,
where too-late regret confuses alternate wills.

SADNESS CORRECTED BY REALISM

Life has its sad moments: Get over them
and leap to embrace a more positive anthem,
so that you don't get overwhelmed.
But that seems like an artificial act.
Sometimes sadness is an irretrievable fact
happening to human beings at a glance.
So take a more philosophical stance
of take-what-comes by whatever chance.
This makes for an easier attitude
widening misery's permissive latitude
closer to acceptance of factitude.

A CULTURAL MAINSTAY

When cops are sleeping, thieves may thrive.
When cops wake up, thieves are fled
with all their stolen loot—
their enterprise's fruit.
So more police are recruited
and their headquarters re-routed,
for night and day protocol,
deputies are on call,

so while some sleep, others are awake,
to prepare for the criminals to bake,
especially the ones on the take.
Thus, the cat-and-mouse game
between cops and robbers plays the same
as always in tradition.
For short, it's the human condition,
with roles to play, in the right position
so that stereotypes will win out
in subtle criminality's essential bout
between all this Right and Wrong
to make the action fit the song.
The cops-and-robbers theme
serves entertainment's dream
in moderate doses, or to the extreme.
Sure, some blood is shed,
as long as the narrative plot gets fed.
Thus, the Wrong and the Right are in the same bed
and humanity celebrates when they wed.
A cultural mainstay, which movies display,
knocks those two together, night and day.

OUR SPECIALLY BRAINY RACE

Love was the first station
toward babies and population.
Don't forget evolution in the mix.
It smoothly mixed the serum of nature's fix,
engendering the match of wombs and dicks,
and the brain's uncanny pragmatism of picks
that filled up the whole universe
with the human race for better or worse
and all the bewitchment of life's curse.
Let's charmingly remain and never disperse.

ODE TO WORDS

Human language
will never languish.
It's verbally vital
and more than an eyeful,
whether in English or not;
knits minds together
through common understanding.
It keeps brains standing
throughout the thick and thin
in league with each other.
Language will create a brother
for every impulse the mind goes through
and every action we all do.
Free language, eloquent,
will show humans the common bent.
People on people then
will make a linguistic dent.
Minds together free us
to altogether be us.
Language binds each mind
to share what we all find
or discover what differences
create new inferences
to patch together our incidents
to generalize specifically
and be ourselves terrifically,
addressing mutually
what affects us crucially.
It does that usually.

THE DIRT-FREE LAWNMOWER

The money I save by not buying
an unnecessary lawnmower
for my Manhattan tenement flat
made all of rotting artifact

in the low-rent district,
tells me not to be too strict
about the spending I don't do.
Be as lavish as green prime grass
in an imaginary garden
without even a real toad
or an ornamental gnome
in your horticulture-filled home
where echoes your rolling lawnmower
sweeping the surface over and over,
and occasionally you bump into a clover
while back and forth you're a rover
with an unpaid-for lawnmower
in your roof-garden upper or lower.
You're an urban green-thumb grower
but no financial ower.

VULTURES OR DOVES

Dear evolution, you got us so far
while history doesn't quite mar
the excellent head start you gave
for rescuing our race from an early grave.
Evolution came first, then history,
which still we're in the making of,
letting vultures fly over our wars
but preparing doves to make restores
and politely dissuade animosity's claws.
Vultures and doves, up above,
fight it out between hate and love
with the fate of the human race
swirling in the air, face to face,
fur flying, to keep up the riot of the pace.
Our planet's beautiful. Let's not deface,
to cast end-history into disgrace.

LOVE'S ROUND

If love makes the world go round,
that fits well: because it's been proven
scientifically that the world is not flat.
That's precisely where marriage and babies are at,
just in case you haven't walked around the block;
and on your brain, perception will knock
that around and around love creates
on this earth the pas de deux between mates.

THE INSIDE WORKINGS OF THE ART WORLD

Oh the art world is full of surprises.
An excuse for a painting, at modest surmises,
is auctioned at millions of dollars.
It makes true artists hot under the collars,
and yet the phony artist has millions of followers
who follow him to museums and wealth.
All in the open! Not an ounce of stealth.
Does this signify any sign of health
for the art world at general at large?
The phony artist and his entourage.
There's no public consensual sensibility.
Taste ignores values of ability.
Aesthetics has no financial stability.
Art is a mockery of utility.
Art is priced off the chart,
known by insiders in the art mart.
But at least gallery exhibits are free
that collectors might not charge prohibitedly,
and dealers serve you wine without fee
upon your feeble little purse.
But hear ignored artists curse.
Art and money together
are hardly birds of a feather.
Poor artists enviously complain

of unfair ratings that award them pain
and celebrity's disdain.
Crowds at galleries gather
to trade the usual art blather.
How ridiculous, rather.

NOT SISTER AND BROTHER

Men and women complete each other,
but not in the way of sister and brother.
Much better that they be unrelated,
to allow romance and love to be stated
as true pretexts to start a family
and biologically fulfill their amity
and avoid incest's calamity
and eliminate scandal's awful damagery
in the broadest human community
of mankind's highest social unity.

IDEALLY, HOW A COUPLE SHOULD BEHAVE

Men and women are of opposite sexes.
Divorced people are now their exes.
But people who are still married
need not be unjustly harried
to hurry up, get a divorce,
if they're undecided who's the boss
between an angry man and his distraught wife.
Equal democracy should protect each life
from excessive bullying and marital strife.
The admirable husband and wife
should be a harmonious pair
and treat each other nice and fair
so that malicious eavesdroppers don't stare.
Maintain social decorum, protect reputation,
to keep our country a respectable nation.

THE DIVIDING LINE

Remembering beloved old friends now dead
makes me survivor-guilty,
privileged to say "better them than me."
"Better me than them"—the same thing,
but with a different ring.
I'm in a better position,
loving them from across the border,
me being a life-hoarder
and them helplessly dead,
different from only being in bed
and waking up the next morn,
the same me who used to be born,
still alive with the ability to mourn
and guilty to survive (I must confess
in my ever-longing distress)
real people I loved, now dead.
I'm spun around in my helpless head.
They were Jimmy, Carl, and Paul,
and not the only ones, not at all.
I stand up while they still fall.
They're only nothing. I can crawl,
but too old to actually bawl.

A BUSY DAY AT THE OFFICE

A corner desk! He has views in both directions,
so he can take care of office matters and make corrections
while from under his desk he can hide his erections
created by an office secretary at a near-by desk
and they both share outside skyscraper views
and also share the inside business news
and she's the one whom he really pursues
in the corporation they both work for
on the sixteenth or seventeenth floor
when by the end today he must finish his chore.
With his responsible job, it's too busy to be a bore,

but he's preoccupied with the office secretary whose legs
interrupt the business figures his responsible job begs
him to finish in time for a deadline
to hand in and then it will be just fine
to continue to pursue the secretary, that's the bottom line
on his personal private scenario.
Then he'll suggest just where to go
when they descend the elevator just prior to his attack of vertigo.
When he recovers, that's the ground he'll continue to hoe.

GENITALIA AND ITS DISCONTENTS

Genitals make all people sensitive
about other people's genitals too.
Then here's to the human race's genitalia
though it sometimes admits to occasional failure.
Shame and self-consciousness proceed
from doing the once-dirty deed.
But now liberation gives consent
for releasing orgasms pent
once the fluidity is spent
on what goes for embarrassed merriment
that grants the body its birthright of content.
Such content then should suffice
to sprinkle on such meals enough spice
and wonder where all the shame disappeared
that Puritans earlier had feared.
History's progress is assuredly weird.
Along freedom's route, we're better steered.
On bodily parts
we jump around to false starts
until experience provides smarts.
It's part of the physical arts.
Let's not be too pert
to require everyone to be an expert.
It all started with primeval dirt.

"HOW ARE YOU?" 'S AUTOMATIC REPLY

A lot of life seems to be in the head
where the brains are, so guard it carefully
from too many crossing ill winds
that strike with sulfur and mercury
from the dangerous outside of where you are:
That's where the evil tides roll over you
and while destroying health, minimize your revenue
with which to purchase any alleviation of your problems
that uglify your outlook with the malice of goblins.
The head is where outlooks turn notoriously inward
and you find yourself lost in the middle of a dim wood
whose misty mis-colors plant you inside
the overwhelming longing to return to the city
except your name is on a list and things aren't pretty
because the National Guard is out to get you
for misdemeanors they claim but just aren't true.
Protecting yourself then is your main issue
in case further problems threaten to ensue.
The scene darkens considerably with its bitter hue
and your many rescuers are reduced to a few.
It turns out that they're spies against you
just at the worst time in your life for that to be true.
What more can you not ask for?
There's nothing left in your ransacked store
to sell in the way of guarding yourself
from hissing misfortune's spiteful elf,
where your files are misplaced on an invisible shelf
not included in your list of furniture
that's your sole property impossible to ensure.
Lady Misfortune seems so attractively demure,
who used to be a hissing and spiteful elf.
The motto of all this? "Take care of yourself."

HOW TO CULTIVATE FRIENDSHIP

If you want to have friends and acquaintances,
make yourself socially attractive,
but don't seem prematurely pro-active.
Win people over to your side
at the point where they'd comfortably reside
within the compass of your companionship
even if just for a small while,
or even longer, if the situation prompts.
Don't force their compassion if you're down in the dumps
nor request their pity if you've been taking your lumps
in your own personal battle with life.
Conversation should shift to their own strife.
If you want to emphasize empathy,
say it's for "you"—not for "me."
Then if you smile, they'll like what they see.
If they give their self-details, then eagerly ask for more,
as if compiling their biographies for their literary store
with facts and tales that drive through to their core.
And if their vanity is fallen, let it restore
within your compassion's radiance
that if they need help, you'll soon come to their aid-iance,
forecasting such stalwart friend you'll be
even without an immediate emergency.
Yet don't let your generosity seem contrived
as if "too much too soon"—it's just arrived.
You're already too strong to see them deprived.
How well together you two will have survived.
Emphasize the personal note
and, though no politician, you'll have his sure vote.

WHAT EVOLUTION HAS DONE FOR ME

Evolution had a solid head start
for my late arrival.
It built up the human race's instincts
with good protein in its proper place
and the organs organized right.
Then when I was born, it was operating smoothly,
providing me with a free ride
in bodily's utmost mighty stride.
Nor did I have to contribute
by fathering a baby on my own.
I got away with bachelorhood.
I didn't put a penny in the collection box.
Nor get married for fertility's sake.
I was a sponge. Even impotence was accepted.
All I had to do was stay alive.
My race had done the work. It would always thrive
as a species fully underway
before I even threw my voice into the say.
I'm proud to be a fully fledged human
automatically licensed to the club,
even voiceless. Someone else would dub.
I was a functioning parasite
and learned the code, the tricks, and got it right.
On evolution's ride, I squeeze my body in
and don't even have to worry about the bible's sense of sin.
Evolution did it for me. I joined in its win.
In the race's family, I'm legitimate kin
and thickly am of the same blood
in affixed authentic brotherhood.
Even without vanity's perk,
I'm in the good. I'm no jerk.
Only on death do I have to carefully lurk
while evolution itself carries the load.
The earth is its and my fancy abode.
My impeccable pedigree makes me family
to join majestically in the ancestry
just simply and only by being alive.

With that admission ticket, what remains?
I bear the mark of a race without stains?
No, I wouldn't go that far.
Immorality blots out a perfect record
but gave everyone an opportunity
to acquit themselves with a sense of immunity
for the sake of our entire coalesced community.

THE ADULT STREET WAIF

Relaxing seems to be an idle hobby.
I can practice it in any lobby
or foyer of a hotel
on a soft and easy sofa
where no one would bother me so far
if I'm dressed anonymously enough
so I don't look like an unshaven street tough
trying to take off from living in the rough.
But now I'm being approached
by a hotel guard with a mean demeanor
in a military-like uniform
who's hastening his stride like a storm.
I wish now I resembled more the norm
like a proper hotel resident
groomed enough not to make a dent
on suspicious management.
Well, the hotel is now behind me.
So is relaxation. Where to go
occupies my current stress,
lacking an appropriate address.
The local Shelter is an option.
"Any port in a storm," I always say,
merrily making my way
to occupy the remainder of the day.

A PLACE OF LAST RESORT

If life keeps on turning against you,
then look for something to defend you
against the plenty of adversities
that spew their venomous fleas
against your life despite your pleas
to convert outside threats to inside ease.
Whom are your pleas directed to?
Your personal protector, that's who.
Is he a live human being? Or an image?
He's someone hired to minimize the damage
that life unfairly inflicts on you;
and crumbles up your any issue
into solutions that solve your ills,
reducing all remedies to a bunch of pills
that are mere metaphors for happiness
that turn out to be superficial sappiness
and merely prolong your distress
without providing any redress.
Where help comes from—what's the address?
Is there any such place in the whole outside world?
Write it down on such stationery
that so quiets my ills, they're all stationary
and allow me their fate to bury
that changes my grim mood to boisterous merry
and allows me to catch the ferry
to that magical place, Fun Isle
that extends, like life, into a small mile
but elicits every second a perpetual smile.
Oh please, what does it symbolize
that ideally replaces your ears and eyes
with visions that admit of no compromise?
It symbolizes hope and fulfillment
and elimination of any illment
into a beatific stillment
of any complaint about life
and its implicit tendency toward strife.
Is that possible? Not on your life.

REPAIRING

Don't be lonely. Pursue company
through the agency of talk.
If you have a conversational opportunity
that grants you some community,
jump right in and don't balk.
But what if you and that other disagree
to the point of boredom and dislike?
Then pay your social fee and take a lonely hike
to a true friend's house, on foot or by bike.
Or in the big city, go by train or bus
for assured company to erase the sour fuss
of words failing to bind. Fall back
on the tried and true, and you've hit the right track,
repairing to where you're always welcome
and your wounded pride will get help. Come.

Where to go once a venture fails
is true relief. Everything else pales
unless you resort to the hopeful mails.

AVOID LONELINESS

Social life you shouldn't ignore.
Without people you'd be a bore
and have only yourself for company
which lacks variety from other sources:
All the people who are not you
could each provide you with a different view
of altogether the multidimensional "True"
meaning the compilations of experience
that makes a common universal sense
to broaden you out from being too dense.

STATUS RAISING

Try to load up on social prestige,
even aspire to noblesse oblige,
and give your girlfriend a good squeeze
in public view to gain admiration
by your whole social circle
who cite you as a true real man
glorifying in his social span
with true assets and talents galore
on which popularity will take store;
and socially your prestige will soar
beyond the deep blue azure,
much to your pride's intrinsic core
where you've already struck the public vein
to justify your right to be vain.
Any more do I need to explain?
I'm wonderful. Isn't that plain?
(If this is conceit, please don't disdain.)

MILD CONFESSIONS OF A SEX WRITER WRITING TO WEARY ADULTS

Genderizing your study of human observation
spices up your findings into sensationalism
to maximumly alert your readership
that entertainment is now being served up
of amused gleanings of how the sexes operate
in direct relation to each other
but not quite like sister-and-brother,
which waters down the human interest
into a lot of trivia to report
and the time of reading it must invest
before sleepiness closes the pages
of your printed recordings of sex relations
in every shade of demeanor in all nations.
In short, what's the sexual dimension
that you thought ripe and ready to mention

to grab up all the readers' attention
about prurience they never knew before
short of me in the role of an authorial bore?
I'm afraid that what I have to report
deserves merely the ironic retort
that readers shouldn't have to waste their eyesight
on the subject matter of sex in all its usual blight.
I can't conjure up what's ordinary into a fright,
nor put it in the grand and blazing new light
that readership would greedily demand.
I'm a scribe operating under financial command
and shrink to be fired for coming up with no fresh twist
stuffed into no new list
of the dull and usual literature
that's supposed to be amazingly mature.
We've all been through this before.

ODE TO GENITALIA'S MECHANICALLY REPETITIVE CYCLES

Hail Parental Genitalia,
the springboard for early infants
in a decent distance
from their mucky making,
who show Minute Genitalia versions
even before they're virgins,
when they get their urgings
before burgeoning
into the overt ranks
of Mature Genitalia,
before they're exponents
and self-opponents
of the Withering Genitalia
just before corpse time
which is lost time,
called Ex-Genitalia:
life's finally duly genifailure.

A BRIEF EXPLANATION OF EVOLUTION

Evolution has got us so far,
why should we slow up now?
But no one has personal control.
Reproduction is on a roll.
It's the race, not the individual;
so if you get killed by accident,
or even by lonely old age,
which is currently all the rage,
it will make exactly no dent
as an isolated incident
in our abiding group membership
of biology's self-repetition
that has automatic control.
You're a digit in the whole,
numerically bearing a minor role.
It's genetic,
so don't get frantic.
You're a facet, an aspect.
No need to inspect.
Evolution doesn't oversee.
It just is, the basic "be."
For your membership, no fee.
Try to imitate evolution
and just continue to be.
How long, I hope?
Well, we'll just have to see.
The evolution and the individual
are two almost unrelated things.
One is assured,
the other desperately needs assurance,
hoping for extra durance.

A CLOSE RECOVERY? IT BETTER BE QUICK.

Lack of equilibrium make you dizzy?
Don't get yourself into a tizzy.
Straighten yourself up and pretend to be busy.
Then you must find just where to go
opposite direction of vertigo,
which turns out to be your internal foe,
which if you don't relieve, will issue you much woe
and on your heart a stroke could bestow.
Avoid that calamity
and walk away brain-free
able to communicate, even with me.
Congratulations on your recovery
which if it hadn't happened would necessitate
a community announcement for a funeral date
and the determination of your estate.
To what does that equate?
Avoid calamity for your own sake
and resume humanity's give and take.
Above all, keep yourself upright
to forfend the stark fight
between being faint in the head
and being mournfully dead,
ripe for grave-habitation
on an impromptu invitation.
It's your life's exit station
but you wouldn't know it
even if inspired by a poet,
whose information arrives too late
to readjust your now sorry state.
A stroke is an instrument of "fate,"
an anonymous accident of no-one's hate.

PUTTING INSOMNIA TO SLEEP

If anything's wrong with your life
(that already meets its quota of strife),
then of course remedy it.
Be an enemy of it.
Attack relentlessly
with full intensity
and stamp it off the earth
never again to resume birth.
What is this miserable curse
that you want to eliminate
to resume your old normal state?
Insomnia.
(This poem pauses
to review its causes.)
Just sleep it off? That's easily said.
It's not automatic when you place your head
on that infernally restless bed.
Well, just try as hard as you can
with your fists utterly clenched
and your pulse rate eagerly tense.
Putting insomnia to sleep
is placing its solution in your keep.
But if you over-try, you may just weep
pursuing such an alien thing like sleep
lost somewhere in the deep
where time is huddled up in a heap.

MEMORY'S DISCONTINUITY WITH "NOW": TWO DISTINCT SEPARATENESSES

The temporary "now" whizzes by
so quick it's soon gone,
to bury itself in memory.
But its memory gives a false picture.
The "now" and the memory are built
on two different structures

quite thousands of miles apart.
To unify them is an impossible mental art,
and it's much too late "soon" to start,
you've missed the opportunity by a mile.
It won't do to just grin and smile.
Impossible to unify the "now"
and its later memory?
To answer that problem, don't even begin to try.
If you do, you'll give up by and by.
Go home, and have a good cry,
or drinking alcohol, get high
to restore your lowly spirits
and learn your various limits.
Then your lost memory will be forgot
once after your old "now" has gone to pot.
Then death itself will top off the lot.
The incompatibility of "now" with memory
is nothing like having death for your enemy,
for which there's never an available remedy.

AN IMPOSSIBLY IDEAL FAMILY

Human reproduction gives us babies
each of which is a bundle of maybe's
as to what that infant's future might bring
from which many moods will spring,
tears and laughter both,
during the course of an interesting growth.
Then let's drink a pint to mother and father
who provided the requisite parental bother.
May the grown-up baby show gratitude
for that family-oriented attitude
that allowed him to reach such a stratitude
that they love and kiss each other without a feud
and even expand their dynasty's brood.
An ideal family without a hitch
knows who each other are and which.
They knit up a future, stitch by stitch.

BORNOGRAPHY

Bornography?
(Derives from the word "born"
that rhymes with the word "porn.")
A gynecologist took too many photos
of consecutive babies being born
from different mothers' wombs
and distributed them on electronic media.
The police raided, to jail him
on charges of bornography.
Will those charges hold up?
That's up to the magistrate.
He'll determine that gynecologist's fate.
The whole world is avid to follow this case,
and sheer public morality is at stake.
To know the outcome, don't you ache?
A sensational court case
called Bornography will soon take place,
determining whether the crime is base,
babes and mothers, photos to efface?

THE LAWNMOWER ANALOGY

Being alone together with someone you love
evokes the mythic region of "heaven above"
if only she would requite your love
and not remain indifferently aloof.
Is there a way to change her mind?
Tell her that love is blind
and needs a new pair of glasses,
which you'll gladly provide if she returns your passes
that would unite your respective asses
like a lawn refreshed by buying new grasses
that make mowing it such a pleasure
that you'll ruffle its surface with continual pressure.
Tell her a change of mood would refresh her,
exchanging cruel indifference for love's sweet pleasure

like your new lawn gleaming in the sun
ready for your lawnmower to purr up its run.
That's a better way of wooing than a threat with a gun.
Mutual consent promises a juicier fun.

ANALYZING COMPETING VALUES

Comparing yourself with others
leads to which—envy or jealousy?
Or to smug satisfaction of pride
in which assurance will reside,
but also putting others down?
Status rivalry prevents potential friendship
from ever blooming, with its spiteful whip.
Love is preferable to hate.
Better make someone your mate,
in the sexual sense or not.
Being affable will help a lot
to untie comparison's ugly knot.
And taking others at their own speed
will unpoison yourself of greed,
allowing co-operation to wonderfully succeed.
Don't compare so much,
it disrupts affection's friendly touch.
Instead of endeavoring to compete,
allow good will to reign complete.
What values are the most valuable?
Social life complicates the incalculable.
Some people count more than others
as special adornments to your life.
Others only aggravate a futility of strife.
Let friendship and love always succeed
when people, between each other, are agreed
that to happily consider the other person's need
promotes in the human race a better breed.
On these considerations, don't you happily feed?

KING ME

Protected by a couple of burly bouncers
with their reputation of being surly trouncers,
I, in my big-shot role, lead a parade.
The world cheers, as I march in front
and put on a big, boisterous front
so tyrannical, it's difficult to affront.
And dangerous too, I'm so empowered
(like the ward of a billionaire being endowered)
with rulership authority, over a whole lifetime
of those mired in inferior citizenship
subject to my authoritarian whims
that shackle their freedom that horribly dims:
Atheists forced to sing rowdy, belligerent hymns
of hell being the just reward
for those too impoverished to afford
their liberty to stop being slaves
subject to bloody, horrifying shaves
by throat-cutters with glistening knives
that slice apart their over-protesting lives
that are too liberal for me
and I go on a subsequent killing spree.
I'm the only one in the country who's even free
as the omniscient ruler, in solitary throne
over every politician I've ever overthrown
plus the entire public at large
in thrall to my constant barrage.
A tyrant? Oh no,
I'm the arch protector of my innocent country
that finds it difficult now in being free
due to the ownership that constitutes me:
a private nation of its own accord
that I humbly agreed to oversee
in the patriotic fervor I owe to strictly me.

AN OBSESSION TO IMPROVE MY SOCIAL LIFE BY BECOMING EXTREMELY POPULAR

Popularity is so compelling
to socially achieve,
I'll strive for it mightily
to win it over rightfully
and hold on to it frightfully
by being as charming as I can
among the ranks of women and men.
Any clues how to do it?
From past success, you may intuit
how to progress on this score.
I want many, many people, more
than you could ever believe,
to love me more and more
and even add to this score.
Is that monstrously greedy,
my need too grossly needy,
even revoltingly seedy?
This was considered repulsively overdrive
and was not too likely to survive.
Then I'll reverse my strategy
and appear hard to get
instead of obsessively well-met.
But the new approach succeeded too well.
My number of friends did not start to swell.
Playing hard-to-get rang no one's bell.
The new strategy betrayed me.
Instead of relishing great popularity,
now I'm chronically lonely
and for consolation I have me only.

AN OLD MAN'S DEATH-ATTITUDE, OR, LIVING FOREVER IS NOT POSSIBLE

I'm in my eighties, so the older I get,
the fear ought to grow closer to death
with grim forebodings of my limited breath
with a multiple tremor over my whole body
that narrows itself to be tomb-ready
with the unified stagger of being none too steady.
Yet I'm casually stoical about it.
There's no emergency, I'm not afraid.
Death is not planning a night-time raid.
I'm hiring nobody to come to my aid.
Why is my attitude calm and easy?
Because I can't arrest impending death
since I'm only a human old man,
with ambition limited only to the possible
which living dynamically forever
is not included under: it's only impossible.
Therefore to death I must stay grimly hospitable,
not that I welcome it, but my attitude is tolerant
since it's a very prevalent event to happen,
so I'm not tragically unique in this case.
My death would not crash the headlines
nor even the ordinary obituary deadlines.
So no big deal. If it comes,
may I have done all I could to prevent it;
And no greeter is there to present it
as something newsworthy. But I'm worthy.
I earned my entitlement
by longevity's accumulation of years
which grants me the honor of having no fears.
Being invisible, death never appears
as anything marked with a special image.
I can see right through it.
Yet, in prospect, I would rue it.

WARNING TO ATHLETES AND OTHERS

If you put yourself out,
don't do yourself in.
So if you want to win,
don't try to be too stout
and wear yourself too out,
thus giving yourself exhaustion,
allowing fatigue to force in
and upset your campaign to win
by extracting all your energy
and you pay a severe penalty
by lying prone on the ground
while the opponent dances around
singing a victory song
while you snore away along
and snuffle up a little clay
from the losing field where you play.
The coach complains, "You damn fool!
Go back to conservation school
to measure the breath you have left
but now in your lungs lies bereft.
We would have won, save but for your theft
despite your impressive appearance of heft."

TIED ON TO THE TIDE

In population just about equal,
men and women complete their unity
to split in half the human community
and breed together to engender sequels
of babies also divided by sex,
performing according to biology's text.
And the future summons us with "Who's next?"
after packing away the ones newly died.
Evolution's non-purpose sweeps along the human tide.
And you and I join it on our own impersonal ride.

A VERY COMMON THEME

By the holy stars above,
the way to go is love,
just like the crooners remind us
in vulgar night clubs, picking up the fuss
that love also has its downside
which they colloquialize as "blues,"
referring also to fabulous screws
love causes and is caused by,
that go up and dominate the sky
with meteors exploding.
Love wins the day,
having already capped the night.
Love will have its way
if everything goes right.
Love needs co-operation
to succeed in its operation
or else takes an untidy vacation
by way of divorce and grief
and misery beyond belief.
If love goes wrong,
sing the crooners' "blues" song
and hope it won't be long;
or give up in despair,
dissolving in air.

ANOTHER MAN

The old man's mind closed out
before he could review his whole life
and filter through his memories.
It was too late for that final project.
He'd really wanted to think it out
with the breathing energy he had left.
Death had a "right" to abruptly object
and gets the last non-word
to cut out desire and make it absurd.

Meanwhile, here's the world's usual self
without a collective consciousness to give a damn
for the routine ouster of just another man.

A WELL-EARNED EXCUSE

1.

Old age is such an excuse,
you can even claim an abuse
if a stranger knocks you over
by accident rushing for a bus.
You can make a contentious fuss.

2.

Old age is such an excuse,
your anger can light a fuse
if a stranger will still refuse
to give a crowded subway's seat
to you who are old-age frail
and look faint, soon to fail
in the attempt to still stand up
and you spill your full coffee cup
over your trousers to soak,
being subject to a crowd's joke
angering you, but you can't take a poke
at people for fear of succumbing to a stroke.

3.

Tremoring fingers on either hand
show physical weakness at a glance.
The days are over when you used to prance
and lead the cotillion at a dance.

PROVING YOUR INNOCENCE ON YOUR OWN TERMS

My attitude toward cops is: Keep your nose clean
to deprive them of an opportunity to be mean.
Don't do anything that looks illegal
even if, technically, it is so.
Give your morality a chance to grow.
Take an adult college class in ethics
even though it's difficult with metrics
and algebraic formations abstruse
that appear to be of no use.
Your attitude toward cops should be to shy away
but not conspicuously to arouse suspicion.
Be swift-fingered like a magician
and fleet on feet like a stealer of bases
so that cops have no basis
to even suspect such an innocent like you.
In a store if you're inclined toward theft,
lift something light, with no heft
to bulge out in your ample pockets.
Don't even steal light bulbs from their sockets.
Obey Aristotle's book on ethics
but first learn Greek instead.
Then, when you retire to bed
after a long day out on the street,
tell yourself, "I was discreet,
and avoid feeling the pang of guilt.
On this, I've formed a character truly built.
May my innocence never begin to wilt.
I'm a moral being, up to the hilt."

DIVERSE WAYS TO COMBAT BOREDOM WITH AN ASSORTMENT OF ATTEMPTS

Naturally, sometimes we get bored,
which the French have a word for: "ennui."
From that dry patch in life, go get relief
by stalking out what's fascinating

and stirs up your pleasant interest.
Go to an opera or a ball game
or watch children play in a public park.
Or watch airplanes dip or dive
at an airport; or attend a court trial
and for fun argue the jury's decision
but politely withhold your derision
to protect yourself from police scrutiny.
Thus you wage a personal mutiny
against boredom's civic possibility
as you go about an architecture-glamorous street
looking for the odd boredom-resistant treat
and make it unnecessary to yawn
when interesting diversions are born
from society's womb at large,
all conspiring to dislodge
innocent citizens from boredom's acute menace
by such pastimes as to watch a game of tennis
between old, evenly matched players
at a senior center's outside lawn
to provide passersby just like you
with an unusual spectacle to view;
when suddenly upon you it will dawn
that the world can give a gripping surprise
to anyone with a pair of star-studded eyes
and a mind with imagination to consume
with relish an art gallery's room
for which there's added incentive
that wine is free at an opening
which prompts us to kill boredom and just sing
a tune that chases ennui away
while world-wide people all endeavor to play
friendly or private games
like cards, chess, or bowling
or if an old woman, take up the art of sewing.

A DOOMED REBELLION DUE TO UNFAIR ODDS

Philosophically speaking, if we're planted on earth
by the intricate process of birth,
shouldn't we thank both parents
with gratitude and humble humility
to the best of our infantile ability?
How do parents reward us? With spanks.
With such punishment, why should we ever give thanks
plus obedience for their art of creating us
when those two are right now berating us?
We baby crowds in a mass endeavor
should protest with pickets to sever
ourselves from parental tyranny
that amounts to a universal conspiracy
against our innocent diaper brigade.
Like union strikers, we should go on parade
rattling our rattles to request freedom
from the cruel worldwide conspiracy
of universal parents controlling us with misery.
Notice how we wail and howl
as they wheel us around and scowl.
Can't we teach them to tell fair from foul?
They have the height on us
to quell our rebellion with slight fuss.
If only in retaliation we bite them?
Our teeth are too undeveloped to fright them,
with gums soft like our puffy cheeks
from which, for all our anger, no menace leaks
to accompany our innocent tears
in roley-poley admission of impotent fears.
We're subject to the insinuating leers
of the master over the helpless slave.
Yet they complain that they're the ones to slave.
Oh the eternal hypocrisy of the knave!

ADVICE FOR THE RECENTLY BORN, ONLY SO LATELY FROM THEIR MOTHER TORN

Once you're born, you desperately stay that way
with parental help. They're right there
and boy! do you need them!
To get their attention, cry "ahem!"
Then, they'll rush to your help
to avoid another piercing yelp
from your suddenly developed lungs
that seem to have exploded with growth.
Between mother and father you need both
if given a choice at your young age.
But mother's the more accessible one
so concentrate your pleading on her.
But to your father say, "Thank you, Sir,"
when finally he seems to notice you.
Be deferential. Give him credit.
Doesn't his sperm deserve some merit?

A FAMILY GROWS FROM TWO PEOPLE

The human genital
need not be too gentle
in ferociously plying its craft
to produce unity of unison
to get a daughter or a son
from the seeming antagonism
of two competing egotisms
in separate bodily weapons
to shoot each other into a new life
as their baby blesses their sweaty strife.
May they never divorce
as an anti-climax
to exerting their well-fueled force
to create a shiny new baby
in what's now at least a family.

HOW TO BREAK YOUR STUPID SKULL

Some women I had crushes on
but lost them anyway. A crush is no guarantee.
Imagine you could get everything you want!
But first you'd have to sign your entitlement papers
which no authority can ever endorse.
The official bureaucrats would have no remorse.
You're not on a "get what you want" course
which the world is obliged to honor.
Success? That's not always in the books.
The world being rosy? That's not how it looks.
Sorry to be so negative. But don't feel deprived.
I know someone who frequently failed. But he survived.
You too that could happen to.
Stop your foolish fancy to excel.
Philosophy teaches us it's not swell
to dwell in a constant fog of expectation.
Was the world made for your delectation?
Then pack your brains away for a vacation
and give your future a break
by breaking your tendency to earn a heart-ache
when every desire you thirst to slake
is an opportunity you jump at,
but an equally determined wall is there to bump at
which your skull will earn a big lump at.

ABSTRACTIONS IN FRUITLESS SEARCH OF CONCRETE EXAMPLES

The world is littered with concrete examples
that finally illuminate what the abstractions are.
But if the abstractions are too abstract,
they only obstruct, so that distracts me
from just what it was I was trying to get across
to make my point clear, but what was it?
I clean forgot, I'm lost in abstractions
that could construct concrete examples, but can't,

of their finally clearly-put-across construction
which proceeded with a faultless conduction
were it not for the abstractions' being muddled to begin with.
Why? Because the abstractions were messed up by inner confusion
that blocked up the whole point I eagerly sought
within the inner resources of rhetoric that came to naught
despite the fruitless fight I obstinately brought
to the whole mixup unresolved
by my not having a clue to what needed to be solved,
so that by the process of elimination
we finally solved the enigma of illumination.

TURNING IT AROUND (NOT ALWAYS EASY)

When whatever goes wrong, correct it,
certainly don't resurrect it,
before it gets out of hand
like a too-far stretched rubber band
on the verge of a collapse
added to such another lapse
of wrong things piling up
to fill your overflowing cup
of bad news you can't prevent
and horrible things impossible to invent.
Turn your life around
finding stability in safe-and-sound
and let the good times resound
when fortune rises to a rebound
and your feet land plant on the ground.
Fertilize yourself from ground up
and drink from a healthy overflowing cup.
It'll help your digestion to a burp-less sup.

WHAT'S LIFE? A HOPE THAT OTHER PEOPLE WILL LIKE YOU

When people like you, you feel well-liked,
that's a boost to morale and ego.
When people shun you, you feel lost,
lacking admiration and respect.
So then try getting people to like you.
Don't smile all the time, it'll look phony.
Don't frown all the time, you'll look lonely,
forlorn & discontent.
Don't act too smug and satisfied,
people will think you're conceited
and that from humility you've retreated.
Why all this bother about people?
They're worth it, so are you.
You're one of them. Don't you agree?
Well, not necessarily.
To me, I'm only me:
just one little quivering leaf
alongside others such, on a tree.
Maybe I should branch out more
that I'm akin to other people?
And don't they feel the same way?
If I swing in the wind, so do they.
We're all in the same boat—I mean tree.
Why switch metaphors in midstream?
As for life, what is it, a dream?
Oh, don't go to that extreme.
In life, you're wide awake,
and hope lots of people go to your wake
singing all the praises you'd love to take.

FORGING AN IDENTITY OF SORTS

Considering life, it's foisted on you
by generous-handed parents
who then left it to you with guidance
to forge your mysterious future

into what multiple forms it's going to take.
Well, how did it turn out, what shape,
if you can analyze so many intricate parts?
Did nature form you, or genetic mechanics,
or the people factor of nurturing you?
What gave you your essence and character?
What was your social attitude toward other people
to add to your identity with personality
within sudden circumstances
and situational happenstances?
In short, who the hell are you?
"It's me. Do you dare argue?"

AN ACADEMIC TEACHES SPRING

When spring throws its flowers up
in a sprinkle-dinkle cup,
winter knows its time is up
and surrenders to its milder successor.
To know this, you don't have to be a professor,
who delivers a boring, sermon-like lecture
but acknowledges spring with a flowering gesture.

SPRING'S APOLITICAL INNOCENCE

This part of the world opens up
to spring's sweet, modest buttercup
and other dainty, ornate flowers
that demonstrate their remarkable powers
to dare interrupt us
from political scandal and other such fuss,
to dwell upon the serene green
that seasonably upholds its predictable scene
and laughs gaily and doesn't seem mean.

ANY RATINGS DOWNFALL IN YOUR SOCIAL LIFE?

He's obsessed with what people think of him,
probing whether he could have made a better impression
if circumstances had just been twisted differently,
and he'd be blessed with others' good opinions,
or at least they don't think him peculiar
in the crazy sense or just off beam.
How does he fit in with someone else's dream?
Or do other people think of him at all?
Some do, some don't. There's so many of them.
Social life is a distressing jungle.
If he puts one step forward,
well then, where did he bungle?
What is he to them? But which "them"?
During the course of social life,
who you know will count a lot.
But how well do you know them?
And what's their standing, if any?
In name-dropping, be sure you drop the right name.
But what of yourself? What clout do you have?
Because, believe it or not, others could drop your name
and not necessarily just to point out your shame,
or single you out for a fair share of blame.
Gossip could cut both ways.
Just don't let it fill all your sad days
obsessing unnecessarily
over your relative popularity.
Are you thought well of? Or in disparity,
among the common general crowd
within the circles of your milieu?
Do many friends drop you? Or just a few?
But does it rankle? Any regrets?
Learn to cut your social bets,
and whom to chase after, but not too drastically
as to think of him over-fantastically.
Make sure you have some pride left
after being dropped so much makes you feel bereft
of any solid human contact;

but it's not in the social contract
that things go smoothly in your favor.
How do people regard you? Don't quaver
if you're not included in the current social flavor
and the gang will just reject you
after, unfairly brief, they dismissingly inspect you.
How do others see me?
That's too much emphasis in how I be me.
If I'm too indifferent, I'll be left out
when their indifference will overcome mine
in the mutual lack of being benign
with spite and deadly venom.
If you can't beat them, join them,
not to be squeezed out to the loneliness pit
where no one listens to the nuggets of your wit
in your disgraceful relegation to the socially unfit.

PORTRAIT OF A WISEGUY

What's your philosophy of life?
That I take one day at a time
and stay out of crime, unless
I can get away with it
by playing the game with lots of wit
and cunning to be clever
not to be caught trying a trick
on others. In short, I'm a prick,
but I quickly get out of the thick
and outwit the cops if I can,
but reduce risks to a minimum.
With my cereal I crave a little cinnamon.
But at least I'm no immigrant.
I was born right here
in the good old Northern Hemisphere.
So really, what have I got to fear?

GET OUT THERE, YOU FOOL!

I've been around the block a lot, so I know the ropes.
If you've been too enclosed to be out there, you become dopes.
Unless you're conversant with your contemporaries,
you lack the common touch and become a solitary
with your brain's images stuck repetitively
in stale rut roundly consecutively
without going anywhere much.
Learn variety and other people.
See them brazenly straight, not through a peep-hole.
Then the outer world widens up as a whole
and rescues you from your worm-vision hole
and returns your birthright that you narrowly stole.

AN OVERVIEW

Riding the high tide of evolution
quite a bit of time after
our human race started,
we find that the genders are still parted,
like partitions between close neighbors
on geography's claustrophobic scale.
Such an intrigue we'll have to deal with
like family matters between kin and kith.
We?! No, nature does it for us.
We don't do the dealing: we're dealt.
We're given lots of feelings: with them we've felt
and go according to human nature,
what it permits us within its confines.
You figure out what's yours; I mines.
Good. I'm glad we've set the dividing line.
You're open to persuasion while I opine.
What can we do, or are done to,
and felt for, within the human compass?
Compass leads us soon to compassion
for all of us and our outstanding passion.

ARRIVING IN PARIS

Suicide is absolutely fatal.
It wipes out your life promise that began natal.
But at least it showed your capacity for self-reliance.
Suicide-assistance services can be expensive
and their over-all damage can be just as extensive,
as if you eliminated assistance like Lindbergh
who sought Paris to see the high-kick dancers,
all female, who wore period costumes
that revealed as much as they concealed,
until his avid interest congealed
as Lindbergh's head went flop
on the ritzy nightclub table;
for his all-night flight rendered him unable,
by the twin forces of exhaustion and fatigue,
as well as being in the "frequent-flyers" league.
He was dizzy about flying there.
He suffered a case of vertigo
so that he didn't even know "where-to-go,"
but wound up in Paris instead
for if he didn't stop somewhere, he would lose his head
plus the fame he gained
in his all-alone unassisted flight
in the whizzing air of transatlantic day and night
to arrive in Paris and see the follies
that boosted his morale with the jollies,
looking at the high-kick dancers
in their role of exotic foreign enchanters
of whom he soon became a connoisseur
that gave him the phony title of a "Sir,"
and terminated his simple solo tour.

YOUR TRUE SELF

The way not to appear to be a phony
is to reduce so many pretenses to one only,
or even less than one if you want to be sincere
and cut out the mere show of how you appear.
Posturing can screw up the impression you make
with the semblance of something authentically fake.
And all the time you must contrive
to keep your outer aspects fully alive
to what covertly they've been hiding
from all the affectations you've been riding
and what to people you've falsely been confiding
which they innocently have been abiding.
Fooling others can diminish friendship
with a tongue that deliberately makes a slip.
A very detailed pronouncement can be a blip,
thus letting confidence go astray.
Better to wish someone to "have a good day,"
with a solemn straight face for the cliche (clichay),
upgrading your marks into a straight "A"
in polite social civility
for which you've demonstrated ability
to hide your deepest feeling
under the lowest possible ceiling.
Conceal the more, that's what you reveal
to dubiously raise up a false appeal.

MY GENERATION'S TURN

My friends die one by one; when is my turn?
Old age is our primary disease
from which we fall apart and simply decease.
Generationally we're at that unfortunate group
to be allied in age and also its misfortune.
We're guilty of having lived overlong
and blame our parents for birthing us too early.
Well, we had decent longevities

for the most part, but one by one
we find it painfully easy to succumb.
Without anesthesia, we become numb.
Our proud intellects are nowhere "there"
within an enclosed region: no air.

MY LIFE, MY WIFE

I love Candace Watt, who's my wife.
For better or worse, I've shared my life
for the last fifty years
(producing many laughs and tears)
with this same woman into mutual old age,
always in the same book, on the occasional different page.
We've been through all kinds of stresses
but always with commitments to the same addresses,
where our love enlarges as it progresses,
bearing up with some understandable stresses
which each of us in turn addresses.
In short, she means all of love to me,
worth it all through the payment of any fee.

A CONSTANT TRIBUTE

Who do I care about a lot?
She's my wife, Candace Watt.
Of her many attributes,
she's serious, but full of cutes,
though old age now wilts her down,
but me too, we share the same crown,
and will be together always
while life in our veins still plays.
I commend us to further sweet days
while longevity blesses us and stays.

BEING A CONVERSATIONAL ITEM

I overheard being called "incurably sane."
Is that an ironic compliment
mixed with ambiguity,
or just an easy superfluity
in the realm of social humor?
Thus I was subject to rumor.
Gossip is an assumer
spoiling truth like a tumor,
but nevertheless harmless
by celebritizing the charmless
into people talked about,
elevating their dubious clout
in the social whirlwind of "in" and "out."
Flexible opinion need not shout,
nor insult create the excuse to pout.
Keep your composure and remain stout.

WHAT DEATH DOESN'T MANAGE TO EXPRESS BY ITSELF

The airless enclosure of no air
is my area soon.
Then my nose will be useless,
also my lungs will be no use,
not even using them for an excuse.
No use to light a fuse
under my unrevisable body
which might as well belong to anybody.
Once death occurs,
my voice will emit no purrs.
Communication will not be my asset.
Nor will verbal facility be a facet.
As for personal history, I'll be past it.
Results of death pile up.
Not even half empty will be my cup.
As for food, I'll go without any sup
on a pre-arranged diet to the maximum.

As for alcoholism, I'll be sworn off rum.
No beat-beat rhythm on my pulse's own drum.
Nor will people even know where I'm from.
Purely without a self, I'll be left with no sum,
and voiceless emit intimations I'm dumb.
If I had emotions, I'd be grum.

CURING TWO DIVIDINGS IN ONE VOW

Do I have more trouble with myself,
or with other people?
I must patch it up between me and them;
and also put a strong bandage
on the severance of me from me
to cover up this appalling civil war,
thus me to myself restore
and we'll be united as before.
Then with other people I'll cure
that stupid division between me and them
and be in harmony with the human race
and to all of them turn a smiling face
to show I really mean it
to cure alienation and clean it
from the unfriendly people-disease
if the world would grant us that, please.
What an opportunity I'll seize!
Warfare and all that, to appease,
and end all struggles with peaceful ease.
Give harmony a full-bodied squeeze.
Me loves me and them loves them
and I love them, oh glory be!
How ideal the human race can be!

AN UPSHOT NOT AVAILABLE

Evolution keeps on producing new history.
Our race plods ahead, yet the mystery
keeps blurring us with fogs anew
of what to do with our brimming planet.
Or even, in some weird way, understand it.
Meanwhile, expanding populations cram it
and terrifying weapons threaten to jam it.
What's the upshot of all this?
If I knew it, I'd be a whiz
in getting a true hint in what there really is
beneath the surface blur and the angry hiss.
Give humanity an embracing kiss.

OPENLY EXPOSING GENITALIA

The genitalia is never on obvious display
unless at a nudist colony
or in an illegal immorality house
pretending to be an anti-flea place of de-louse
or a decontamination center for a mouse.
So we have our clothes to cover genitalia
to prevent the open view to the public
from opening up a scandal case
just for a sensationalist court trial
protested by political extremists
who advertise themselves as pro-American dreamists
all because genitalia should be kept away
at vulgarity's expense from public display
due to the shame attending it
because it's too close to the pubic area,
creating an atmosphere of sheer mass hysteria
just because of a bunch of Puritans
whose blazing banner was anti-shame.
Now we know where to cast the blame.
It all makes for an ugly scene
that puritans greedily depict as obscene,

calming their nerves and making them serene.
But who are we all to demean
them? Aren't we of their persuasion?
Genitalia should be hidden on every occasion
unless bidden for a private exception
like urinating or defecation,
or creating future babies shorn of detection,
by the combination of vagina and erection
hidden by doors architecturally closed
but not by the bothersome obstruction of clothes
that leave free genitalia's area
closely at the pubic scenery
open privately to the twosome
who together are perfectly legal
but would to prying eyes be gruesome
in together applying fusion
to enjoin nature's highly sought twosome.

THE CON MAN COMPETITION, WON BY A LANDSLIDE (TRUMP VERSUS JESUS)

The world's dirtiest little secret
(that people are afraid to even speak it)
is that Jesus was more of a con man than Trump.
Let colliding dogmas go bump.
Jesus was a salesman of heaven and hell
but those two items were impossible to sell.
So as a con man Jesus knew how to excel.
If humanity wakes up, will it ring a sanity bell?

But adamant christians will consign me to hell
and even escort me there, if possible,
in the face of delusion and the improbable,
that heaven trumps the good news of grace and will.
Jesus knows best. He promises the greater thrill
that Trump will never match,
who's only a bogus political snatch.

THE GREATER THE LOVE, THE MORE DEATHLY THE REJECTION

The shock of maligned expectation
in the face of strong and passionate love-hope
so stuns me; and my emotions choke,
hoping my dear love was mouthing a joke,
when she apologizes: "Martin, I don't love you.
On another man I train my fickle view
and place him in my heart far above you.
I no longer have any feeling for you, dear phantom.
I love him. But you I stamp on.
Now leave me to my faithless life, as I tramp on.
I'd marry him. That will put a legal stamp on
my harsh betrayal of you.
I know you're bitter, but that's my final view.
Now swallow the pill and dismally chew.
If suicidal, disobey that romantic cue.
It'll never work on me, as an inconsequential woo."

A COST WORTH TAKING?

Don't let death scare you.
Maybe it'll even spare you,
making you the first in history
of the human species
ever to escape death's disease
by allowing you never to decease:
the only favor given to anyone
with special exceptionalism that will stun.
But won't you be too old to have any fun?

The price of being too unique
is that you're so dottering that you'll leak
with a frail and puny physique.
Isn't that the lowest possible peak
that you'll still persist to seek
at the expense of being a charmed freak:
strong in history, but in body weak?

THE EVOLUTION EXPRESS

Hop aboard the Evolution Express,
and then you'll soon know what's best.
It'll boom you along at high function
through breakfast, dinner and luncheon
at swhizzing optimal speed
to help you organically succeed.
It's cooked in advance the requisite proteins
and syncopated your reflexes
to co-ordinate your best instincts
by preparing your good old DNA
before your hair even gets gray.
On Evolution Express take a goodly perch
which you don't even have to purchase.
Hop along, look at all the views
through the world's clearest windows to peruse
how the outside looks back at you.
You're fully fit in your whole species
for this well-prepared organizational ride.
Don't fall off the Evolution Express
until at which point you've already died,
having mainly preserved your hide
for family funeral expense.
It was a journey well worth taking
till old age started your aching
and the Evolution Express stuttered to a stop,
urging you and some others "get off," before it whizzed on
to benefit your survivors at high speed,
rumbling along to its multiple democratic deed
on the well-greased tracks.
It takes you away but never takes you backs.
Once you're off, you can fatally "relax."

ASSUMING THE WORST

If life revolves at a dizzy pace,
rearrange the wrinkles on your face
and take a respectable place
in society's status arrangements
and avoid any estrangement
from orderly public procedure.
Don't allow yourself a cardiac seizure
that's untimely and embarrassing.
Don't allow misfortune's harassing,
for bad luck is a curse
that depletes the body and its subsequent purse
and leads only to a lonely hearse
which in poverty you neglected to rehearse.
Just imagine anything worse.
Awful? That's the least of it.
Life's beastly loss of your wit
puts you unimaginably in a fit.
No, not even pride can reclaim you.
As a cadaver, who can name you
with a straight face
to the rhythm of life's normal pace?
Society nudges: you've lost your place.

DON'T CONFUSE ME

Is the world responsible for life?
Or is life responsible for the world?
Don't give me enigma or conundrum.
It's too convoluted to be any fun.
Don't saddle me with puzzles
that make for no easy guzzles.
It's not even intriguing
to be so beleaguering
in what I can't just figure out.
It makes life too weighty a bout
between itself and the whole darned world

to even begin to know what's being unfurled.
(Pause for dramatic emphasis;
for music also, if you insist.)
The cat's graceful posture in being curled
in a dream is easier to contemplate
with my simple eyes on his lovely state.
On that spectacle, let my mind debate.

AN EMBARRASSMENT

The way I was, when not too old
to attract women physically,
I could carelessly flirt whimsically
without the least timidity.
But now, that's another story.
I can't acquit myself with glory
because of the dread disease, impotence.
It takes away my erotic sense,
for which, alas, there's no recompense.
It's like a death sentence
of a vital "part of me."
To all women I say "Pardon me."
But anyway, they're not regardin' me,
since my reputation now stinks.
I don't even get any flirting winks
from women at large
who heard about my lack
and subject me to a mocking attack
at my puny member that's slack,
devoid of a push and shove back
to prove my manhood.
Manhood? That's a laugh.
Alas for my former rigid staff,
of which I retain far less than half.

TO LIVE FOREVER IS TO BE TIME'S THIEF. TRUE?

Uniquely to be spared by death,
given renewable pulse and breath,
is a favor to be denied
to everyone who ever lived.
Would you be the charmed exception?
Sure, but with what objection?
To my body being so broken down
that it's riddled with pestilence and disease
that would perennially never cease
and even get progressively worse,
which is an unrelenting curse.

Certainly, that would curtail my ease
and make it virtually impossible to please
my necessary sense of well being.
Do you call that a "human being,"
subject to pain all the time
in the torture of bodily hell
that no Health Insurance Plan can ever quell?
I'd only try it for a little spell
and then return to usual mortality,
relieved by good old death's relief
and reconciled to an occasional religious belief.
Who are we, to try to be time's thief?

COMPENSATING A MISTRESS

1.

He wrestles with his demon
to pry loose his semen
from ancient cock and testicles
and get a little old-age pleasure
if only the semen could be discharged
instead of being bottled up
in his genitalia's ancient cup
so his mistress could finally shut up.

2.

His impotence has so old-age grown,
his manhood produces a continual moan,
and you should hear his mistress's groan,
especially to her friends on the telephone,
doing his reputation no good
as to where still stands his manhood
after living apparently too long
to sing a boastful manly song.

3.

Before long, his manhood may shrink further.
He may speak to his mistress and urge her
not to despair, she'll get plenty in his will
so her lust for money at least he can fulfill
and hope she'll be thus compensated
for his miserable excuse of a penis
"that can't even come between us,"
shrunk to the size of an infant's member,
leaving only the tint of an ember
from that fiery furious fire
before his youthful days had to expire,
turning an unjuiced cock ever drier
with no cockle pump to even hire.

4.

The embers of his fire
are remnants now for sale
as a total collapse of a male,
making any other disgrace pale
in comparison of what's frail.
Soon life itself is doomed to expire
and the mistress will inherit a money empire
to serve remembrance on the funeral pyre,
whose flame impotently prepares to expire.
(This tale told to me, unless I'm a liar.)

THE MERCURIAL NATURE OF THE "NOW"

Now is so temporary, it soon whizzes by.
Then if you try to retrieve it, you're too late,
it disappeared into the vast past
that recently had just passed,
so we knew it couldn't last;
and at the last minute you bungled,
your aspirations tumbled,
and by that time, you were too humbled
to try to run after it, so you gave up.
You almost knew it couldn't last.
You forgot to hold on to it fast.
It blurred by too fast
to even regret that you had barely missed it
or by a lofty margin
so you had to give in.
Given this velocity, you can never win.
The Now can cause your head, back and forth, to spin.
The mercurial nature of the Now:
Elusiveness in direct flight,
turning recent day into then night.
The time colliding with its own brain;
Dryness dissolved into its own rain.
Nature outpaced, eradicating even its gain.
Now is impossible to catch:
We're blind to the obvious overmatch.
The mercurial nature of the Now.
It's too swift for cumbersome sight.
Its speed even confuses our delight,
that we put up with it without a fight,
left sorely behind
to try to recapture our own mind.
Where did its sequel go? Thence.
Arrival ended with a sudden whence.
I gave myself a terrific wince.

A PAINLESS INQUIRY INTO THE HORRIBLE THEME OF PAIN

What does pain feel like
that the world commonly avoids it
if at all possible?
It just feels awful and dreadful.
Will that limited description suffice
to make you see that pain is not necessarily nice?
No, because there are all kinds of pain
which you'd have to codify into a lengthy list
to break them apart and persist
from the general to the specific
in many numerical cases.
Of my investigation, that's the basis.
It also includes the severity
of pain "from one to ten."
As an inquiry, this is painstaking.
Nevertheless, it's worth taking.
This sun is too hot, I'm baking.
And my insomnia is a miserable unawakening.

WHAT REJECTION DID TO ME

My girlfriend rejected me and I was despondent.
I wrote her a begging letter but she didn't respondent.
So I had to shred my love for her
because she persistently ignored my letter.
She had apparently found someone better.
The doldrums I plunged into
amounted to a dizzy spin to
the dissolving of my sanity glue
that had held together
the parts of me that needed to co-ordinate
to keep my brain from being inchoate.
Thus resounded the fatal drooping of my fate.
My smashed love left me only as the advocate of hate.

GENERALITIES ABOUT—WHAT ELSE?—LIFE ITSELF (MIXED IN WITH ADVICE)

The world is where so much can happen
and some of it happens to you
in a global population not few.
Some things go wrong that you can't sue
because litigation has limits
when lawyers clash, with their trained wits.
Take your choice of life's best bits
but also be generous to others,
since we're all sisters and brothers
on our whole race's family tree
that branches out to more than you and me.
Treat others kindly. But don't forget yourself
whom you identify: neither giant nor elf.
Don't die out and land on the shelf
like a dreary discarded good
in a shabby neighborhood
where previous better times had stood
and now looks like another lump of wood.
Preserve yourself if only you would
and some chance events allow you a "could,"
the way things can turn out
between polar extremes of lean and stout.
Duck devastating blows
and see how life goes
in its practically fatal bout,
and tell me what it's all about.

AN ABRUPT TERMINATION OF FRIENDSHIP

I was tempted today, but resisted it.

Oh, too bad.

No, don't be prematurely sympathetic. It was actually good for me, as it turned out, in the long run, to resist that original temptation.

(WARMING UP TO IT) This may be intriguing. but I need a full explanation. Go ahead.

Should I start with the full set of circumstances?

That would provide the background information, to clear the path for my full receptivity of your narrative.

Don't bother to build up any preparatory suspense.

But you set me up. I'm impatiently waiting.

Well, first stop your impatience, and then stop the actual waiting altogether. It'll avail you nothing, since I won't oblige you.

That's a perverse turn of events. Are you willfully frustrating me?

Yes, since it's within my power, and I don't like you.

But what happened? We were friends.

Just impulsively and arbitrarily, I end our friendship, for the fun of upsetting your two expectations: First, the expectation of my explaining why I resisted the temptation today; and secondarily, my startling, plus puzzling, peremptorily ending our whole entire friendship, which arbitrarily cut across many years of our harmonious times together.

Just like that? I'm shocked.

Well, you ought to be. I manipulated you thus.

But is that fair?

Now you're introducing morality. I won't play.

PROBING WHAT KIND OF LIFE A STONE LEADS IN HIS AUTHENTIC REPUTATION

A stone inherently or intrinsically has a hard life.

Yes, he makes it hard on himself. By essence, it's his own fault.

Can't he break his internal "essence" mold?

No, because then he would not really be himself.

He would stop being his true and authentic self?

What else can he be? He's not a soft-bellied cloud with break-through vapor mechanism.

No, that sounds wishy-washy.

Sounds!? It IS, you dolt.

ENOUGH OF THE INNER LIFE

Does everyone have an inner life?

Sure. Especially the secretive, the anal-retentative, the introverts, and anyone who harbors something in concealment or shame.

Is an inner life an impediment to an active, functioning life?

Not necessarily. It can be a pause in normal decision-making, to deliberate on what to do next or later. It can facilitate an inspired choice, a breakthrough in stalled activity, and other encumbrances that bottle you up for momentary lapses in motor activity of engagement with the outside world.

So it's okay I go ahead with deep-thinking subjectivity as long as it leads to something beyond its current stiflement?

No law against an inner life, so long as it doesn't brood up a plot of atrocious inhumanity which it then gives vent to without moral bonds.

Sounds like a police state.

No, we police ourselves: on the honor system.

But don't people occasionally cheat?

Oh yes. That's why it's so covert and furtive.

Then people with inner life are cowards?

Oh shut up. I can't go on like this.

A NON-REVELATION

How are your wants today?

Well, one of them reached an emergency level, to the intense extent of urgency.

Oh, do tell.

It started with a situation, and a set of surrounding circumstances.

That's reality for you. How did you face it?

With desperation.

Of course. What actually happened?

Well, the situation got out of hand.

Of course. I understand. Could you retail the specifics?

I'm at a loss.

Have you repressed it? Was it that bad?

It's all repressed. I can't supply you with information.

Thanks for wasting my time.

That ironic tone increases my helpless guilt.

(WALKING AWAY) Here I am, angrily departing. You teased me, seeming to promise me an interesting event, but the telling stalled with permanent interruption. Was it a ruse you planted on me? (BUT NOW TOO FAR AWAY TO HEAR THE ANSWER, WHICH WASN'T FORTHCOMING ANYWAY.)

PROBLEMS SEMI-SOLVED

In general, what is life?

Being alive.

Doesn't that definition lack detail?

Plenty of details it lacks. But we don't have enough time for all of them.

In that case, what is time?

Keeping things in order. It prevents everything from happening all at once, in a chaotic coinciding of events, a mish-mash.

You're right. Neatness counts. Everything in its proper order and proper place.

Otherwise we can go crazy, right on the spot.

Let's take the time and space to sort things out. "One at a time" is my motto.

One WHAT at a time?

Everything, just about.

That's all inclusive?

What's the point of disincluding anything? That's ungenerous, not to mention illiberal.

Also inhumane?

Humanity is a minority race.

That figures. We're outnumbered.

CALLING THINGS BY NAMES

Are you in need?

Always.

Also in want?

That too.

Want is more urgent than hope?

Want is more optimistic than hope. Want has more expectation of succeeding, whereby hope is nebulously partially doubtful of getting what it hopes for.

Do we have to be careful of what we want?

Yes, want is risky. Failing to get it can lead to disappointment, frustration, anger, despair, and in extreme cases suicide.

So we have to hedge our wants?

I'm not a gardener. What do you mean by that?

Not get our hopes up too high, by assessing in advance the probability or possibility quota of the realistic prospects of attaining this wish or that wish.

Is wish a synonym for want?

Yes, both can connote the arrogance of entitlement, the robust satisfaction of semi-assured success, once we survey the field.

We assess the realism of arriving at satisfaction as opposed to failure, and estimating how devastating the failure might be, depending on what's at stake.

Do we estimate those things instinctively?

Sometimes. Like a bird or squirrel whose instinctive reflexes make wise decisions to dare this or to dare that—avoid accidents and other mishaps or disasters. But at other times, we mull over this likelihood or that one—not only mull, but obsess, accompanied by anxiety, fear, desperation, and other fierce emotions.

What do you conclude from all this?

Conclude? No conclusion. Life carries on, let's follow it to every step along the way: achieving partial success or partial failure, and learning lessons that point morals in the process of incessant learning, revisions, and attitude changes.

All in one person?

All in any organic being, even amoeba, along the ranges of the simple and the complex.

Is this called "philosophy"?

No name-calling, which, if not impolite, is at least rude.

WHAT ENVY DID

If by chance your timeless death has the good luck to be interrupted, grab that opportunity for dear life and hold on desperately, for that chance may never come your way again.

Your advice is futile—it's meant for if I'm dead in the first place, which I'm certainly not. Look how alive I am! (PUNCHES THE OTHER MILDLY ON THE SHOULDER.)

All right, don't increase your evidence. I withdraw that useless hypothetical advice, especially in light of your insulting response.

Which you deserved. Don't play games with fancy. You postulated my already being dead, which is a crazy liberty you took with me. Are you concealing a hidden wish that I'd be dead?—Since you appear recently to have resented me?

I confess. (HEAD SLUMPS.) I envied you.

What a severe punishment you had in store for me, due to your envy! Now explain.

Your pretty wife is alive, and mine (PAUSES IN MISERY) died.

Oh, what a petty reason! Accompanied by my wife, I went to her funeral, didn't I? And I even cried for you!

At the wake you ate too much.

Does hunger deserve such punishment?

Look, we're human. Let's forget it. (HANDS AROUND EACH OTHER'S SHOULDERS.)

I knew you'd come around, some way.

SPECULATIONS IN THE REALM OF THE UNMISTAKABLY DEFINITE

In general, is life our state of being?

If we're lucky, yes.

What if we're not lucky?

Then we're either dead or yet to be born.

Better yet to be born, because then you still have a chance, even though not yet. But death means that for you it'll be all over, without recurrence, on the strict principle of "one to a customer."

Are you being metaphysical?

Not the least. I'm nothing if not practical.

Then if you're a realist, what do you mean by realism?

It means that what's out there is not lost to—or on—you; that you take in strict account what, including other people, shares the world with you. It means you're not just in your own head. It means you're taking part in the out-there, wherever that is.

In fact, where is it?

Somewhere. When I figure it out, you'll be the first to know.

I appreciate this privilege you grant me. But can I rely on you?

Truth is what I'm made of.

Truth? What are you talking about?

THE MOTHER

As my son, you'll always have to obey me, despite your being middle-aged and me doddering.

But I'm not a child any more.

No matter. My wishes come first. They always did, and must remain so, especially as your father selfishly abandoned me so that my consolation is to tyrannize you.

But by so imposing your selfish will on me, you inadvertently retard my adult maturity development. You're holding me back. I hold no reputable standing in the community, and it's your fault.

Don't pile your blames on me. I am what I am, so let's leave it at that.

But I'm ridiculed as a dead-beat all up and down our critical community.

Don't be so self-conscious about it. Even put it out of your mind, so you won't nag and complain, which annoys me to an extreme length.

But don't you care at all that I'm a laughing-stock and they gossip that you're to blame?

"They?" Who are they?

The community, with which we live.

At this rate, you leave me with only one alternative, which is to excommunicate you as my son; so from now on you're on your own. Leave our house, I don't care where.

But I have no money, not even a bank account, to afford to rent an apartment or wherever.

You demean me as a mother.

I don't "demean" you, because you ARE mean.

Don't let's word-quibble. Out! (WITH THAT IMPERIOUS AND AUTOCRATIC GESTURE, AND FINAL CLIMACTIC ONE-WORD, PIERCING UTTERANCE IN A DRAMATIC TONE, SHE CAUSES THE CURTAINS TO FALL IN WASHING HER GRIMED HANDS OF ALL REMAINING MATERNAL RESPONSIBILITY FOR HER BY-NOW RETARDED SON. CONSEQUENTLY HE SUFFERS; BUT WHAT'S *SHE* FEELING? WHATEVER IT IS, SHE REFUSES TO ALLOW ME, THE SCRIBE, TO INCRIMINATE HER. SHE WANTS IT BOTH WAYS, TO AVOID BEING PENNED AS A VILLAIN, WHICH, IN THE EYES OF THE COMMUNITY AT LARGE, AND IN MY EYES TOO AS THE SCRIBE, SHE CERTAINLY IS.)

FATHER VERSUS DAUGHTER, ARGUING OVER HER RECENT TATTOOS

I being your father, and you being my currently thirteen-year-old daughter, don't I have a perfect right to, from the point of aesthetics, object to your inflicting your temptingly lovely thirteen-year-old body with these vulgar tattoos, all the more conspicuously displayed now that the current month of June's hot weather allows your public clothing to be reduced to openly display the vulgarity of your inappropriate tattoos, paid for by the monthly allowance money I painstakingly earn and paternally hand over to you?

That's it, Pop: "hand." You "hand" over the money to me, but it's your very "hand" whose molesting I object to. Why must you paw my burgeoning body, however tempting?

I don't intend illegal incest, if that's what you're driving at. But why do you expose inappropriately your twin juicy thighs in increasingly immodest postures that dangle from the upholstery of living room couches and chairs?

Pop, don't you see, or are you morally blind?

I sure see, in your open display on view.

I'll be honest with you. The very reason I adorn my young body with the tattoos you so vehemently object to on aesthetic grounds, is because they disgust you: in order to actually discourage your inappropriate paternal lust from obscenely manifesting itself in outrageously criminal behavior of an intimate nature.

What a prude you are! Did I bring up my daughter to be a prude?

In self-defense, Daddy. In self-defense. I don't want your ugly old body to give itself fatherly permission to illegally rape me.

You prude! You're rationalizing!

Don't I have a perfect right to do that? After all, you're my father, you big brute.

Oh yeah? Your mother doesn't think so, and she ought to know.

She's a pathetic chronic liar!

Look who's talking!

Oh what an unruly family I find myself innocently involved with! Why do you wolfishly exploit my being a helpless teen-ager?!

Oh, don't give me that drivel! I first accused you of flaunting your temptability upon my helpless masculine vulnerability. Are you turning the tables in this exploitation switch? Or are we speaking the same language?

Far from ME exploiting YOU, you actually exploit my helpless daughter role with your vulgar and unseemly lust as a mere helpless male!

I now punish you by ordering you to go back to that same infamous tattoo shop to get a total wholesale bodily erasure of these revolting tattoos.

But the tattoo artist needs his recent art to have time to dry off my lovely adolescent body, otherwise its premature removal would painfully jeopardize my precious health.

You fraud! No wonder our family is an outrageously dysfunctional mess!

Don't act so innocent! You're involved!

YOU'RE the one who pretends to be innocent, you tempting little morsel!

Daddy! Through and underneath all this, I secretly suspect that we really love each other, if truth be told!

Could we secretly elope?

(DEMURELY AND COMPETITIVELY:) No. Mother would object.

A REVELATION BETTER NOT SPREAD

By now I've actually accumulated enough arithmetically additional years to almost convince myself (shaking my own shoulders with my own hands) that I'm no longer 1. a child, 2. an adolescent, 3. a young man. Did it really happen to me that indeed I'm old (as of this present writing, being written down with unmistakable ink in my own now increasingly shaky and wobbly handwriting, evincing tremors)? Old enough to get and keep worried that my valued consciousness is no longer guaranteed to be permanent. This is disastrous.

Should I spread the alarm to my still-alive old friends and acquaintances? No, I'm sure they've already heard this uneasy and unnerving rumor that one day there'll be no tomorrow, which used to seem like an incomprehensible abstraction, an algebraic equation required to be memorized in order to approximate the required heft and hang of its internal mystery willfully untranslatable.

What a revelation this is!—an epiphany. But maybe I better keep this insight to myself. If told, it seems to be dripping with the ugly stinky juice of unpopularity serum, which could diminish my already slenderizing social status in the surrounding community into a shriveled, virtually disappearing wisp.

THE PRIDEFUL WARNER; THE HONEST DIE-ER

What's more important than life? Save it.

But it's in no immediate danger.

You never can tell. Be prepared anyway.

But I feel perfectly healthy.

"Feel" is one thing. But you can't tell what's going on in there. You're no doctor.

(FALLS DOWN, HAND TO HEART, WITH SLURRED SPEECH.) Hey, you had a point there. You were prescient. I credit you with warning me. Can you go a little step further, and foil this seeming emergency by saving me, provided, of course, there's sufficient time? (COLLAPSING, DIES.)

Well, I was right saying "You never can tell." You illustrated my point surprisingly quick. But I won't make this a boasting point. Why take advantage of a man when he's down? But I sure feel on the ball.

(REVIVES BRIEFLY.) Better you than me. (THEN RESUMES DEATH, THIS TIME PERMANENTLY.)

He shouldn't have inflated my tendency to be righteous. The bum spoiled me in his final act.

A GIFT CONVERSATION

I interrupted my death to say, "I wish I was back there. My nostalgia is acute."

Did anyone hear you?

No-one was around. It was a social desert.

How unlucky. You were merely talking to yourself, like a psycho.

Then I dropped back into my death, with an uneasy resumption.

Are you okay now?

No. Death is hell. You should try it.

Why should I? I'm better off here.

Here? Where is that?

Where you would love to be, you lump of shit.

I'm already down. Why pile it on with an insult?

Does it matter? This conversation is unlikely anyway. We're just pushing our luck to be in it.

Yeah. We should thank our poet who put us here.

OBSESSED WITH DEATH? JOIN THE CROWD

(scene: 2 gabbing men, anywhere.)

Is death real, like for example a fire engine?

That's a wrong comparison or simile, because a fire engine is by popular reckoning loud-clanging and rip-roaring like a charging bull lurching at the red cape on its socially imperative duty in the grip of alarm and acute alert; while death is notoriously sedate and even signifies nothing, according to ancient poems of a contemporary aspect.

Death and a fire engine? They're two different things entirely. They're in separate and don't fit in the same bracket.

Death has quieted things down and snuffed noise, whereas fire engines are loud and blaring in their frenzied pursuit.

But death is divisive with EVERYTHING, not just something like a fire engine. That's how non-inclusive it is.

Yes, it calms everything down to a uniform pallor.

It goes even beyond, or less than, pale.

We're giving death too much discussion. Stop referring to it.

It might jinx us.

Let's just call it bad news and leave it at that.

No, you can't leave it, once it gets its hooks on you.

No, not literally leave it—leave it as a SUBJECT.

Sure, better than subjecting yourself to it.

Death doesn't run on a pun.

Get death out of your head or else smile its image to death.

What image? Does it even have an image?

It's too vague and metaphor-empty.

Are you calling it nothing?

Substantially, yes.

QUIBBLING OVER WORDS

Never visit death. It's like a no-escape trap. Odds are, you'd never get out of it alive.

You advocating I become a coward?

Yeah. Demeaning to be a coward, but uplifting for your cowardly reward.

Better safe than sorry?

That should be your permanent motto.

Permanent? NOTHING is permanent, you fool.

Yeah? Then try death.

Try it! A little sample could prove fatal.

A little goes a long way?

Yes, it travels direct to nothing, by way of paradox.

Paradox is only a word.

Rhetoric is safe. But I can't say the same for death.

Yes. It's its own fatal sentence.

LIVING IN THE COZY SUBURBS

I live on the outskirts of death.

Then is death a city and your outskirts are the suburbs?

I'm safe and sound there in the suburbs. The "city" is merely an enlarged cemetery where you dump death's pestilence victims.

Better to commute than to be mute?

Better to stay clear, and never commute.

But if you never commute, how do you make a living by not going to the office where wholesale commerce thrives, not just the cemetery business?

That's a metaphorical, not an actual, problem, which deals with city planning and avoids the central death dump.

A metaphor is a safe distance to discuss a subject that if you're subjected to it, you're too already dead to play around with the metaphor game.

Keep it as a discussion subject rather than you as its subject.

Literal-minded life keeps you out of the central harm of death, whose actuality is effaced by our social linguistic ironies while we can still play around.

Don't get caught in the inescapable literal actuality, where being a victim ends the fooling-around game with its humorous references from a snug perch as we intellectualize our fears.

IT WAS FUN

Death rejects interruption without a special permit, which I managed to get on a once-only basis through influential contacts I'm not at liberty to disclose. I rubbed my eyes like a baby to take the blur out of them and went on a staring expedition, partly for nostalgia reminiscence and partly for the sad fun of observing the outside world which I hadn't revisited since my permit got activated. Some things had changed and some looked familiar from the years before my death, which now reclaims me forever again. What had I learned from my special permit interruption? The world wasn't mine any more so I saw it through death-eyes in a double-vision distortion that was eerie. I was in a weird sense of time. Other than that, I'm now re-thrust into death's "care," which I term "imprisonment," using living terminology. My permitted death interruption was without reportable incident, due to my glazed-over eyes. But I had felt privileged. Now I'm back to "jailbird duty," irresponsibly dreary, which I can't describe. I'm granted no future privilege, so that's it, folks. Your once and nevermore correspondent signs off mournfully forever. It was fun.

AN ANTHROPOMORPHIZING CONVERSATION

Death is so scary. I'm petrified with fear.

How would you know? You never tried it.

I'm reluctant to ever find out. My idle curiosity would kill me.

Oh, what the hell. You stink with fear.

I'd rather fear safely than plunge disastrously. If curiosity could kill a cat, why not me too?

What! Compare yourself with an animal!?

But aren't I one too?

You low-life skunk!

TIME SOLVES THE PROBLEM OF WHEN DEATHS ARRIVE

Does death scare you?
Out of my wits.
Then simply avoid it.
Yes, but when?
Don't ask. I'm not a clock.
You seem all wound up about it.
It scares me. Both death and the clock.
Differentiate them.
I will. In time.

THE FUTURE FEARFULLY FRETTED ON

Death is scary.
Sure. It's the end of you.
It's unthinkable.
Then shut it out of your mind. It could make you sick.
I'm already sick of obsessing over it.
Change the subject. Quick.
Then let's discuss politics.
You're right. It restores us to life.
Feel better?
Oh, not so much. The political situation sheds no life on my impending death, which I can't get away from. I'm just stuck.
Differentiate between thinking about it; and discussing it; and being in it.
In it? Inside?
Far in.
Can you only be slightly dead?
Same with being slightly pregnant. Either or.
A little goes a long way.

The long way that a little goes is quite enough, as far as that goes.

How far do you have to go till the road ends?

Till there's no measure. Suddenly you're out.

WHAT LIFE COMES DOWN TO OR EVEN DOESN'T

What's the essence of life?

I don't know. It's hard to tell.

You seem lazily uncommunicative, on this score, even labor-saving. Can't you come forth instead of giving up, which you seem prone to do?

You ask me to express the undefinable, which is a pointless task that I heartily absolve myself of undertaking. I'd rather just live life bit by bit, a moment in, a moment out, than put life into a vague heap of words.

You seem woefully inarticulate.

Why not, facing this impossible task you've inexplicably assigned me? Who are you anyway, to impose such a burden on me? Since my refusal is staring you in the face, why don't you give way and endeavor an answer yourself?

Sorry. I'm not capable.

In that case, the solution seems obvious. Let's both or each be life's illustrative example of representation. Instead of verbal explanation, let's each in our own way be living illustrators?

Yes, isn't living itself more natural-seeming than puzzling out an ineffectual verbal blank?

Will literature be the poorer? As a huge body, it will be forced to survive our equal non-contributions.

We'll not make a dent on the awesome granite of its successful archives that claim fame?

Nor will it make a dent on our ambitions as scribes.

Do we admit defeat in the face of ambition?

Do we have the ambition? It would be less woeful to be cowardly ambitionless than to bravely have ambition but abysmally fail in shame.

Should we both, or even one of us, give up, or go ahead?

Choices! Is life a bundle of choices?

METAPHORS AS A DISTRACTION FROM TACKLING WHAT'S TOO DREADED TO ADDRESS IT TOO DIRECTLY

Death is like a plague, that's why I try to avoid it.

No, you avoid it for its own sake, not for being a verbal metaphor.

You're right. Why am I so indirect?

Because you're skirting around the issue.

You mean the issue of death?

Yeah. Be glad it's only an issue now. Being an issue means it's not yet ON, or IN, or WITH, or OF, you.

Do you issue me a warning?

Yes, to stay clear of it itself, in the real.

Then is death real?

Not to you, if you're "it."

What is "it"?

That which it's better to discuss from a safe height, moving around.

Better to discuss what is devoid of substance? You don't dignify death.

Why should I? There's no significance to dignify. Fuck graves.

You're bitter, and without social grace.

NATIONALISM (Dialogue between two Americans)

Long ago, an English poet made a nice phrase: "the bread of friendship and the wine of love."

I agree. It's well put. And applies at all times, including tomorrow.

Yes, it shows that human nature, despite changing historical and local circumstances, is pretty much the same always.

Throughout all times.

The human race is terrific. Honored to belong to it.

A privilege. Whose guest are we?

Evolution's. That's our common ancestry.

UN-common. Let's not put it down. Let's extol it. A terrific legacy.

"One touch of humanity makes the whole world kin."

That's another nice English phrase. Boy, were they good at language, those English.

Some were, more than others. Every ethnic or national group has very varied members.

You're right. I won't generalize, and oversimplify, by assuming national characteristics.

Let's not split the world apart.

No. The better for everyone if it's cohesive.

"United we stand, divided we fall"?

That's a good one too. But it's American.

Good for us. We're no slouch.

DIALOGUE, BASED ON A FAMOUS QUOTE

"Man's inhumanity to man" is an Alexander Pope quote that speaks through the ages how horrible some people are to others. Why is it still going on?

That's human nature, I suppose.

Can't we all get together and stop it?

Things are not that simple.

But it's awful.

The world is too complicated to rectify it.

What about activism?

It makes short bursts of improvement when successful. But human nature, in its global complexity and rival unities, is too vast to make an appreciable dent on its malpractices, as a whole.

So Alexander Popes's quote still not only reigns true but is extremely likely to remain so? That's lousy.

Lots of things are lousy. But that's a major one.

BESET UPON BY MY CURSED MALEFACTOR

All I want to do is lead a good life. I assume obstacles will befront me, but they're overcome-able by the sheer willful force of determination, since my heart is in the right place and I know my place in the world, if luck backs me up.

But isn't luck an unpredictable factor, by its very precarious essence?

It is, but I'll be undaunted by setbacks and fight to the very end of my capability to rectify what's wrong and reinforce my right to be right.

You sound dangerously optimistic.

How so? You mean I'm riding for a fall?

Yes, it's a dis-spiriting formula. Unduly optimistic, failure might—will—plunge you into an overriding depression that will plague and harrow your life.

Are you putting me under a curse?

No. I'm just putting a realism pill into your deluded mouth.

Then I'll clam my gritting lips so tight as to operate as a shield against your realism pill that you would jam down my unwilling throat.

As your menace, I'll force it in.

Well, we're in the essence of conflict. But what's your motive for opposing me?

I'm your evil twin.

But what occupies your OWN life? You don't just waste yourself as my private nemesis? How do you get paid?

In spite.

Despite your own life? You devote yourself to being my plaguing imp?

Sorry. I'm good at it. Beyond that, no further justification is needed.

Imp, go home.

You're my home. I'm your devouring parasite.

WHAT TO PUT BEHIND YOURSELF TO KEEP AHEAD

I love a woman but she rejects me.

That's so common throughout the known world at large. Then if you tried hard enough and always fail, just give up. At least you tried.

That's no consolation, that I only tried.

Are you inconsolable?

Admittedly.

It's common sense that if you keep harboring a failed desire, you keep your loss going. Some desires have to be given up on, if you want to maintain homeostasis and equilibrium. Try giving up on her. If you maintain loving her in vain, you'll go on suffering like a fool. It's like, if you're old, wanting your youth back.

But at least I DID once have my youth. In the case of my loved one, I never had her at all.

Pathetic. It's wisdom to know which desires to retain (if they work) and which to let fall aside and give up on, for your own sake of being comfortable in your own skin.

I can't get her, so now I don't give a damn about her. She can go to hell, for all I care.

(CONGRATULATORY TONE) Smart boy! I knew you you had it in you!

I'm changed! For the better!

Knowing what to put behind you is the very basis of survival.

Well, I must have a big behind.

But that's better than being an ass.

HUMILITY BELATEDLY REALIZED

The truth that I may actually die sometime is no new news, more like a noose that's dangling, ripe for my neck. I'm at death's beck and call, I can't claim a prior appointment as a legitimate excuse for delay. If death says "Today," I'm bound to obey. After all, who am I?

A MAN'S DEMAND, WHICH "REALITY" DENIES

Why are women always rejecting me, when all I ask is unconditional love?

Maybe you come on too fast, with desperation. They may detect that you're too needy to discriminate from among them. They like to be thought of as individuals.

Those tempting little monsters! Who do they think they are, that they give themselves such a privilege! They act like spoiled and entitled princesses!

Well, tough luck on you. You have no choice but to accommodate them in their concern for their own egos. Otherwise you have to do without them.

Tough shit. I'm not giving in, to spoil them!

That's YOUR loss. Then do without.

(OUTRAGEOUSLY) Do without women! But I'm a man!

(LOGICALLY) Well, you made your choice. Suffer.

That's quite a tall order. Suffering, by definition, is too unfair.

Sorry. That's human nature's reality, on the whole.

Human nature is tough enough. But reality too?! This dilemma is a torture!

(WITH FINALITY) You got yourself in this mess. Now dig yourself out. Use your own brain if you have one.

Sure I got one. But it's in the wrong order.

A DIFFICULT GENDER PREDICAMENT

The song said, "All you need is love." But I don't have any.

Well, find it then. I'm not your daddy.

Easy for YOU to say. You're young and handsome. But me, I'm old and ugly.

Can you blame women for your tough predicament? They're only human.

Not in my case. They're merciless.

Oh those poor dears. Can't you go easy on them?

Not in my case. I'm only human.

So is everyone.

All I want is sympathy.

In your case, give up on love and aim for sympathy.

Who's going to give me it?

Sorry. Not me.

A lovely woman, then?

You hope. But reality has strong odds against that. Don't bet your life on it.

You heartless reality-pimp!

DIALOGUE BETWEEN TWO FRIENDS AND THE UNPAID DEBT BETWEEN THEM

To seize an available opportunity to want something and get it can be very self-benefiting. But if the opportunity turns sour, then be wise enough to relinquish it, to avoid the mess of wanting something in painful vain.

Some wants I've had briefly and then wisely had to give up on them. Other wants I saw were successful to maintain because of the pleasurable benefits I got from them. So you have to know which wants to keep and which to get rid of, and above all when, in each case.

Good. You've made your point. To change the subject, you owe me money, so discharge your debt.

I see you want me to honor my monetary indebtedness to you. I advise you to stop your desire, in order to spare yourself the unpleasantness of my refusing to honor my debt. If you don't, then your penalty is to lose my friendship, which is more valuable to you than to get your money back.

It's true. I value your friendship and hate to lose it, so I give up requiring your repaying me your debt.

Wise choice. I love you as a friend, and simultaneously rejoice in the money I've just saved.

I don't begrudge you keeping the money. As a friend, I love you. The money I lose, I gladly bear.

Thanks for both our sakes. If only the big financial corporations could emulate our admirable joint spirits. Too bad for the world. Good luck for us.

DIALOGUE, BUT ONE SOON LEAVES AND THE REMAINING ONE MAKES DO, ETC.

Are more things similar in the world, or different?

The scope of your question is much too vastly large to venture a reply. The range is too amorphous, and the result is an abstract vagueness whose borders are indefinable.

Should I then retract my question, now rendered impossibly unanswerable?

Yes. Let's switch to mere trivial topical chit-chat, like tomorrow's weather and today's extensive consequences of yesterday's alleged political corruptions.

How much time for these topics do you currently have?

None. I have a hair-dresser appointment. (LEAVES HURRIEDLY.)

(SUDDENLY ALONE.) That was abrupt. Well, now I'll resume my on-going self-conversation, which I had left in mid-progress. There were many loose ends of dangling subject matter. Being alone, I'll take on both voices, with fairness of equality promised to each party of conversational disputes. I'll be like a third party—an umpire, needed like a referee to soothe out passionate disagreements and prevent angry discord. I want my internal debates civilized, conducted almost at a parliamentary pace. Being alone, time is no issue, considering that death alone (I'm middle-aged and healthy) stands between me and my summing up, if it comes down to that.

(CHANGES MIND.) Or I may drop this solitude altogether, and seek the convivial ease of another social companion, to break my lonely monopoly of my own tedious thoughts and their voice-divisions. (RESORTS TO PHONE.) Hi, Doris. Just me. You busy? Oh, I'm very sorry.

TAMPERING WITH HUMOR

I need humor to comfort my life from my ravages and insecurity.

You're using humor as a medicinal remedy? You're stretching humor's use beyond its true capacity, by straining its resources to an unnatural abuse of its true nature.

What is its "true nature"?

Freedom from pressure.

I thought pressure forced humor into its funny practice.

Humor defies your stupid analysis. You're just a pedant. Humor is foreign to your nature.

Who are you to presume on defining my nature by cataloguing its lacks and imperfections?

You're presumptuous to contradict me.

Where are we heading?

It's not funny. (THEY SQUARE OFF, IN BELLIGERENT STANCES. MERCIFULLY, THE CURTAIN FALLS TO SPARE THE SCARED AUDIENCE FROM VICARIOUS DANGER.)

AN INTERCHANGEABILITY DIALOGUE

If you're burdened with unfulfillable wants, you're better to give up on them, to avoid various degrees of disappointment and frustration, which can eat away at your "indomitable" spirit and leave you miserable and destroy your good mood, until at last you give up and instinctively say good riddance to those pesky persistent wants.

That's good advice. I'll take it.

Then pay me.

You better give up on the foolish desire to want pay from me, in order to avoid the position of frustration and disapointment and useless, futile, self-defeating anger.

You've thrown my advice right back in my face, as if illustrating it in your own case.

Sure. We're interchangeable, when it comes down to it.

At least we've salvaged our friendship, despite it rankling me about the knotty debt issue.

Oh forget it, pal. I can use that extra cash.

Generously, I don't begrudge you. Shake, pal. (THEY "SHAKE" HANDS, WITH CORDIAL AFFECTION, THUS EASING THEIR "SHAKY" TRANSACTION.)

GIVING THE WRITER A BREAK IN A FEW MERCIFUL CASES

What are the special differences
between wanting and deliverances?

(1) Sometimes you want something so eagerly that, paradoxically, when you laboriously manage to achieve it, that very achievement becomes an anti-climax.

(2) Contrarily, sometimes we only moderately want something, but when we do achieve it we burst into extreme ecstasy and immense delight.

(3) Give examples of both these propositions.

(4) Give contrary examples in both cases of wanting and FAILING.

Sorry, reader. Provide these examples yourself, from your immense past body of living experiences and memories. The writer shouldn't have to do all the work. Let the reader helpfully exert him- or herself and give the writer a break. Believe me, he needs one.

ARE YOU WITHIN MY IDENTITY, OR A STRANGER?

(Dialogue, gradually leading to possible interchangeability:)

Who's the real me? What is life?

Do you doubt your very existence? You sound "beside" yourself. Do you weirdly glimpse yourself as a stranger? Don't you feel unmistakably safe in your own skin?

How can it be otherwise? Stop messing with my head, sewing seeds of mistrust? I'm purely and only me, from a whole body—as time goes continually on—of living experiences and memories that secure and legitimatize my only very identity myself as the only living me.

Then who am I? Why am I dialoguing in your own vicinity? Am I your self-doubter? How am I in your company as an intimate outside stranger—your other self?

You're weird. We shouldn't be having this conversation.

Am I an interference? Or an essential companion, your alternate?

Do we habituate even the same planet? Is my security being invaded by you at a private entrance?

Am I entitled to take this liberty? Am I your living, breathing brother?

I don't need you. Am I empowered to banish you? Are we actually kin? Is this "soul talk"?

If one of us is a spook, isn't that you?

I don't identify as such.

My parasite? My living "other"?

I feel doubted by you.

The feeling is mutual. Are we woven into a common bond?

It's a certification by assumption? It's all so uncanny. Are you the other me, or have I gone too far?

We're two, or one? If we do the math, would we arrive at separate sums?

Maybe we're cross-bred?

Is evolution our only family, or can we name an actual mother and father?

A GROUP OF OLD MEN DISCUSSING CELEBRITIES' RECENT SPATE OF SUICIDES

Truly, we ought to be glad to be alive.
"Ought" is operative. What about suicide,
whose victims seem unable to thrive?
That's a mystery in the hidden self
which newspaper reporting can't squeeze out.
Life can transcend examination
and can't sum itself definitionally
into what is really a matter of what it's all about.
Comments whiz around the subject
but are themselves subject to counter-criticism.
No wonder substance is confused with witticism
in the parlance of making your opinion known.
Anatomize life down to the last bone
but where can we hear the missing flesh moan?
The end was spontaneous. Too late to change
for a done act on the death exchange
within the body's own personal range.
Suicide's arch perversity.
A mystery of the wrong choice
by a swift decision of will.
A broken body devoid of chill.

SUBJECT: LIFE ITSELF

Life is not always easy to explain.
But sometimes the meaning is just only plain.
Do you have a definition handy?
I do. Isn't that dandy?
Life is only what it really is.
To understand, must you be a whiz?
The summing up of life's business
is to abstract it into an "is"-ness.
More an essence than abstract?
Life changes but remains compact.
Motivation turns feeling into an act.
That act is seen by others as a fact.
Puzzling life into an uneasy definition
verging on lazy oversimplification
is not my idea of a true analysis.
But mentally, I'm in paralysis.

TO MY LIFELONG FRIEND

My old friend is dying, full of forgetfulness;
and whatever he does remember
he mangles by obsessing over,
as his brain out-rots his rotten body,
twin travelers along a plunging heedless route
that drops nowhere through the earth,
where consciousness loses connection with his birth
and the toy animals of his innocence.
I was there with him, in our early days
growing blindly into what we will become
when the robust prime of manhood
enlarges us into a head of sperm
in the danger zone of headlong love
turning tragic or turning triumphant.
Later, there were even worse things to confront.
Now my health is holding out, but not his.
I kneel and weep, while his bedside spins.

DON'T FEAR, LITTLE BOY

1.

The night is associated with dark
and not just for a lark.
The sun momentarily absent
is the causative fact sent
from way up there to way down here
to prove that we need not spherically fear
a rude emptiness in the sudden sky
as a fore-message of doom by and by.
Scheduled is the upward sun while the hours fly.
Go back to sleep, little boy.
If necessary, hug your furry toy.

2.

This then be the lullaby
that nothing's wrong with the everyday sky
that chronically endangers the earth's health.
No miserable surprise is dealt you by stealth.
The reassuring sun promises future wealth
if daddy goes out and makes a bundle
to guarantee prosperity that's not too humble.

THE TRIO

Laughter came regularly
from what Jimmy and I created
from mere conversational material.
This was the invitation
for holy lifelong friendship.
There's me, there's Jimmy, and then
our third companion: friendship,
forged by our laughter together
through youth, manhood, and thereafter,
the happy product of our laughter.
Now Jimmy is on his death bed
and I kneel beside him with a funny head.

OUR FRIENDSHIP ON THE ROAD

Al Lehman drove me in his car
throughout the years, near and far.
The various cars have been long sold.
He's dead. His passenger remains old.

DISREGARD THIS RUBBISH

1.

What I forgot
must now turn to rot.
What I remember
lasts as far as today
with tomorrow a possible maybe.

2.

But back to what I forgot:
now discarded to the basement bin
destined for the garbage truck
that collects prime varieties of useless muck
in dismal miscellaneous array.
What's forgotten, then, has run out of luck,
put aside in the rubbish heap
and needn't cost you any sleep;
regarded as memory's official retard
and deeply assigned to the "disregard" pile,
carried far away to the lost mile
in night's fatigued lost vision,
by a nighttime moaning garbage truck
with heavy worn-out wheels
repressing its cargo's unheeded squeals
begging for one last grossly deprived meal
of smelly leftovers meant to be ignored
by the already professionally bored.
My goodness! Oh lord!
This putrid crap is what we can't afford.

HOW LIFE BEGINS

Boys and girls together
come out to play.
They certainly do,
combining to mutually woo.
Coy maidens don't say "maybe,"
thus awarding life to many a baby,
giving the maternity ward
many a fertility award
to ward off underpopulation
and carry reproduction's archaic formula
into a rate of growth more than normula,
all because coy maidens don't say "maybe"
to gender-division's partiality to a baby.

THE SELF-CONTRADICTORY HISTORY OF A CATHEDRAL

A religion-free cathedral was crowded with non-believers. The crowd got so large, it stampeded like a gun-shot cork from a repressed wine bottle, out from its pinching doors into a festival-raging street that wildly cascaded into a jamboree of rioting free-spirits in an orgy of untrammeled freedom for its own nihilistic sake. This created a backlash, so the fashion of the multitude reversed into the severe repression that had initially architected the cathedral in the first place, where now piety held reinforced tyrannical sway to a tortuous medieval extent, defying recent liberal emancipation of the sullen obedient masses.

DUTIES AS DO-DEEDS

Sex without love coldly proceeds
to get a baby that maternity feeds.
Love with some sex warmly proceeds
to get a baby that maternity feeds.
This is how the human race breeds,
evolutionarily specific in its deeds.

LISTEN TO ME. HERE'S WHAT YOU MAKE OF IT

1.

These relentless bouts of insomnia,
like lengthy safaris in Somalia
seeking a lost skull from an elephant tribe
worth plenty on the market,
wrestle to no avail
with the problem of inefficient energy
put to use beyond its means
to come forward with enough evidence
to put paid to what's falsely made:
In common decency, SO WHAT!?

2.

Stupidly stumbling on solutions
to problems devoid of necessity,
I peer forward into the unknown
and come up with the cumbersome cumulations
at least dealing with the halloween hobgoblin
worth its weight in confusion.
I swear, this is no delusion that I can currently discern.
Let me level with you. And you be the believer.

3.

Might as well stick to the hackable trail
scything through resistant leaves of bamboo stick
with canteens of gallons of the water freshly minted,
collected from neighboring brooks,
seeking to disguise my unmeasured footprints
to avoid the influence of mafia crooks
with their atrocious but swarthy looks.
I'm not a bigot. But everyone else is.
I can't turn them all in.
So you calculate with that.
I'm merely ridicule's doormat.

INDUCING JEALOUSY: THE WINNING FORMULA

(MAN:) In case this audience is curious: to bring them up to date: For a long time I've been trying to impress you, leading to high approval and admiration, which in turn is aimed at winning your love.

(WOMAN:) You're barking up the wrong tree. You over-attempt these assaults, which are getting you nowhere. You're trying too hard. I suggest a better strategy: Try being hard to get.

No, that's too phony. It wouldn't work, for I've already played my hand.

Much too much so, you naive fool.

I have a great idea, an enlightenment. My new strategy for winning you is to make you jealous. Betty will be my instrument.

(CAGILY:) What does she look like?

A stunning beauty. (PAUSE:) Is it working?

Is WHAT working?

My strategy for making you jealous.

(HUGGING AND KISSING HIM DRAMATICALLY:) I can't abide Betty, that hussy. She's not fit to be your wife.

In that case—.

Yes, my only darling, I will marry you.

Let's hurry, before your jealousy wears off.

What's your hurry? (PAUSES:) When's your next date with Betty?

As it happens, tonight, actually.

(HASTILY:) City hall is open for the next few hours. Let's hark there.

But I'm not suitably dressed yet, for this abrupt occasion.

Oh, don't belong to the bourgeoisie set. Pretend to be a bohemian.

(OUTRAGED:) What do you mean, "pretend"? I am! Don't I have a free living style?

(COMPLACENTLY:) Yes, dear. (THEY HURRY OFF TO GET MARRIED.)

NO PLEA, NOW YOU'RE FREE

(Scene: divorce court:)

The attraction between the sexes
is reduced when they become exes
due to the detumescence of divorce.
They still love each other, of course,
but only in a remembering way.
Unfortunately, their remembering is not going to stay.
Each will get out of each other's way
to make room for wife number two
and, respectively, husband number three.
They lose the right to say "you and me,"
pause, and kiss each other regretfully.

THE IDEA I LOST

I lost what I had meant to say.
Where did it go away?
Into my very same head
from which I had meant to say it.
Did forgetfulness betray it?
Of course that's the culprit.
I was already on my pulpit
ready to pronounce that very thing,
which darkly flew away on a lonely wing
so that my prepared announcement
was a gift that I could not bring
into the audience's attention
despite my very noble intention
much worth the very mention
that had not taken place.
How vacant was my frozen face!

THE LANGUAGES OF WORLD LITERATURE

All the words come together
in a screeching sound.
Better to keep them apart
to make the best sense
in literature's fund of verbal art
that keeps codes in their right order,
each in their truly sequestered border.
Appreciative readership is the best lauder.

THE HARD LIFE OF A STONE

A stone's life is so hard, yet bearable, since it is what it is, so the only self-approach it could make is, however hard, this: its life must be endured with the stoical, no-nonsense fortitude of accepting what it intrinsically is, living within the bounds of its means, and being comfortable in its own skin.

It has no skin.

Well, there's visiting skin, like algae or mineral residue, or environmental coloration, or bronzing, or neighboring plant rot, or sunshine on its surface, or the moving hatching of shadows, however elusive, lightly shifting.

You're romanticizing a stone. Can't you just say what it is, and leave it at that?

That's too hard.

Well, your attitude reflects the true nature of the stone. You're both hard-bitten: IT as your subject, and YOU in your reaction.

We're hardened to what we are, and can hardly say otherwise.

You just smiled. I'm glad you're not stone-faced; and bear human, reactive characteristics demonstrating the condition of your own fluid nature, as opposed to—

(INTERRUPTING:) Put it at rest.

You just identified it. "At rest." No wonder it's the stuff of tombstones.

That's a dead issue. Leave it.

THAT WICKED POISON, ENVY, OR, DOES THE CAMEL BLAME DARWIN FOR ITS HUNCHBACK?

Part of envy is wishing that others weren't so fortunate as to enjoy what you envy them for. So envy is implicit bad will or bad faith. You wish those fortunates wouldn't incite your unpleasant envy by having something you highly value but don't yourself have: such as more money, younger age, superior looks, a more successful career or more promising prospects, more popularity, better opportunities, moneyed parents and relatives, more esteem and prestige, a better looking mate, a better sex life, and general status superiority in whatever community you have to operate in.

You resent having to feel being forced to feel inferior to those damn lucky bastards. They got the breaks, why couldn't you have? But why do they have to rub it in?

However, it's not really their fault for your own dissatisfactions. They were just trying to better their own lots; can you blame them? They didn't intend their comparative successes to be misery points for poor you. Did they ask you to compare? That's your dare. So go on suffering your resentment.

But better keep it to yourself. You'll humiliate yourself further if "everybody" else knows and secretly mocks you or pities you. You poor fool.

But don't feel ashamed. You couldn't help it. That's just the way you are. Can you blame the camel for his hunchback? Does the camel blame Darwin? Poor Darwin. He already got hell from the bible set. Why does history have to be so jealous of him? Didn't he work hard enough? Give him a break. Anyway, he's aledy dead. Envying someone dead is the height of folly. Be glad your lungs can still fill up, bad air and all.

YOU CAN'T REJOIN THEM

Death is not a party; so you can't "rejoin" former friends and loved ones "there," if unfortunately you eventually follow their deaths with yours. There are no companions in death; no one qualifies. So: so far as loves and friendships go, better hurry get your fill while they're still accommodatingly available. Now's the time, or maybe tomorrow, but don't wait too long, or it'll cost you. Meanwhile you try to save your own precious skin by trying not to emulate long dead or freshly dead friends or loved ones or even family. Hold on for dear life. If death divides you from them, accentuate these divisions by "living it up" with a vengeance, if you still have the energy left. Let their deaths be a lesson to you: You're never too old to learn, you damn fool.

DEFINITION: TO THE LIFE

Life is not always easy to explain
but sometimes its meaning is just only plain
like a clear glassy window pane
that you can easily see under penalty of pain,
unless your sight's fuzzily gone to wane.
Then please explain life's spotless meaning
to give your explanation a severe cleaning
of all excess and inadequate matter
down to the last infinitesmal tatter,
so life is left neither lean nor fatter
but just centrally exactly what it only is,
having prepared for your any further quiz
like lips having surrendered their picture-perfect kiss.
Life's meaning, given its fullest explanation,
sharply delineates "holiday" from "vacation,"
so that it leaves you without an annoying reservation
of lacking or excess subject matter
to squander on an empty meaningless splatter.
Life under an impeccable magnifying glass
describes itself perfectly, from nose to ass.
Life's describable meaning, no less,
is just what I rendered, so give it a bless
for delineation resembling itself, more or less,
that so gives its naked theme its least irrelevant dress
even if it must go local to so express.

TO A FORMER LOVE

What has memory done?
Having once been everything,
your reduction to nothing
in my emotional head
makes the loss of sentiment sad.
We were once each other's permanent darlings.
Such diminishment into indifference
on my part is betrayal. Is it yours?
In retrospect, have we become bores?

CONFUSING HOW TO FORGET. (INSOMNIA PLAYING A REDUNDANT ROLE TO DEMENTIA'S PRIMARY DOMINANCE)

Due to dementia, among the things I forgot
was: "Did I have insomnia last night?"
Or did I just sleep it off, and now
mere dementia interferes with my sleeping bouts
where all my sweet dreams must fall prey
to forgetfulness now that it's turned day?
Who needs redundant insomnia
now that I landed in my forgotten today
where memories forgot to come out to play?
Or were they only overlooked
in my puzzling schedule that's not entirely booked?

A BIT MORE

What's left of me
(since my life has mostly been spent
with only a problematic few years left)
has some good things to enjoy.
Sex and flirtation are not among them.
A few privations won't hinder me
from resisting a few tugs of pain
while life still spells out the name of gain
while dim horizons start their readiness to wane
amid loads of remembrances to dump away,
and despair undermines the old days of play.
Night penetrates harder into the day.

MASOCHISM RELISHING IN ITS HOPE, BEING LAUGHINGLY DENIED BY THE CRUEL LOVED ONE IN WHOM HE WALLOWS HELPLESSLY

(Man:) Loving you doesn't seem to make you a copy-cat and love me back.

(Woman:) Why should I? I'm reserving my love for someone else, whoever he may be.

I'm already reserving my jealousy for whoever this candidate might be. Any clues as to his eventual identity?

Nothing except that you're not it.

You mean I'm not he?

No resemblance.

You block me out as a possibility?

You're not my type. Put it that way.

Your cruelty takes the air out of any hope.

Why does hope remain in your sunken breast?

To prevail on you seems all my poor life can muster as I lay the poor luckless corpse at your stubborn feet.

Is rhetoric your only recourse?

I can't believe this is pathetically happening!

Well, enjoy your disbelief. Take consolation in it.

Thanks for considering my end of the bargain. At least I was in your mind.

As far as you ever could get. How dare you enter my conversation in the first place?

Did I pressure too boldly?

You had nothing to go on.

Then what am I doing here? At least we're on conversational terms.

Terms? Your term is up. (LEAVES HIM.)

(LEFT EMPHATICALLY ALONE:) Well, at least I scraped up this try. At least that far I got somewhere. Even her true future love hasn't yet made the dent I never will. My failure is relative to comparison. By the process of envy, I'm already conditionally related to her eventual husband. It may be minor, but it's a plus in my life—no, a subtraction. When will my negatives ever stop, in my uncannily star-crossed excuse for a pretense love life?

DIALOGUE ON THE FLY

(BEWILDERED:) I don't understand.

Oh you poor guy. Let me help you out. Just what is it that you don't understand?

Thanks for your sympathy.

Yes, but what am I sympathizing?

I'm always being rejected by women.

Oh, I see why.

At a moment's notice?! Don't keep me guessing. Why?

The zippers of your trousers, your "fly," are carelessly open, and I can see your skin dangling.

Yes, but in my defense, it's dangling INSIDE, not outside, my dear, rumpled trousers.

Nevertheless, it makes you seem uncouth, and even over-eager with the women to get into action as swiftly as you possibly can, vis-à-vis those darling female creatures. It makes you look so desperately needy as if you've been heavily laden with years of cruelly enforced celibacy.

Then wouldn't women be all the more willing to relieve me of my by now aching overload of desperation-tingling sperm?

Maybe they're afraid of being overwhelmed, as they hear your panting breath and see blushingly how prematurely open your unruly lower clothing are "champing at the bit."

But at least they can estimate whether my member is suitably fit.
Surely with their seeing what my open fly exposes,
they hopefully gasp, "Holy Moses!"
Then teasingly, the gap closes.
Then gushingly they'll declare, "Clothing maketh the man,"
estimating an imaginary span.
My trouser creases are impeccably neat.
Doesn't my open gap promise an entertaining feat?
Just tailor-made for it.
Something not the least to forfeit.

I can't argue with your open scheme.

It's the adolescent stuff of a sure-fire dream.
Your pants will make every gal pant
for what the pants have an unruly promise for,
admirably kept in stock, and in store.
Let's praise where sex finds its masculine core.
Nor is the female part precisely a bore.

HEADING DOWNWARD

The time is running away from me
from when I used to be able to breathe easy
and conduct my life "normally,"
with habitual free-flowing bodily function
in the usual pace and manner
to perform simple tasks routinely,
even briskly, formally,
as was always my way formerly
since I began manhood's voyage.
But lately, old-age destroyage
seizes my body with a network of tremors,
quelling the old buoyancy
from my former boyhood wizardry
and displacing it with destroyancy
in an over-all breakdown seizure
as opposed to vigorous procedure.
This of course is a new unwelcome feature
in the latest edition of my life's picture,
introducing an annoying new fixture
in an obvious downhood direction
and upsetting all dreams of perfection.
I may not be here for the next presidential election.
Not knowing who won won't faze me.
My intellect for politics will become lazy,
and historical memory very hazy.
You won't hardly be able to place me.
Erasure from life is bound to displace me
with a new baby I'm not related to,
the latest addition to evolution's roaring zoo.

LIFE—DEATH, IN A HEADLONG DICHOTOMY

When the whirlaround is directionless,
I know I'm heading deathward
which is a bold and solemn move
that cuts through the surrounding dread
that sits us staring stark while in bed
and by morning grows a big fat sore head.
With all this fuss about life
with its socially boisterous parties,
doesn't death cut through it
and laugh backwards at the left-behind bullshit?
Death is a real preoccupation.
Life is its foremost distraction.
Now that these priorities straighten out,
what are the "favorite" odds in the life-death bout?
Well, those two are dichotomies.
Let life precede death, for priorities.
Make room, put life first
to slake your enormous biological thirst.
Sequence will solve the problem
of including both in a problematic equation.
They're unified, like a sovereign nation.
If time has room enough, they both fit in
and neither has to lose for the other to also win.
The life-death bout, for eternal stakes:
Let them alternately sleep, while the other wakes.
Life versus death, to a draw,
keeps us on our toes, till the other pleads, "No more."

LIFE VERSUS DEATH, TO THE FINISH

Life and death—what a pair!
The world is their referee,
with no holds barred—keep it fair!
What a tussle, relentless and pressing.
Is it boxing, baseball, or wrestling?
Even an umpire has to be required

to keep the peace between those adversaries,
both formidable competitors
for journalists and their editors
to give daily newspaper reports
for the excitable public to keep up with
from stark tabloids or stately papers of wider width.
The life-death clash—follow it in the sports section
and decide for yourself under full inspection:
A fairer result than a political election.
Life versus death, to the finish.
Is it a losing tussle, or a winnish?
It depends on who eats the most spinach.

HOW LOVE TURNED OUT

It's a romantic necessity
that a young man and a young lady
should adore—but beyond that—
LOVE each other to bliss
so that Cupid cannot miss
with his junior bow and arrow
to make them stay strictly on the narrow
as a newly wedded couple,
almost each other's double
in mutual outlook supreme
to be each other's dream.
If not, I'll prolong my scream
that true romance is unrealistic
as though adoration cannot stick.
Sad years later, divorce destroys the past
with its almost dehumanizing blast.
The romance so quickly got shattered
as if those cherished dreams never mattered
and retroactively now bear tatters
all throughout the HOLY fabric.
The house tumbles, brick by brick,
showing the divorced husband to have been a prick
with his promiscuous use of an unruly dick.

A POLITICALLY METAPHYSICAL PROTEST

The eventual death of anything that lives
is the unwelcome announcement that philosophy gives.
And it also includes yourself too
like all the rest of the biological zoo.
So carry a "protest" sign, warning of that news,
and picket everywhere, protesting those views
as being radically unfair.
Preach a more shining air.
It's too much of an overworldly scare,
something that my nervous system could well spare
before I start my Denial campaign
to ease my cowardly exit-stential pain.

BIDDEN? OR SMITTEN?

Your helpless fear of death
puts a glitch into your breath
as an over-all forecast of doom
that shows you've almost run out of room.
Immediately stop fearing
while death grows ever nearing?
No, your whole system is overridden
by a palpable fear of what can't be hidden.
Meekly you must fall prey to what's bidden.
Perversely reverse it? Be by death smitten?
Oh, you poor pussycat little kitten!

PEOPLE, SELF, AND WORLD

It's fun to be friends with people,
but being alone can also be fun,
allowing your brain to free-associate
and remembering the course of life's events,
and whether you succeeded in your intents.
Altogether, being alive is a swell place to be,
provided you and your health can remain so free,

and also money will help you along
to be in the chorus of life's open song.
Avoid death as long as you can
to be a proud member of women and men.
After delving into "then," prepare for your "when."
Meanwhile, share generously this great den.

WHERE I "GO," IF PHILOSOPHY WERE GIVEN A VOICE

You don't have to be bold
to get too old,
which proceeds so naturally,
it quite overtakes you
not to mention taking your breath away
and other internal diseases
which old age is heir to.
But I have to bear up to
the toughest of all realities
it'll be my outlook to endure:
My advanced old age
bears the gift of mortality
I'm not allowed to refuse.
To it I simply must yield
and go alone to the death field
whose expanse is practically infinite.
Admittance there is my priority
due to my seniority
and enforced invitation
I'm ill-advised to snub.
But society will snub me,
and not visit solitary confinement
which is my sole solo alignment
and free to perform no other assignment
in aimless non-specificity
and deprived of other baseless activity
in the non-being I'm destined for
that's too vacuous even to be a bore.
Anyway, there's mythology's empty lore.

HOT AND PLENTY

Boys and girls together
on the sidewalks of New York,
eating lean meat or sloppy pork,
ignoring the use of a civil fork,
while the band goes marching on
and sings a happy song of wedding.
Then comes the fateful bedding
in the good old summertime
when nature bides its time
bearing children by the bunch,
from a mutual fertile hunch,
sweating out the good old summertime
where the temperature continues to climb
and boys and girls intertwine,
being the products of what their parents did,
generations repeating nature's common bid
planted in the good old summertme
on New York's street-lined grid
and nature pops its oozing lid
producing kid after kid after kid
as children repeat what their parents did
on the melting sidewalks of new York,
eating lean meat and sloppy pork,
where sweat pops off the slippery fork,
nourishment for future use
to light again reproduction's fiery fuse.
Considering such mechanics, who can refuse?
As the climate continues to climb
bearing children's rise to their prime,
saving every dolorous dollar and dime
for the blinding summer's sweet melodic sunshine.
Oh what a glorious time.

MARRIAGE, AND ITS ARBITRARY INEVITABILITY

Of all the thousands of possibilities,
the marriage-carrying connection never occurred
to our separate mentalities that oozed and blurred
that a bonding could intervene, so we conferred,
and just so!—we made it happen
by abrupt joint decision,
even risking others' derision.
We overcame an overwhelming division
between thoroughly opposite personalities
that rejected all the actualities
and ignored the practicalities,
so we became united in a kiss,
merging in mutual bliss.
So we embarked on marriage
and now wheel a baby carriage
whose wheels squeak,
as a symbol, so to speak.
Of what? Yet to be determined,
on the basis of alignment in the firmament
far above the squeaking carriage
bearing an infant, product of our marriage.
What will that infant become?
Somewhere between the zones of brilliant and dumb.
Right now, sucking on its thumb.

A FRANK ADMITTANCE

All I wanted was to be thought well of
by all the members of my community.
I tried too transparently hard.
For consolation prize, they made me eat lard.
I only say this confession now
so my poor example won't be followed
and others' swollen dignity won't be hollowed.

REGAINING DIGNITY

Preserving my dignity is my number one motive.
But others ask humorously, "What dignity?"
I tried to prove by example
that the community shouldn't trample
on my poor unworthy self-respect.
But nobody was eager to co-operate, I suspect,
by swallowing my eager plea and taking it to heart.
My community standing now is that I'm not too smart.
They ask me to play the fool, but I won't accept that part.
Who do they think I am? No, I won't go into that.
I turn my back and ask there-on to please pat.

A DEPRESSING EVENT

Such a lovely affair it was supposed to be.
But it didn't get off the ground. The cause was me.
My sex member resorted to old impotence.
The failure was at the wrong time. It didn't make sense.
I supplied the wreck. There was no recompense.
Mentally my erotic zone went dense.
Embarrassment was my only defense.
She accepted the apology and said goodbye.
I went off alone and had a good cry.
But out of masculine pride I hid the tears.
This had gone on occasionally for years.
No wonder woman after woman disappears.
To rub it in, I have more mortality fears.
The whole me, not just my member,
is reduced to low flame and soon the ember.

DOWNGRADING THE SOCIAL RANKING IN TERMS OF UTMOST HYPE

I need to be highly famed;
If not, somewhat famed,
If not, then esteemed,

If not, then acclaimed,
If not, then admired,
If not, then respected,
If not, then accepted,
If not, merely tolerated,
If not, then rejected,
If not, you get scorned.
If not, you're never borned.
What grade's your popularity standing at?
Standing? Hardly. It's fallen flat,
skinny frail, not robustly fat,
compelling poor pity's passing pat,
not where the posh folk patronize at.
I've been shot down, rat-tat-tat,
I've bottomed out like the low-cast rat,
weakly striking out at the futile bat,
writhing in ugly twist at the wrestling mat,
arithmetically sucker-sacked,
presented with the actual non-stat:
A living legend whose time turns apt
and whom destiny has officially capped.
On history's register, the tune is tapped.
In steel marble, Fame is permanently trapped.

THE REPLACING GENERATIONS

East side, west side,
all around the town.
Me and my gal dance
a timeless tune, perchance,
in old New York
under the summer moon,
reflecting the good old summertime
while the centuries gently climb
on the sidewalks of New York
that get a new paint job
in front of a whole new mob.

SOCIAL LIFE

Social life is so valuable
to be a part of,
full of art and manipulations.
We have friends to different degrees,
some close, some casual:
a big part of life, as usual.
Who less values who
than the other one?
Who more values who
than the other one?
Those are dilemmas we go through
in various ratios, now and then.
Social life is intriguing.
Social life is boring.
We go to- and for-ing.
I find it most restoring.
I'll always give it a fling
unless I'm a hermit.
I don't need a permit.

PEOPLE AND THE PERSON

Politics (lots of people) leads to sociology.
Sociology leads to psychology (the individual).
People, that's what we are
in the aggregate.
The individual, that's what it comes down to.
Some individuals are part of couples,
which can be romantic.
Living together is an art.
Each one is a separate part.
Each one is an integral part.
Joining together is a risk.
If you take the plunge, don't be brisk.
Come with a smile, not with a fist.
You join one person, not a list.

Treat her on an individual basis.
Zero in on who it is.
Is it life-changing? Or a fizz?

THE SOCIAL NECESSITY FOR REALITY (SECRETLY DISGUISED AS A LOVE PLEA)

1.

The nature of reality is very problematic.
Sometimes its delirium is almost hypnotic.
Reality is what we all have to go through
to have some kind of idea as to what will ensue.
And so we can make a reasonable prediction
and prepare for what is not intended to be fiction,
but the actual event, more or less what's to be,
and meet it head-on;
let the experience occur,
in its own real shape, not a blur.
That's reality, sort of. You concur?

2.

Reality is based on what's "true."
That's the bond between me and you.
Those who deny it are very few.
Reality is what we agree upon,
consensual, however subjective.
At least that's our mutual objective.
Co-operate. Don't be defective.
It's not mandatory, but elective.
Be wisely wary, and be selective.
If I say I love you, shouldn't you love me?
On that sort of reality, let's both agree.
The ultimate reality is you and me.

BOYHOOD MOVIES

In the deepest dark of the night,
under conditions of fright
and shifty shadows,
crime careens between cars
and shots are shot out
from illegal or law-enforcing guns
while the cops go chasing the crooked ones
and money is the source of nefarious crime.
Economic stability
will war against impoverishment
while the drama unfolds
between those eternal foes:
the bad guys and the good ones.
Box office tickets for the drama ride.
The case is on and cars subside
to cinematic thrills and more beside.
No stars, but the highest noir
with the lights deeply down
and the stakes are out of your mind
and the death trap keeps you on edge.
Spectatorship requires imagination
and imagination is blown to bits
while movie-goers get the shivering fits.
And it only cost two bits.
From boyhood you'll soon grow up
having taken morality's lesson.
Nor will your patriotism lessen.
Oh the wonderful movie house.
You look avidly and learn not to be a louse
but if you can, a hero
while you grow up to manhood from the time of zero
under the dark influence of noir.
And from deep down, your adrenolin will purr
and next Saturday you'll ask for even more.
Saturday boyhood at the movie in nineteenfifty.
You're growing up in innocence nifty
and learn direct honesty, not shifty.

A SPECIAL ENTITLEMENT

Oh please grant me immunity to death
whereby the usual loss of breath
doesn't apply to very privileged me,
thus avoiding mortality's exacting fee.
If I could escape so uniquely,
and directly dodged death, not obliquely,
I'd be accused of being undemocratic.
But so what!?—I would love to live longer,
and thus retrieved, I'd have a song for
the stupendous beauty of human life
that despite old age's ravages
can be conducted with great sophistication.
I would love this prolonged vacation.
An extended term, no matter what the price,
till finally death claimed me—through fire or ice
or whatever the means, to meanly suffice.
The roll of a gambler's unlucky dice,
depriving me of life-itself's role
to which I was granted entitlement sole.

A LIBATION TO THE PAST

The past bewilders me
by being so forwardly present.
It grants me itself as a present.
I open the package and behold
the past all wrapped up
but spilled out now in a new cup
for current drinking to accompany my nightly sup.
The past jumps forward, so down is up.
It embraces the Right Now, which it must interrupt.
The past in its interrupting mode
inspires me to write this poetic ode.

AN ETERNAL TRADE

Death is uneasy to ponder
and difficult to contemplate
and uncomfortable to consider.
Then trade it to the highest bidder.
But he turns you down,
prefers life instead,
and he'll take life in your stead.

THE CHILDREN'S REVENGE. THEN PARENTS WILL AVENGE

All children know
that their main duty is to grow,
to spare their caretakers from overwork.
But from such benevolence children shirk
and do whatever damn pleases them
like discharging from the chest excess phlegm
or from their cute little mouths
expectorate to show their droughts.
Of mothers' and fathers' "sacrifice," they have their doubts,
claiming their parents have full control
in abusing the parental role
and parenthetically are on a roll
to torture their offspring
for unruliness in anything.
Children ought to form a union and rebel,
condemning both parents to an approximate hell
that denotes a permanent holiday from life.
Thus ends this intergenerational strife
in theory. But what if some parents were good?
On that note let a good father brood.
Parents? At least spare them
for kindness to children after they bear them.
In that case, don't be quick to condemn.
Content children from kind parents stem.
Reversing the curse, I say "ahem,"
and apologize for an intemperate phlegm.

My own sperm was sweet and kind,
preventing my kids from a nasty mind
that avenges parents unjustifiably.
I rule. I'm treated undefiantly.
I'm not wrathful, nor am I liable to be.
My conscience is clear. My brats are in school
daily learning the good old golden rule.
Neither they nor I is a gullible fool.
Our reflections cast well from an indifferent pool.
For this relative harmony, I drool.
It's all in the family, I guess.
Let's not be adversarial, but bless.
Reality might disagree, nevertheless.

TO AL LEHMAN

Goodbye forever, my dear friend.
There was a turning in the bend
from which I never saw you again.
It signaled to me an end most definite
to define my loss of hope forever
with whatever futility I still endeavor.
It clamps down on the word "never"
(end of a world, end of a word,)
aloft in the lost clouds, like a bird.
The whole thing is too sadly absurd.
What meager power remains in a lonely word?
The word "never" takes its occasion
to hurl itself on me, with abrasion.
I must submit to its persuasion
now that it alights on its true occasion
by putting to an end my friend
coming around the dissolving bend.
Now my mourning substitutes for him
but barely succeeds to penetrate the dim.
Mourning can go only so far
but halts right there at the imaginary bar.

THE LIMIT OF BEING WITH HIM AGAIN

My dear friend, you're inside me
as memory, as far as memory can go
compared to when the friendship was live
on both ends of us
or shall we call them sides,
when our united lives coincided.
But you're not here to continue
with spontaneous co-operation.
I'm here to write this.
You're sunk into abstraction,
and I bear you entirely on my back
through my pen and computer machine
to drag you back into where I live.
That's all my friendship allows me to give.
If it were more, I'd dig you up,
fill the wine glasses, and then we sup.
Periodically, we let laughter disrupt.
Only the other world would dare interrupt.

A SLICE OF MUSIC

The band goes marching on
playing a hectic tune
under the sunny moon
as delirious as a lune.
Keep in time to it.
Rhythm out your whole shakes
and watch the oven while your cake bakes.

THIS TIME MAKE IT WORK!

I did all the remembering,
you did all the forgetting,
when we broke our romance up.
That was unfair distribution.
Can't you be jolted too

by that miserable break-up?
As far as your heart goes, what's up?
Can't you share some part of the burden,
to take away from me
the whole blow of the hurtin'?
Let's get together, and lower the curtain.
We'll start again, with renewed flirtin'.
You don't have to keep your whole skirt on.
We won't skirt around the issue
to start a marriage, with a baby to ensue.
You co-operate. This time be true.
Let's keep our arguments minor
and reduce their number to few.
Now it's for keeps, between me and you.
No more weeps, or only a few.
Destiny married me to you,
so be alert, and hark to your cue.

TWO FORMS OF INEQUALITY

The rich have too much money,
the poor not enough.
Financial equality is an ideal
to solve that "inhuman" gap
between the haves and the have-nots.
It ties up statesmen into knots.
But worst still, in a way,
is the still-living and the now-dead gap.
It wipes other inequalities off the map.
An example is my loved one.
Why would she "have to" be dead
and only me still living instead?
Am I thus privileged
with unfair entitlement?
I leave it to metaphysics
to dip into that insoluble problem.
If it's a privilege, why the unhappiness clause
in my predicament? It grants us all pause.
I'd unravel this knot with helpless claws.

BAD TIMING

Your friendship overwhelmed me.
This is your only tribute,
for your value came to me fullest
when totally you were already under dust
and modestly then out of hearing
from my words, which would have been cheering.
But tricky time prevented that.
But still it counts that we actually met,
which partially redeems "our" regret,
which only I can experience.
And for you, nothing more makes sense.
My consciousness alone bears our recompense.
That's a metaphysical irony.
Can anything iron it out for me?

A DISTANCE BOAST

I never had a dog,
I never had a cat.
Nor did I adopt a pet bat.
Instead I went to bat
and hit a ball so far
it broke the distance bar
between where I hit it
and where it finally landed:
in a sand pit.
But I wasn't playing golf.
But there was a big gulf
between where I hit it
and the unintentional sand pit.
Enough to throw me into a fit.

RESTORING VIRTUE AND EQUALITY

While others burp with ample food,
you starve with a miserable bone;
and with a low and desperate mood,
you liberally ask, "How could the world atone?"
But the world turns over no stone
to restore equality for democratic stomachs.
The world is a great big stupid lummox
to allow poverty to kneel at wealth's feet
and beg for the bare minimal philanthropic treat.
So I advise poor people to steal wealth
and not be caught, while attaining good health.
Then their stomachs protrude from a stretching belt.
It's enough to make virtue's heart soddenly melt.

MAKING FRIENDS: A FINE ART

To get friends, first try to be popular;
and if you get angry, don't try for the jugular.
Have good grooming and make a good impression,
then you'll get friends without any question.
Don't be tedious and boring when you speak,
and always the other person's point of view be sure to seek.
Don't ridicule others if they display a sign that they're weak.
Get a reputation as fair and mild, just like the weather,
to make it easy that you and others get together.
Be sure to be likable and attractive
and inclined toward peace, but also active.
To be a good friend, ask "What's your point of view?"
Then say, "Oh, by coincidence that's mine too.
Surely our souls are linked, nice and sweet and true."
The science of making friends
should lead us to perfectly sociable ends.

CONTRAST, AT YOUR EXPENSE

When your friends succeed and you fail,
hide your envy, pretend that you don't ail.
Assure them that you're not jealous at all
that while they rise, you should dismally fall.
Then they'll pat you on your "noble" head
that while they shine with gold, you droop with lead.
While they feast with an expensive meal,
your intestines rot with hunger's squeal
and you get the raw end of the deal.
What a difference with how they feel,
blessed with proud success; and you, cursed
that your whole life has crashed into the worst,
after once with optimism your head would burst.
It's bad luck that they happened to come in first.
How do envy and jealousy differ?
Your ruined pride turns out that much stiffer.

GUIDE TO IMPROVING YOUR MOOD

When you feel lousy, try to improve your mood
(Not by standing on your head: you're no acrobat.)
by eating a lot of wholesome food,
with a varied diet—some of this and some of that.
It goes to your stomach and then your bowels.
Wipe your mouth with embroidered towels
to prevent dribbling with former saliva
that got caught between your loathsome teeth
but your tongue was unable to extract.
Follow these prescriptions and do it exact,
and your mood will undoubtedly come around
and produce from your anus a cracking rowdy sound.
Then we'll know that you're safe and sound,
and your mood will be uplifted
and suitably your attitude shifted
from rotten to good on the opposite scale
so your sleep won't be disturbed by a self-pitying wail.

Upwards on the thermometer your mood will sail
till it reaches ecstasy and euphoria both;
so as to change your mood you'll now be loathe.
To not one doctor do you have to avail
if your current happiness doesn't get too stale.

TO AL LEHMAN, FOREVER

Once dead, Al Lehman can't revive.
How lovely when he was alive.
I was his passenger in many a car ride.
Not where we were going, but he was by my side.
When it came to a car, he knew how to drive.
But his own body ran out to gas
so out of my life he had to pass,
but lives always in memory's loyalty
in his primary prime and eager old buoyancy.

THAT VITAL ELEMENT WE CALL LIFE

Life is full of substance, not just mentality.
It has a physical basis, in reality.
So treat life as a solid essence
and you'll enjoy its very material presence,
but also suffer its pains.
But set that against its gains.
Be mentally fit. Don't join the "insanes."
Live it up. Until life unfortunately wanes,
and the whole you will be shoved in the drains
and fill the nebulae's deserted lanes.
While it lasted, life showed its evidence
before succumbing to its decadence
that it was really something to reckon with.
I'd willingly return, if beckoned thus,
to repeat the lively mystery and make a great fuss.
I'd arrive happily by any long-distance bus.

MY MOOD PLUNGE, AND HOW I GREW OUT OF IT

Always try to be happy. If you can't,
try different assorted tactics
to make your good feelings active,
even if you have to take a laxative.
If still your mood drags down,
submit it to a television clown
whose wit and charm prevail
to make the audience chorus hail
his quite original humor
that gives an occasional victim a tumor.
If he doesn't improve your morale,
certainly you can't call him a pal.
Then pick up the phone and call your gal.
"No, I can't have a date with you
because you're too morose.
That's the way it goes,
I won't let you get too close
until your mood improves a lot.
You sound like you have a blood clot."
With that rejection, my mood disimproved
to a downright depression.
In desperation, I tried a session
with a sympathetic psychiatrist.
He gave my treatment a slight little twist
by warning me against suicide
and begged my depression to subside
and put gloom off to the side.
He failed. But I'm still here,
banging at the steel doors of good cheer.
They reverberate but don't admit me.
Then suddenly suicide hit me
as a very pragmatic idea.
But I rejected it, due to the fear
of death itself, whose dingy hole
dismays me with revulsion as a whole.
So backwards to life I stealthily stole.

CASTING BLAME

1.

Parents are unfair to children,
so children voice their complaint
in loud and raucous tones,
piercing the listeners' bones.
But children are unfair to parents
and work them to the bone.
Both complaints are justified.
It's a generational barrier.
My wife's fault. Did I have to marry her?

2.

Who to blame doesn't necessarily solve the problem.
As for my innocent kids, I'll have to absolve them.
They're too young to blame,
so my wife will have to do.
Sorry, wife, it's a shame
the scapegoat title belongs to you.

WHOSE IDENTITY?

You have to signify or dignify yourself with an identity in order to be entitled to an existence? No, just help yourself to an existence and let others worry or bother about who or what in social life your identity is. Go ahead and be. Let others identify you. Just hope they don't insult you, belittle you. But don't give them reason to. But don't knock yourself out hovering over and protecting a special sort of identity in particular. Be other "people" if you want, at different times.

If somebody says, "You're not yourself today," don't be deterred. It's your privilege.

SOCIAL LIFE'S COMPILING OF FRIENDSHIP RATINGS

People are so valuable in my life
but to different degrees.
I have a hierarchy of variations
of friendships going and coming.
Some mean more to me, others less.
Luckily I'm popular, so I can choose,
and vary the priorities I offer.
I'm the object of preference:
with some a priority value,
and regarded by others more tepidly.
In my zoo of friendships
I compile a "Who's Who"
and I'm included in others' "Who's Who."
It's a jungle out there:
sink or swim in anyone's lair.
Social life needs friendships.
Differently in and out they slip.
Not all can board my ship.
Nor does everyone welcome me
to the highest tier of the tree.
I may fall out from a low branch,
and to others I avidly entrance
though I wear the same pair of pants.
I can't pretend a neutral stance.
Oh Friendship, we all need you.
But to different lengths we heed you
from the many to the few.
Oh what a promiscuous view!
Hurry up. Be on cue.
Where do you stand among the many few?
And to what degree
by choice or being chosen?
Are you among the favorite dozen?
It's all an elective mandate
and none will exactly equate.
Be a bum, or be a mate.

But some just won't compete.
Their life is already complete.
Isn't that a wonderful feat?

HOW GOOD GOVERNMENT WOULD WORK

This whole world is out of whack
when people are forced to exist with plenty of lack.
What do they lack? Too much.
Food, freedom, and happiness
are just three examples
provided in minimal samples.
Let's correct the politics
and try for a more efficient fix
drawn from the model of how a person's heart ticks
when his personal prosperity gets in some good licks.
All people would feel more benign
when the slogan "I want to get mine"
is a goal many would preach
but not out of people's equitable reach.
"More for you, and more for me,"
is how the world should operate.
Then let's have a Minister of State
to administer this goal that's great.
Work hard, to improve people's fate,
and you'll call everyone your lovely mate.
And they'll call you the same thing,
causing each to each to bodily cling.
Out of this, some people get a fling.
The benevolent government allows this,
and citizenry can barely contain their bliss.
Our round world would then be one big multiple kiss.

DOES THE EARTH FAVOR US, AND THE WORLD CO-OPERATE? LET'S FIND OUT, WON'T WE?

Is the world ideal for human life?
Are the earth's natural resources enough?
Will the sky be on our side
and also the water?
Do plants and mineral life
add enough to our well being?
Does the magnetic field help us?
Do animals, fish, and birds
benefit us, just like literary words?
Will the climate raise the hot tides?
If the earth is insufficient in these,
must we pluck fruit from the trees?
Oh earth, be kind to us.
Otherwise we rise and make a fuss.
How about human nature?
Psychologically, does it create warfare
and put our whole lives in a snare?
Should we tamper with it, if we dare?
What would the sun and moon advise
for our common fall or common rise?
"Man's inhumanity to man"
were Pope's words, and they scan.
Will the world set us free
to exploit our divine mystery
and learn enough magic tricks
to solve the intricate conflicts?
Can the computer help us to survive?
On earth, is it possible to thrive?
This ordinary question is now alive.
Evolution is doing all right
thanks to Darwin's inventive might.
Let's go as far as we can
and even penetrate eternity's ken.
If not now, then precisely when?
Our welfare depends on just where?
Then must we try another planet?

If a new scheme, then plan it
and get it right this time.
If soaring doesn't work, then try to climb.
Put survival as priority
and try every authority
despite their contrariety
in our great big common society.

A BIG REGRET FOR A CHEAP CAUSE

All those memories are there for the getting.
But some of them I'm most regretting,
and are worthy of immense forgetting.
But will I be able to repress them?
Or at least suppress, if I may?
Which one has a sharpest bite
that gives me utmost pain I have to fight?
When a letter from Jenny I got
that if lucky I would have forgot,
where she announced she's taking our two kids
and instigating divorce proceedings
and will stop my daily feedings
contrary to my hungry needings.
Now I'll miss Jenny's cooking
and at my kids I won't be looking.
Please feel sorry for me
if you have compassion at all.
My disgrace is my major fall.
Did I deserve it?
I can't swerve it.
I was unfaithful,
betraying our wedding ring.
Thus I'm subject to regret's bitter sting
for the crime of having a paltry fling.

THE PROPER WAY TO KEEP TIME WITHIN ETERNITY'S RULE AND NOT SIMULTANEOUSLY MAKE YOURSELF A FOOL

Memory cannot raid the future,
only prediction and expectation can,
and also a word like anticipation
which presumes too much on the future's virgin innocence
and as yet unreadiness.
Future is an unfilled page
waiting for its scribbling sage.
If the future hasn't happened yet,
then till it does, memory is premature
and has to abide its time and place
and put on a totally neutral face
so as not to be too influential
in tampering with the essential
order that the future has to be waited for,
or else time's corruption for everyone is in store
and penalties will grow for interference.
Impatient for the future? Then wait your turn.
Obey sequence and continuity, or else you burn
and become a charcoal unless you finally learn.
The future needs to be waited for
or else you're a dope for putting "after" before "before."
If you try to argue, you're just a miserable bore.
At what point is the future ready?
Don't hasten yourself. Be steady,
or you'll be accused of meddling,
which even for a professor is unsettling.
Preparing for a slow future?
Don't jump ahead too quick
and rush through to back up your pick
with speed that's much too early.
It's enough to make an honest clock surly.
Have due respect for sequence
and prepare to be orderly in its defense.
Your wristwatch will burn your wrist
if you reverse chronology and persist.
Keep Time honest, obey its rule

or else you're a damn misbehaving fool,
and need to go logically back to school,
having been stupidly left behind
for interfering with processed Time,
which is considered an anti-temporal crime,
not temporarily, but for all time.
Or else lose your head and become sublime.

KEEP THE GENERATIONAL FLOW.
IT'S INSPIRATIONALLY NECESSARY, YOU KNOW.

Thank you, parents, for begetting
me, whose life is owing to you.
Some day I'll properly acknowledge it,
for extracting me from non-being's inactive pit
and giving me young manhood, so fit
that in turn I'll help a baby to be born
who I'll be the father of, and blow my own horn,
while not forgetting to credit my lovely wife
for aiding in the true being of our child's lovely life,
whose future also contains children plenty
once he passes the fertile age of twenty.
My role in life has been to pass generations along
while crediting my wife for harmonizing our song.
Darwin thanks me: "You've done nothing wrong,
advancing evolution so it's so big and strong.
Your lovely wife you must credit too
for assisting in the act of performing a zoo
limited to only human beings
who are the race best worth seeing
from our own same human eyes.
Surely their birth furnishes us with no surprise."

COUPLE-ATING

The angry male provokes the resistant lady
to coyly retaliate and act shady.
This inflames him to an aggravated ardor
that dominatingly he pushes even harder
so she submits with superior thrill
to tease him further up and down the hill
of their doubled-up bodies
to consolidate their mutual regard
to an ultimate pitch that they dare not to retard,
and go wildly ahead as expected
just as nature dictated and directed,
leading to pleasure on both sides of the coin
where heads and tails, true to formula, will splashingly conjoin,
lust inviting love to spill itself over,
to go from France to the wild cliffs of Dover.
They pant and relax. Then to do it all over
hardly hurts if they have time enough
with themselves again to obligingly pull out more stuff.

THE BODY OF MY THANKS

Life is such a wonderful gift,
let's extend its length with thrift.
If we die too soon, we're miffed.
So live long as a lovely lift.
Who deserves thanks the more?—
mother dear or father dear?—
who both together provided good cheer,
but APART never would,
but just be two blocks of dumb wood?
Their combination was for the good.
Mother and father combined
provide the mastermind
that invented the birth of me
when their two bodies went on a spree.
And virtually it was all for free,

resulting in that magic mystery of me
whose life I'm charmed to live.
I have enchanted thanks to perennially give
to dear mother and father both
who supplied the impetus to give me growth.
To acknowledge them forever is to be my oath:
responsible for me, for good or ill
in the immense ecstasy of their good will
which I dearly hope to fulfill
to the very best of my reproductive skill
once I get a sufficient wife
to replenish the destiny of our family life.

LIFE'S PURPOSE INVESTIGATED

Who can figure out life's mystery
and simplify it into a lengthy history
of the whole philosophical deal
that makes us sit up and squeal?—
Or take cover from life itself
and consign that latest tome to the shelf
where it gathers the usual dust
which any inferior book also must?
It's enough to make me cynical
that the game of life is not winnable.
What I write now reaches its last syllable
and my empty brain is no longer fillable.
All you writers who try to figure out
life—tell me what it's all about
in words of such simplicity
that it suggests an evil conspiracy
of a bunch of literary scribes
who puzzle a mystery that no one ever describes
to the fullest of satisfactions—
What's the purpose of our actions?
Maybe it's to end our distractions.

BASIC ANTI-WAR REASONS FOR ALL WAR-LIKE SEASONS

Life is on very uncertain terms
with itself, when it's still spent on waging war
which puts the self in danger
by the enemy's self-defense.
Therefore, let's abolish war
so as not to endanger the wager
of that aforesaid war.
Put self-safety before
the killing of the enemy
if he doesn't kill you first.
(We agree that killing
could be done by THEM, not just YOU.
And that would be curtains by all thus engaged
since killing is caused by being enraged.)
Instead, let's all be engaged
in peaceful kissing of each other
and the calling of each other "brother,"
or "sister," for that matter,
to protect our clothing from a blood-drenched tatter
and a bandaged head from your fancy hatter.

THE VALUE OF POST-ACTION TALK

Disappointing results tend to outstrip initial boisterous, fervent hopes, souring people on life's ornate promises.

Yes, it spoils life's public image as a self-promoting advertisement claiming that life is an unalloyed, unsullied good. People take compensation in cynicism and make endless jokes alluding that life is never or rarely what it's pumped up to seem to be. From within, that may corrupt life's implicit value as a voice of good valuable tidings and something positive rather than negative.

Enough about life. It's enough to live it. Must it dominate conversation?

Living life isn't enough. It should be analyzed, to complete its voyage from mere crude living to the refinements of exquisite philosophical discourse.

Are we capable of such?

Sure. It's written down in this concluding or conclusive poem:

> First living, then giving it verbal extension:
> We labored for our wages, justifying our pension.
> Further talk? Go into another dimension.
> I'll dimention this, you dimention that
> to prolong indefinitely our chat
> covering all territory, from this to that.

FOOLS, TAKE HEED.
(ADDRESSED TO THOSE OF YOUR BREED.)

Human life is a sacred blessing,
so be polite to those you're addressing,
even a criminal who's not confessing.
Though he's so hardened, you be gentle.
He may be handicapped in mental
normality, so be his liberal helper,
but hope you're not his target in his role as a scalper
who pimps in disguise as women's developer.
If you meet him, discuss the weather
but don't stay near him in criminal tether
nor be accused of being his bird of a feather.
Be suspicious that he may do you in.
If opposed to tough guys, pray you may ever win.
Everyone dangerous you should avoid,
even if his excuses come from the book of Freud.
Your whole life may be smashed and destroyed.
Depending on who you're with, don't be too nice.
A gentle balm may be chemically mixed with rough spice.
Heed my urgent warning, which should enough suffice
if you don't want to be life's martyrly sacrifice.
Watch out. Don't be taken in.
You should know that fools like you could never hope to win,
and then your sacred human life would be worth a pin
that magnetically sticks you in your precious skin.

WHO DO YOU ROOT FOR?

I show a criminal tendency
to at movies identify with the bad guy,
also on television and in books
to sympathize with the actual crooks.
I can tell by their looks
who's the evil one and who's not,
then I place my empathy bet
on the lousy louse who's now my pet.
I'll somehow correct my choice yet
to avoid being in debt
to morality pure
that will always endure.

WHAT'S STEWING?

Evolution automatically arranges
that its mutational changes
be registered on the official chart
of reproduction's empowered art
so that lots of babies will be born
to add their multiple names and addresses
to the amount of humanity's power
to enhance our generation's towering hour
so that terrific history will journalistically flower.
This overwhelms me quite
to conceive what's going to ignite.
I hope it's not an appalling blight.

POSTING A PUBLIC WARNING

Watch out for a stranger
who may represent danger.
His cruel aspect on display
may warn you safely away.
He has an indeterminate look
but underneath he may be a crook.

So if you value life carefully,
be warned preparefully
to dodge and duck as much as you can.
To thwart his homicidal tendency,
get him jailed to put an endency
to his alarming and severe threat.
He may be a drug-addicted vet
slightly crazed from the war
that tragically ruined him before.
Now he constitutes a menace,
but you can beat him at tennis.

EXUBERANT ABUNDANCE PROSPECTIVELY GIVEN TO US IRRESPECTIVELY

Is life mysterious?
Of course. Be serious.
Mystery is just one element
from tail to trunk of the elephant
which we as life's celebrant
take voluminously to the heart
to solve any puzzle and still become smart.
Diversity and variety abound.
Thus we go swirling around
tasting this and that from the treasury box
that mere curiosity openly unlocks,
sampling trivia and items deluxe
just for a minor expenditure of bucks,
and the world unfolds profusely,
surrendering tightly and loosely
rich gems and poor trinklets,
high surprises along slight gifts,
to do our deep lives such uplifts
that toward mystery just about anything tilts,
even to the point of wearing kilts.
Hurry up before all before us wilts,
and to catch up, we awkwardly skid on stilts.

WATCH WHAT YOU SAY? NO.

As for the meaning of life, opinions vary.
One affirms THIS, and the other the contrary.
Everybody has the right to disagree.
Free speech doesn't exact a nominal fee.
You're entitled to what you think.
Even if outlandish, you don't have to blink.
Some opinions are suspiciously attributed to drink,
others even to a way-out drug.
But if you've got the opinion bug,
belligerently affirm it, don't be a slug,
though others accuse you of being a stupid mug.
Democracy advocates free speech.
Take the required liberty, but don't belch a screech
to blast others' ears off; it's open to each,
like a wild wave that floods the surprised beach.
For you, hope that others don't prescribe bleach.

TEMPTED TO LET GO?

Strain as you must to make sure
that precious Life is what you secure
to dearly hold on to, with all your might,
against the dragons and horrors of fright,
if Life seems vulnerable to loss.
Keep it near you, you're the boss.
Then relax. You've got it secure
against death's pernicious lure.
Death declares itself the more pure.
But I retort: "I'm not so sure,
but aim to hold on, for dear Life,
to my dearest asset: my Life.
Otherwise, I'm turmoiled in strife."

WATCH OUT

The frank fragility of life
needs us to steer clear of strife
so as not to endanger ourselves
amid the grim peals of funeral bells.
So "safety" is the operative word.
The lack of it is too absurd
even to safely contemplate.
Don't put poison on your plate
to tempt yourself deathwards.
Keep air going breathwards,
and stay well out of your perverse death-wish.
Peril is not always an easy escape.
Keep your eyes on the lovelier landscape.

IF THE BLADDER'S TOO FREQUENT IT'S SOMEHOW DELINQUENT. THE BATHROOM I FREQUENT.

My bladder is my sleep-ender
and makes insomnia my betrayer
because I have to be a bathroom player
with my periodical urine
at too early in the morning
as a suitable warning
that I'll be sleepy all day
and droop when I should work or play.
The bladder is my sleep spoiler,
my peaceful-rest soiler,
my peace-of-mind destroyer.
Yet I'm grateful that my bladder
keeps me going up the ladder
of organic consistency
without the onus of disability,
and opens up the world of pissibility.
Better to say "urine" than "you're out,"
as long as your system is holding up stout.
A later nap restores you, no doubt.

SELF-CONSCIOUSNESS IS OVER
WHEN YOU'RE NO LONGER A ROVER.

I can't remember if I have dementia
as my life creeps into this last venture.
Old age sure seems like a deathly trap.
For losing my youth, I have to take the rap
and fold up my non-existent tent
and proceed along the terminal bent
devoid of my usual old merriment
and drearily dissolve without intent.
An ending too weak to protest
is appropriate, but not the best.
The penalty for hoarding too many years
is to succumb to all the usual fears
and don't worry about how it appears
because now you're out of society
subject to people's promiscuous variety
of critical observations of you.
Pointless whether they hit the mark and were true.

WHAT MEMORY ENDEAVORED
WHEN WE WERE SEVERED

Jimmy Stagno, my old friend,
when his body failed, he had to bend
and reluctantly face death in the face
and had to give way, his whole being
losing everything including memory,
which was my component, left to me
to do the memory business for us both,
including starting out young, before our growth
accelerated, and now look at us:
He's not there, and I'm there for both,
bearing up a double burden.
He spoke, I heard him.
When I speak, he doesn't heed.
Our friendship made us the same breed.
We ate together. He has no stomach.

It's a one-sided friendship now.
He lies underneath my brow,
or else far within
where the past in its entirety lurks
spread before me, avail it or not.
I'll dip in reluctantly, shot by shot.
The record is all but complete.
To devour us both is a gourmet feat
with tears sprinkled as a side dish
(or maybe saliva, to put sentiment aside,
which doesn't technically spoil the dish).
I pluck him bodily out, like a caught fish.
It slips away. I bungle my only wish.

RECOMMENDED READING

As if life isn't confusing enough,
philosophers keep introducing new stuff
for us to cogitate, mulling through
books, articles, treatises
to probe along the intricasies
of the brainy literary businesses
allied to science, of course,
to reduce romantic sentiment
and specialize on reality itself
to include among the books on your shelf.
Thus biography has a stake
on all this eye-fatiguing intake,
giving you new mental pies to domestically bake
to prove that sincere endeavor is never a fake.
On all this intellectual activity, what's your take?
I'd tell you mine, but that would help you cheat,
like someone who substitutes white bread for whole wheat.

MAKING THE IDEAL REALISTICALLY PRACTICAL, AND GETTING CREDIT FOR IT

If you can't have the ideal,
then make an appeal
for something more realistic.
Then make it tick,
so you're on the better track,
but you can't get idealism back
(having already abandoned it,
because it just doesn't fit)
except in other circumstances
wherein you'll have to take your chances,
depending on the situation
close to opportunity's occasion
to pounce on an idealistic chance
which offers itself in a better stance
of winning the contest
where the idealistic best
will win in the practicality test.
Make the idealistic practical
when the ground is ripe for its actual,
to convert the ideal to a realistic factual
when stimulated by opportunity's realistic perk
to make idealism realistically work.
No wonder your lips indicate a successful smirk
defying anybody to call you a potential jerk,
when your alertness won success with a quick lurk.

ELEGY FOR JIMMY

What we used to do is no longer possible
since one of us is dead—you.
You can't drive me in your car any more
nor I be a passenger therein.
The ingredient was that we needed each other—
spoiled by your death.
Do I blame you? It wasn't your fault

that being familiar together
in friendship's cosy assumptions
is now strenuously ruined
on whose ruin I pour my grief
and stagger alone in disbelief.

MY OLD SCHOOL BUDDIES

If I'm old, and my boyhood schoolmates are dead,
where does that leave ME?
I'm now absolutely free
to join them in non-existence,
which doesn't console me an inch.
Death is totally negative. That's a cinch
that makes the still-living wince
if they're eligible candidates
to adjust their future dates
to join old school buddies
in irretrievable consciousness loss.
The teachers died earlier,
now the students follow.
I find it increasingly hard to swallow.

THE UNINTERFERING SNAKES IN THE BOTANICAL GARDENS ON A GORGEOUS DAY IN THE JOLLY MONTH OF MAY

When the merry month of May comes along,
the world breaks into a blossom of song
along this side of the Atlantic,
so it's time for magicians to get frantic
to accompany flowers with sounds
synchronizing melody's botanical bliss
at which hidden snakes would be reluctant to hiss
because they don't want to spoil the effect
and break the ecstatic mood with a slithering defect
that would interfere with a paradise that's so perfect.
Thus those snakes combine with idealism
to keep out of sight with their sneaky wisdom.
Otherwise the guards would haul them into prison.

SOME DRAWBACKS TO LIFE

Life being too complex to analyze,
I'll stop trying to cut it down to size
and simply accept reality
as a true pure fact of actuality,
but not along the lines of conformist normality.
I must really be myself.
How can I choose among my many selves,
like an embarrassment of unearned riches?
As a comedian, I'll have you all in stitches,
but a medical surgeon can also do that
provided you're truly injured to offer your skin
and have enough pain to wince when he punctures in.
Pain is only a partial essence of life.
There's plenty more, including mental strife;
also marital disorder, if you take a wife.

HOW ARE THINGS GOING?

Old age is a deathly trap.
In life's lengthy race, you're on the last lap.
My school classmates succumbed
so I'm left alone and feel numb
except for arthritis' constant ache
and the more than occasional stomach ache
which I can't pretend is only fake.
Other ailments also pursue me.
And people I owe money to are too dead to sue me,
so that's a huge life saving,
since unequal democracy
is what we're braving
in the bad- or good-luck sweepstakes.
Do you by accident have what it takes?
How things turn out is what makes
people relatively calm and happy
or else dead or they feel crappy.

ME, MY WIFE, AND OUR BABY BOY
CLAIM EACH OUR PART OF LIFE'S AVAILABLE JOY.
WE HOPE THE WORLD'S END IS NOT "DESTROY."

I gave my sperm to evolution
via its reproduction agency.
Not that it's an emergency.
Evolution can do without me
and keep perpetuating itself
without my spermatic help,
which resulted in a nice baby boy
who gives both wife and me such infinite joy.
But we can't regard him as a toy.
He's very real in his own right.
If we disobey him, he puts up a fight
until we must give in.
He puts up two cheeks for wife and me to kiss
on both sides, so we can't miss.
To cap success, we give each other a kiss.
I'm glad my wife is no longer a miss,
so the baby's legitimacy is beyond doubt,
though he'll grow up without a capitalistic clout.
But we'll train him not to be a lout.
After all, what is life all about?
Not just money, but prestige too,
to avoid making humans a mockery zoo.
Good luck, reader, from me to you,
and my dear wife salutes you too.
But not that darling, my boy.
Right now, he spits on his toy
and is easily forgiven by wife and me.
Long live his lovely life, and he's free
despite his obvious dependency.
He'll apologize or forgive later
and find a wife and mate her
to make evolution slightly greater.

A WALK IN THE OLD HAUNTS AFTER JIMMY STAGNO DIED

No more Jimmy Stagno.
Now I don't know where to go
except to compensate with nostalgia
by walking along the same grounds
we used to both frequent for so many years
united in conversations along the way,
including the merriment of verbal play
ending in rounds of plain humor
and then a restaurant where all this continued.
I tried to repeat that in the same mood.
But tears interfered along the way.
I enjoyed the nostalgia. It was a good day.
One thing was inevitably lacking.
I didn't get his personal backing.
The mood turned to extreme blacking.
By now it was lonely night
fraught with the bitterness of blight.
I thought I glimpsed his sight.
The world went on. It was all right.

A VOTE FOR LIFE. LET DEATH TAKE A BACK SEAT. UNADULTERATED, I'LL TAKE MY LIFE NEAT.

Is death the opposite of life?
It quite is, but bears some resemblance too.
In life, we have periods of quiet,
lying down, and stillness,
not to mention the bother of illness.
But being voluntary is a different matter
than all your faculties lying in tatter
with you not even "you" any more,
something that you can never restore,
having lost all your identity
in addition to the body entity
in which you enjoyed so much plenty
but had to endure it too.

Better by far to go back to being "you,"
which is the greatest gift you ever received
if the witness of me is to be believed.
Don't lose it. It can't be retrieved.

ADVICE TO MALE BABIES BORN TO WIDE-HIPPED MOTHERS

Women's hips are wider than men's
to make room for baby embryos
who fill out, and need the whole space
to wail, while about to be born,
that life has a reputation to be forlorn
but it's too late to opt out
from nature's plan, whether or not
that reputation is correct
and is exactly what we must expect.
Those embryos got large and were born.
Life turned out to conform
to the prediction it would be forlorn.
But go ahead and live, and blow your own horn
to make your lungs young and strong.
Then marry a wide-hipped girl
like your mother and give it a whirl.
Let whatever happens go ahead and unfurl
despite the forlorn tendency
of life from beginning to endency.
Surprise yourself. Life won't be too bad
but first try it out, and see if it's that sad.
If it is, then go ahead and be mad.
At least you're alive, so be somewhat glad.
You'll get a baby girl from your wide-hipped wife,
so proudly you've produced a whole new life.

WATCH OUT

1.

Life is frail, life is fragile.
Protect it as best you can.
Being free and easy with it
should be a lifetime ban.
Be tight and restrictive
to protect its tiny precious inch.
If you see danger come close,
close your fists and flinch.
Don't let life's distance shrink
from oblivion—don't dare blink.
One careless slip, and then
the door's slammed shut—don't ask when.
Try to analyze it, but too late:
Your thinking's gone, and so is your fate.

2.

How close to the edge life can be!
Give me your pledge to be cowardly,
after taking due care
not to do what you don't dare.

3.

Watch out, be quick.
Life's easy to unstick.
Don't take peril for granted.
If you're rich, your tomb may be granite
unless the cemetery keeper will ban it.

TO JIMMY STAGNO, AS IF HE WERE STILL ALIVE

Is your memory the same as mine?
Oh that would be really fine
that our memories intertwine,
since friendship is a sharing

between two volitions on the same daring
as they go on eternally comparing,
so the conversation is endless
and we'll never be friendless,
having each other
as the mysterious other brother.

COMPARING LIFE WITH ITS OWN MEANING WITHOUT TO EITHER BEING DEMEANING

The meaning of life? I'm not sure.
Somehow life seems too obscure,
not to mention of course complex,
to deserve a plain meaning.
That seems mean of life to so demean
the actual meaning of itself.
So let's call both equally obscure
in their complicated rearrangement
of a bodily organism and its attendant word
to keep their wrinkled separateness from seeming absurd.

AN ENDORSEMENT

Deep in the throes of a mental breakdown,
he decided instead he'd be a clown.
So he studied humor and jokes
and satirically made some pokes
at the vulnerability of people
whose proud self-illusions
insulted reality with confusions.
Then he tried to go on the stage
of nightclubs and was all the rage.
He forged ahead a good career.
As a popular celebrity he won the public cheer.
This is a good-luck story
without a moral, to the hero's glory.
It's a heart-warmer, at least for me.
Go to his shows. It's a minimal fee.

MY LAST PLAN

If life comes to an end one day,
how would it be possible for me to convey
a sincere thank-you for the life I had
which divided itself equally between good and bad?
I'll bid life a silent goodbye,
then allow my friends to cry
over the demise of Marvin, a nice guy.

**TITLE IN REVERSE FOLLOWS TEXT,
SO NOW YOU KNOW WHAT'S COMING NEXT**

Al Lehman and I were innocent kids.
But he was more worldly-wise than I.
So he provided the guidance
and I followed as a disciple.
We learned soon to get an eyeful
of girls, whose feminine charms riled us
to begin the adult business.
Hence our apprenticeship replacing kid-ness.

    **TITLE IN REVERSE
    TO NOW REHEARSE:**

Growing up, with help from a buddy,
so that our early life wouldn't be too muddy,
we also learned not to be a fuddy duddy
but take a manly stride toward maturity
and earn our livings for security.

THE "CONSTRUCTION" UNION

If you have any singular woe,
don't double it with extra trouble.
Detonate your trouble
to a heap of demolished rubble
by a good demolition job
by a hard-hatted construction mob

wielded together
by a corrupt organization
that gets double pay for taking a vacation.
With an outfit like that,
who wouldn't want to be a hard-hat?
So if you have a woe, enlist their service
and pardon them if on your shoes they take a piss
when "bargaining" you out of that and this.
Soon they'll embellish your woe
but put you in their permanent debt.
If you think you can get out of it,
including your shoes, you're all wet.
Do turn down their offer of a "bet."
That'll give you much more to fret.
But you don't dare to turn it down:
Their protection racket is offered with an irresistible frown.
If you don't take it, they'll tab you as a "clown,"
and increase what you owe them to simply an outlandish amount,
offered at a surprisingly low "discount,"
signifying how your woes are bound to mount
by a significant degree.
To save your skin, be sure to agree
with their "outstanding" terms,
or they may slip into your drink some meddlesome germs.
You can't trifle with such formidable firms
or they'll squash your face down among the worms
while lisping their list of "exacting" terms
which to disagree with is ruinous.
Their "violations" are numerous.
No pity for the consumerist
if you happen to be on their list
and be pulverized by a pure right fist
through which your shoes will be further pissed.
The luck you never had should be "goodbye" kissed.
Goodbye is the right note to find yourself missed.

SHOULD WE MAKE A FILM ABOUT IT?

If there were no philosophy, would there still be life?
Sure there would. The intellect is extra
to cement down the substance of this lecture.
It's essential we be rational
to make sense of the actual
in relation to the prevalent irrational
that runs through the entire universe
and runs back again in reverse,
whether in blessing or in curse.
If I had extra money in my purse,
I'd sponsor an investigation
into the joint mentality of every nation
and find out how the whole world ticks.
There's a lot of benevolence. They're not all pricks.
Let kindness be our social substance
to combat our rampant inhumanity
that corrupts the purity of our sanity,
and helps psychiatry to thrive
to keep mental illness alive
or else cure it
just slightly bit by bit.
It would make a terrific movie hit,
especially if provided with wit
and mechanical technology for extra effect
to add dimension to our study of intellect.
Add everything else, just to make it perfect,
devoid whatever of the least defect.
Whatever mistake, be sure to correct.
I'll choose an expert to inspect
the damages and the revenue,
then be sure to get back to you
to put you in the picture with a cue.

**BAD SELF-NEWS
WITH PESSIMISTIC VIEWS
OF MISERABLE MISFORTUNE
OVERWHELMING YOUR FUTILE CAUTION.
OF BAD LUCK, YOU EXCEED YOUR PORTION
TO AN ALMOST COMICAL DISTORTION**

If life gets you down in the dumps,
at least you don't have a case of the mumps;
and you're ahead of the game in finance:
you won't go broke till the near distance
like two months from now, for instance.
True, you're all alone with no love,
and you have no religion, so no help from above.
Your prospects of a job have turned nil
and you're burdened with an unknown kind of inner ill.
Your "friends" have abandoned you
because you can't repay their loans,
and periodically you discharge spontaneous moans
that acoustically are confused with self-pitying groans
attributed to endless gloom
living in a barely furnished room
at rent economically cheap
so you feel like a failure and a creep,
anonymous to all of society
who only pretend to propriety
when you show your unwelcome face
that looks like a familiar symbol of disgrace
in the lack of public esteem,
being a bum who ran out of steam.
This is negativity, to the extreme.
The way you dress qualifies for bumhood,
and you stink up the neighborhood.
No wonder you constantly brood.
You even subsist on inadequate food,
diminishing health and vitality both.
Useless to take a suicidal oath.
The only "solution" is to live a dream
that breaks apart how things seem.

THE DYNAMIC LIFE CYCLE
ENDING ON DEATH'S STALLED BICYCLE
COLD AS A BURNED-OUT ICICLE

As a kid, first you have to routinely grow up.
Once you're in the doldrums of that hurdle,
when your glands are still romantically fertile,
you start beginning your path to grow down
past the puddle of a middle-aged muddle
which leaves your wits zithered in befuddle.
Then having completed the standard lifetime round,
you plummet mercilessly into the death-time ground,
which plays right into the philosopher's notebook
that meager mortality gets everyone on the hook,
whether you're a legal advocate or a crook,
or a saint or a knave compiled in a library book
where dustily that's where you're referred to
as a former denizen of humanity's crowded zoo
that rises in population up from the original few.
Meanwhile down-below's population also grows
to add non-statistically to death's fallen foes
who used to be in wild life's glowing throes
and end past melancholy's posthumous woes
when life's primal thrust
went completely bust
and you too, if you must.

EVERYTHING AND NOTHING TOGETHER
IN OUR MIXED METAPHYSICAL WEATHER

Life may have started at nothing
and made its way through
in the full course of evolution
to arrive at you and me too
who are substantial beings
full of hearings and seeings
not to mention other things
too innumerable for these listings,
there being insufficient room

to accommodate this insurmountable zoom
and the flickering constant boom
of humanity, everyone avoiding doom
to the individual extent
of private longevity's precious extended length.
Compared to others who die before you
due maybe to diet or the flu,
you're lucky or envious or both.
Farewell to all that preceded growth.
To ourselves and friends we take the most sacred oath
or else don't because of bitterness.
We're all each other's constant witness.
Or indifferent, as the case may be.
There's so much to overlook in what we see,
and how disappointed we may have felt
when deep desires go out to melt.

THE COMPOSER'S EXPLANATION

If something is wrong, then do something about it,
attack the problem, and fix it.
Address yourself to it,
don't let it just rankle there
and fester, and get even worse:
put the knob into the reverse
and bring things back to normal,
make the problem go away,
relieve it from your chest,
void your system of it,
get rid of it,
put it to rights,
give it your best fight.
Take care of it, all right.
But first identify the problem. What's wrong?
Oh, I lost a chord from my incomplete song.

PRAISING A WIFE STILL YOUNG ENOUGH TO OUTSHINE A REALISTIC PORTRAIT

The love I bear for my wife
exceeds the limits of my life
within the bounds of natural nature.
If I were an artist, I'd commit her to portraiture
that attempts to compete with the human original.
Still I prefer herself over her copy-cat art.
She definitely enjoys the realistic part
in her natural human guise.
She's also preferred by all the guys
over the poor unfortunate art
that wastes its frame in an empty hall
where her true glow is in a state of stall.
Actually, there's no comparison at all.
Her texture adroitly stands out
from the flat stiff canvas pout.
But what if she grows older?
Then art's artifice should become bolder.
I pack this up, and put it in a folder.

THE RUINED PICNIC, INCLUDING ITS PARTLY REDEEMING AFTERMATH

If you're about to have a picnic
with a blanket covering the grass,
and good friends to try enjoying themselves,
what if distant thunder is heard,
not to be mistaken for the chord of a bird?
You're under threat of a rained-on picnic,
directly contrary to your fun-loving mood.
Your friends are scattering away from the blanket,
not bothering to carry food and wine away.
Thousands of clouds are covering the sun,
which ran away just like your friends.
You're left alone to pick up the wet waste
while the eat contents of the blanket are reduced to paste.
Has your mood turned into angry thunder?

About such a reaction there's no need to wonder,
when such a lovingly planned picnic turns asunder.
But the raindrops now are getting more sparse
and belatedly the sun tries returning.
Too late. You've already been abandoned
by your scattered band of "loving" friends
whose unanimous betrayal you're left to brood on
and with nothing dry to put the destroyed food on.
The left-over bottles of wine
will help you and the returning sun
to escape misery by getting drunk
as the world turns aglow in swoon-like twilight.
You're left alone to brood your unpopularity, by dry night.
What can you do about your departed friends who took cowardly flight?
But the world reverberates with a semi-holy sight.
The day concludes its verdict with a partial blight.
But now the cosmos is shrunk to an uncanny height.

WHAT'S MISSING AND WHO BY

Since Jimmy Stagno just died, where does that leave me? Missing him. That's the way things go, when a lifelong friendship of eighty five years is broken and destroyed with the remaining one helplessly ready to carry on conversation as usual, but without the uniquely irreplaceable dialogue partner. All their mutual references accumulated over the decades now suddenly untouched, unconfirmed, discontinued, barren. I'm left holding the bag—the whole contents of which are pouring down drainage. The seeds of furtherness drowned out forever by an abrupt severance of two partners into that eternal division that inflames the weak survivor's leaking head with leftover vital points unaddressed and turned rancidly fallow, would-be. The cow's milk-leaking udders at the flaccid helpless shattered lips of her calf's early corpse hours in a meadow that carries on as usual with successful others of their slow-moving species, however the weather may vary that scene of many locations.

THE WEATHER PULLED A DAMPER
FROM THE FOOD READY IN THE HAMPER
FOR A GLORIOUS INTENDED PICNIC
BUT UNWELCOME RAIN CREATED CONFLICT

The picnic is all ready on the prepared blanket.
But what of those pops of distant thunder?
Will your rising spirits then wetly go under?
Your planning schedule has unluckily turned up a blunder.
Your pack of friends runs away from the rain,
leaving the abandoned food to turn into paste
and undergo the ruined spectacle of abysmal waste.
Your popularity is insulted by your friends' betrayal.
But wine bottles remain that the rain doesn't harm.
You pop them open, turning the lonely day into a charm
of drunken solitude, questioning your social prestige
that's sodden-ly been punctured through and through
by invited friends unanimously abandoning you
to a drenching downpour that seems to mock you
as if nature had a venom of its own
as your prepared picnic has scattered and flown
and you're angry at human nature
as if weather allied itself with fate sure
to break your sobbing heart
as if you're supposed to be mature
with such wet adversity to dryly endure.
Such generosity to be rejected
before the clouds above could be inspected!
In your mind you had a different scenario to play,
but the cue came too late on a ruined day.
Into every life expect some rain,
but not when timed wrongly and produces pain.

A NEW SLANT TO JUSTIFY SELFISHNESS. IT TOOK A LONG TIME TO GET THERE. ALSO, A DENIAL OF THE GENTLE MYTH OF "SURVIVOR'S GUILT."

(An essay in defense of old-age well-earned selfishness.)

The world in its original origin is way beyond me in the past. All I have to deal with is one Now at a time. That takes up my time. I go on from there.

To be continued. The empty future is peopled with what may be, images I only learned from the past, and actively apply.

I'm too old not to be afraid. My friends are gone. How does that apply to me?

Well, I'm still here, here I am. I survived my friends, but without guilt. I'm actually happy about it, though I feel sorry or indifferent about them. The main thing is in the Me, which in its increasingly venerable state I even rejoice and gloat. Hurray!—the same old me, just a bit shopworn.

All right, so I'm selfish. What else can I do with my remains, but to exercise the still-young colt of my selfishness, let him jump over fences, subject to self-renewal while my good fortune holds out?

So I exult in my Selfishness, which Society had so misunderstood, underestimated, and depreciated. Long live to it.

This loyal defense of the simple subjectivity of Selfishness had to be earned, through long years as a survived reward. That's how Society will tolerate it: It's scared not to, due to its respect for Time.

P.S. I'm waiting for my comeuppance.

TWO LEGITIMATE WORDS AND ONE NOT, IN DESCRIBING THE HUMAN MENTAL APPARATUS. BUT RELIGIOUS CLERGY WILL GET AT US, AND IF WE WERE A BALL, THEY'D BAT US.

The human being is counted a body at a time,
with each body having its own independent "mind"
including of course the well-esteemed "brain"
that has attained scientific validity.
But the "soul" is too mystical a term
to deserve respect as a viable entity
with a well-merited separate identity.
So "soul" doesn't exist, but "mind" and "brain" do,
from the atheist's superior point of view.

SAFELY LIVING LIFE SO IT DOESN'T GO AWAY AND GET OUT OF HAND

Life is too important for us
to let go of it too easily
by accident or negligence.
So maintain your tightest maintenance
and compulsively obsessive vigilance
to keep alive your acquaintenanceship
with that existentially essential entity
we worshipfully call life
and don't let it carelessly slip
from your strenuous clenched grip
and scatter itself like a vase
with its bouquet of flowers falling loutishly out
leaf by leaf and bloom by bloom
all over the disarrayed room
to upset the neatly arranged carpet
and all the chairs where you used to snugly sit
near no receptacle in which to eject a polite spit
which society would reject as not fit.
I'd already learned the finesse when to quit
bad behavior and not to repeat it.
It's uncouth to irresponsibly spit.
So I keep a dry mouth to when I drink
with a breath sweetener so my alcohol doesn't stink
except when I'm fortunately near the kitchen sink.
Life is so dear, I dare not wink.
It's bother enough to have to repeatedly think.

LET IT BE A FILM, NOT REAL, THAT YOU FLASH A WEAPON OF DEADLY STEEL

Pointing a gun gives you dominance
of your situation along with prominence,
in a masterful position
to insist with precision
what you require the poor victim to do
in his fearful submission to gun-authorized you.

All you have to do is point
and his will power gets out of joint.
He succumbs with obedience
to your any and every expedience
as your dutiful slave for the occasion
with you holding the total maximum persuasion.
His trembling dislike of you is hidden with evasion.
I hope it's a film, and not in real life
that we're beholding this bout of uneven strife.
As for the outcome, who can tell?
I hope your trigger finger doesn't ring its bell
and send your victim for a spell
of being permanently unwell
if he survives the trauma at all.
What punishment will you befall?

HEARING A YOUTH'S VOWS,
OPEN YOUR MOUTH FOR SOME SURPRISED "WOWS"
ON PARDONS HE LATER PROFESSIONALLY ALLOWS

As a young boy, I want to do my parents proud
by having an intellectual manner but not too loud.
I want to cultivate the best assets
to win all of life's major bets,
and that's about as good as it gets.
I don't wish my parents worries and frets.
On my boyish behalf I'll be a responsible young adult
but not adulterated to be a dolt.
Nor do I want to spitefully revolt
against middle-class values my parents proudly hold.
I'll refrain from being a brat obnoxiously bold.
I'll earn as much money as income can hold
by cultivating a money-making profession
as a priest who condones a murderous confession
but stipulating indulgence of his harmless sexual obsession,
with a curtained booth concealing an intimate session
bargaining severe rules on physical possession.

**THE COMBINATION OF MONEY AND LOVE
KEEPS THE WORLD SWIRLING ABOVE.
THE COMBINATION OF LOVE AND MONEY
KEEPS ME SNUGGLING WITH MY HONEY.
THAT MAKES SENSE, IT'S NOT FUNNY.**

Life is going from hope to hope
and all you want is satisfaction
in return for all this action.
Not all our hopes get realized
but still we go on hoping
even to the point of eloping
if her parents don't consent
to formal marriage ceremony
or just Justice of the Peace.
Why? Because you don't have any money.
"Isn't that the truth, honey?"
I say to my snuggling wife.
Luckily, she has the dough
independent of her parents' opposing
her marriage, which she completed
with lucky me—her parents defeated.
Money makes the world go round,
but love too. Isn't that sound?
They both come from the same ground.
Money cushions the marital bed.
Would you prefer a park bench instead
right next to a squirrel who's dead?

BALANCING DEFT POLAR EXTREMES

What can cure melancholy
that came seemingly from nowhere?
Convert it to being jolly
and dig up your extra laughter
from jokes long leftover,
revive them with new flair,
dancingly leap to the air
with merriment's burst from nowhere,

just exuberant spirits
that combat and win over
melancholy's relinquished reign,
shifting sides on the same plain
of neutral capacity
handling emotional opposites
ejecting one, pop! from where it sits
and situate to the other side
to seesaw the same ride
like a counter-espionage agent
smoothly turning the adjacent
with a magician's suave patience
without the slightest wastage
and no loss of face-ege.
Melancholy to happiness is a ride,
but back to melancholy in a landslide,
and your hopes must momentarily subside
until you reverse this embattled tide.

REVENGE ON PARENTS FOR MAKING US STRONG ENOUGH TO AVENGE THEIR EARLY PARENTAL WRONGS

Thank you, parents, for being strict with us
helpless little children, but now we're grown up
to reverse the balance of the power
and we've won the victorious hour
of forcibly transferring your throne
to us, having overthrown
your vicious bully crown
to our own heads, thank you very much.
And when you're doddering near death,
we'll vow to keep in touch
and stand on your respective graves
and give you powerful survival waves
in gratitude for those roads you paved
toward your conquerors, you knaves!

CONVERSATION'S OCCASIONAL GIFT TO IDEA FORMATION, TILL YOU GET IN THE SOUP

Between two people, compatible to different degrees, a conversation may produce meanings and understandings that neither of them could produce alone by himself. The combination of two minds through conversation can give special access to multiple idea formations denied to either of them alone. Conversation can be a creative engine different from individually concocted ideas in solitary communication with one's own mind, however fertile.

Sometimes two idea chefs are better than one—they produce an otherwise never known soup, which may even appeal to the world's collectively approving appetite through gradual savorings resulting in recipe savings, that go beyond the mere experimental fad state into universal staples—I don't mean horse stables, but that's a horse of a different color, a neigh-sayer.

Anyway, see what soup gets invented by talking with your friend, but first wear a napkin to catch a possible overflow: but short of a deluge if the pan or pot had only moderate dimensions to begin with, so you don't find yourself flailing in your own collective soup with a failed chef partner who unfairly blames you for lacking seasoning and then you question his reasoning, but he's already out of your listening range, having quit before being deranged. Anyway, marketing of the soup can be arranged.

AVOIDING PESKY CARS ALONG THE WAY, THAT'S CITY LIFE IN WORK OR PLAY APPLIED TO YOUR OWN NEIGHBORHOOD WHERE ROUTINELY YOUR CONCERNS HAVE STOOD.

When you cross the street, be very careful.
Gulp in your mouth a tense airful
till you make it to the other side
and then you can regain your normal stride
and take your casual thoughts on an inner ride
and you restore your bunch of priorities,
planning what to do as your life proceeds
into the realm of your active deeds
lying before you in the future
for whose safety you made sure
when you cross every street with a green light
to keep your head free of abnormal fright.

Safety is your first priority.
Then all proceeds without alacrity.
After all, this is a big city
even if it seems so small to you
with a neighborhood vision
to narrow it down to your needs of precision.
Go along, street by street
at a casual pace normal for you
in your friendly eyes of brown or blue.

IF ONLY.
THEN YOU WOULDN'T BE SO LONELY.

If only I could go back in time
to reclaim opportunities I once had
that I casually rejected
but today would be ultra desirable
and intoxicatingly obsessive
if only within my possessive.
Examples? Offhand I forgot them,
but remind me another time
and I'll remember them with a vengeance
and pour all my recollective engines
to retrieve what I was on the verge of
if only today I could regain the nerve of
at the moment of direct impulse
that, lacking it, I would convulse
and medically damage my pulse.
Human desire takes place within time.
Let opportunity thenceforth chime
with desire right on the spot
to claim ecstatically the whole pot
that gleams in evidence that it's there to have
if only you realize it's dear to have
in the ready clutches of what's near to have
with the great Now that it's here to have
without the fear:—of losing it
if you departed from your silly wit
and dropped the ball in an ugly fit.

**THE AGE OF DECISIVE CHOICES.
RAISE OR LOWER YOUR VOICES.
THE DANCE HALL IS A WEIRD DEVICE
TO BE MERELY FRIVOLOUS OR PRECISE.**

If only one of you loves the other
but the other doesn't,
then the situation is problematical
and romantically possibly mathematical
with the odds rising or falling,
ecstatic or appalling,
as to how "they" wind up together
or quite possibly not,
and the issue dissolves from a knot
with one of them being forgot
and the other going on to a new one,
from an old moon to a new sun,
and the game is on with a new heart
to be broken or not from the start.
Do they stay together or do they part?
One thing is sure. A flirtation
is sure to happen all over the nation.
Love and sex are here to stay,
but who's the victim?—and who may
be the deciding one
for a serious bout or merely a case of fun?
Will an affair go on, or will it be done?
It may be light-hearted; or it weighs a ton
for the broken-hearted losing one.
Romance could be a slippery dance
depending on a dangerous game of chance
and luck or timing, perchance.
Serious stakes are at issue
for a frivolous heart or one that's blue.
Most of all, it resolves around you,
and what's involved is false or true.
In the central role, you're the creature
which the narrative is bound to feature.

Are you now the highly sought, or are you the seeker?
Let them coincide, so nobody's weaker.

RUNNING FOR OFFICE?
WITH WHAT ORIFICE?
YOU BARELY GRASP THE CORE OF THIS.

Birth is a free gift. You're given a body.
It's an outright gift. But along with it
comes an extra bonus: a brain too
with which of course to do your thinking
as your eyes are there to do your blinking
not to mention at times your winking.
Your brain may be disposed
to be a conservative or a radical
or perhaps go between them
to be moderately liberal,
depending maybe on how you figurable
to reunite the miserable
with the ultra haughty rich.
Perhaps you have the political itch
to run for office for a hitch?
I laugh myself to a stitch.
You of all people!? Son of a bitch!

WHAT TO BE, ACCORDING TO WHAT NOT TO BE

Birth is free.
All you have to do is "be,"
and also acquire an identity
but steer away from eccentricity.
Don't be accused by society
of irrationality
verging perhaps on insanity,
which is catastrophically devastating to your vanity
as a social human being
decently worth others' seeing.

**FOLLOW THIS ADVICE TO THE HILT,
HOPING YOUR LIFE WOULD REDUCE THE TENDENCY TO
  WILT.**

If you push hard, life might oppose you
and leave no clear path ahead.
So ease up a bit, and life
may not retard you with too much strife.
It would like to be co-operated with,
so time your pulse rate and give it width.
Use your brain to coalesce with
that temperamental being, Life,
and appease its perverse disposition for strife
if you want a relatively friction-free life.

**EXPECT CHANGES.
THIS IS WHAT LIFE ARRANGES:
TO FEEL ONE WAY, THEN ANOTHER.
OTHERWISE WE'RE CHOKED INTO A STERILE SMOTHER.**

If you feel lousy, try to improve it
and boost yourself from a lowly pit
by getting to feel wonderful next.
Follow this chronological text
so you won't feel awfully vexed
that your mood is stuck in a dim groove
and is unlikely right now to improve.
If melancholy, force yourself
to jump off the misery shelf
into the grand old light of day
feeling so wonderful, you want to play
the futile game of remaining the same way,
which is really against the law of nature.
No human is such an unlikely creature
that a continuous mood is his only feature.

THE CRUCIAL RACE OF TWO CONTESTANTS: WE KNOW ALREADY WHICH IS BESTANT

Life is our continual Number One
in our list of priorities.
Only other contestant in this race
is Death, with its much inferior pace.
Who of all people would choose the latter
as being more valuable to pursue?
Suicidals and depressants would,
those addicted to melancholy,
those with an aversion to pleasure,
those of a self-destructive incline,
and such others might decline
to back Life as the evident winner
in the special priority sweepstakes.
Those whom cancer is wracking,
and those whose heart-power is lacking,
and those already at Death's half-way door
might choose Death, in their doomed defeat
sprawled on the floor at the heart-warming feet
of triumphant Life, mourning for the losers,
and those pitiful or benighted choosers
of emptily vacant dubious futures,
weary of being generous Life's moochers.

A VERY WELCOME TOPIC

Human pleasure takes many forms.
Some are unusual, some are norms.
How hard it is to generalize!
All pleasures are not of the same size.
But why quantify such an elusive thing?
Pleasure is pleasure when it has the right ring.

**GIVING PARENTS THEIR DUE
FOR GUIDING US THROUGH
YOUTH'S WILD TRAVAILS
LEAVING NO CRIMINAL TRAILS**

Us children are grateful to our presiding parents
for guiding us through the roughs of childhood
into the toughs of adulthood
with consequences not too adulterated
because they were parentally consecrated
to our safe growing up
looking at life as a flowing cup
brimfully being fuller than empty,
signifying that life is full of plenty
and our poor little plates need not be empty
but heaped to the very top,
all the better for our growing up,
and not arouse the suspicion of a cop
despite professional cheating
covered over by special pleading
and sneaky such illegalling.

**THE SECURITY OF THE COMFORT ZONE
PROTECTING PLEASURE ALL FOR YOUR OWN**

Everybody should perfectly own
an exquisite comfort zone
ripping and roaring all your own.
It only admits pleasurable feeling.
And as for pain, there's quickish healing.
The car for joy is greased for wheeling
and it heads into wonderful times
to the happy tunes of merry chimes.
And your ecstasy neatly rhymes
with no need to resort to crimes,
since there's quite money enough
to get your honey and other stuff
and live so smoothly, you're out of the rough.
Perfecting your own comfort zone,

no need to live too close to the bone.
Just make sure life is happy enough,
it's really true—no need to bluff.
A legitimate comfort zone is the real stuff.

STARTING WITH PLEASURE, BUT THEN WHERE?

Pleasure is so nice when it's happening to you.
Sustaining it is your eager aim;
even, if possible, increasing it.
Or is that too arrogant to ask for
when you greedily come back for more,
even though you had so much before?
How much of it are you going to keep in store,
hoarding it as if you're starting a store
to sell the goods to yourself at a bargain rate,
going from gluttony to a commercial state,
till finally pleasure loses its edge
and suddenly moderation is your new puritanical pledge?

MY SIMILARITY TO OTHERS

What's the essence of life?
On that I can shed no light,
with no shred of insight.
I leave that battle for others to fight.
I just want to go home
and let my mind infinitely roam
into various diverse ideas
leading to the mood of hearty cheers
and the elimination of morose fears.
With this attitude, I have many peers.

**PLEASURE AND PAIN—WHAT A DICHOTOMY!
OPPOSITE RESULTS OF OUR ANATOMY.**

Sometime, at your open leisure,
contemplate the nature of pleasure
and you'll see it comes in different forms,
so let's differentiate: there are no norms.
But yes there are: Pleasure can be orderly.
Pain too. But that's another subject
which I'll not open, if you don't object.
Its associations are far from perfect.
Pain should always be relegated to the past.
If it's too recent, you may still be aghast
and your tolerance may not last.
But better THEN, than NOW.
Let relief rejoice along your brow.
Get human nature to show you how
to be happy that pain is over:
But still you worry—it may reappear
to endanger your much preferred pleasure dear
whose reassurance hopes to obliterate fear.

**TRYING TO INVESTIGATE LIFE TO AN EXACT EXTENT,
TRYING TO SEE JUST WHERE IT'S GONE ON A BENT
FROM THE TURNING POINT OF WHERE IT HAS WENT.**

Is life an abstract subject?
No, let's approach it head-on,
and feel its nitty-gritty in the palm
of a hand grasping at its concrete
real stuff—life's sure being, itself.
It's dynamic and vital, you bet,
it's truly organic, like dry and wet
which go only half to describe
life's pure essence—but I'm only a scribe
hoping to capture its true only vibe
that characterizes our grand old human tribe.

TIME, CHANGE, PAIN, AND PLEASURE: CONTEMPLATE ALL THESE AT YOUR LEISURE.

When pain proves unbearable,
then avoid it if not too late,
or else acutely reduce it
till it's easily tolerable
at pleasure's onset and pain's demise
at a sudden reversible surprise.
Pain and pleasure are allies
through the agency of time
that allows a transition period
that's so naturally weird
and much changed from what it appeared.
Doesn't time have you sweetly endeared,
installing happy promise for the dread you feared?

YES, WHAT ABOUT LIFE?
IT HARMONIZES STRIFE.
YOU CAN CUT IT CLEANLY WITH A DULL KNIFE.

I depend on physical health
to extend longevity's old age
as my narrative lengthens to my final page.
Of details, there's an enormous wealth.
May physical health prolong it
to add memories that belong to it
to join everything in a whole "novel"
while I pick up crumbs and grovel
for inspiration to include
what was my life's sum's over-all mood?
Was it slickly sophisticated? Or merely crude?
Neither. I cheered and boo'd
to what stern memory allows me to conclude
that left me in a dizzy swoon
and a giddy frolic to the slumbering moon.

WINNING THE PARENTS-CHILDREN TUSSLE
WHEN PARENTS GROW WEAKER AT THE MUSCLE
AND CHILDREN ARE QUICKER TO HUSTLE
TOWARD MATURE STALWART BUSTLE
AND END UP WITH THE WHOLE STOLEN RUSTLE.

Parents have to be forewarned
not to be tough on us children
or we threaten revenge when we grow up;
and instead of gratitude to our parents
we'll cause them suffering plenty
till the scales of revenge turn empty
with our winning fair play
of consolidated overturn;
and in old age they'll cravenly cower
with demeanors so grandparently sour,
and transparently the hour is ours.
We'll buy them courtesy flowers
in farewell's transference of powers
to us, their "dutiful" children
now grown larger to build on
advantage of having inherited from them
the ascendancy of the conquering monarch
from standards they set, turned to our succeeding mark.
Do you sense any ingratitude?
Sorry, we're spoiled in our insolent attitude.

ALLOWING LIFE MY IGNORANCE

Does life have a special secret?
If so, I'm not privy to it
and am completely out of the know.
I don't consider this a terrible blow.
A little ignorance does me no harm
and doesn't feed me with false alarm.
So I'll sit quiet and remain calm.
Socially considered, it's part of my charm.

HOW NOT TO BE TOO FRAZZLED ABOUT LIFE

Life is a really special thing
that in my case is too personal
to even figure out.
I take it subjectively
but try to share it with others
as a social impulse
uniting me with the strange world
and everything with which it's embroiled.
I acquire only a smattering of knowledge
which barely carries me to the cliff's lonely edge.
I'm crowded with others on the virtual ledge.

HOW TO SPEAK PHILOSOPHICALLY ABOUT LIFE

Is there a correct philosophical approach
to life that's beyond reproach?
No, say anything you want
and give it a slight philosophical twist,
and of the matter you'll never quite get the grist
even if your brains should stubbornly persist.
Like a watch, you might as well wear your heart on your wrist.

IN SUMMARY, WHAT WAS IT ALL ABOUT?
I'M YET TO PUZZLE IT OUT.
I RETREAT IN DREAMS, AND POUT.

I'm building up toward the end of life,
trying to extend its dwindling middle.
Is my conclusion that it was all a riddle?
You can put it that way—yes.
But what remains to confess or bless?
In actuality, what was it nevertheless?
Certainly more tidy
than a total retrospective mess?

WHERE AM I GOING IN HIS RETROSPECTIVE?
BUT I'M NOT HIS INTERNAL DETECTIVE.
I STUMBLE STERNLY ON SOME SORT OF PERSPECTIVE.

Jimmy Stagno being dead, I have memories at my command
of our more than seventy years together.
He remains dead, as I survey what happened,
picking this or that at random
that adds up vaguely in a blur,
reaching at this, then stirring the other one out,
but incoherent. Who was he?
My best friend. And I—who was I?
His best friend. Well, those days are gone,
having, in due turn, been lost and undergone,
from this distance, alone without him.
The days whizzed by, as if on a whim.
The details fall apart, and I'm blurred.
The over-all impact? I'm always stirred,
as if suddenly in reminiscence we've conferred.

LIFE, DESCRIBED FROM ITS OWN ANGLE
SO THAT DEFINITION DOESN'T HAVE TO DANGLE

Life goes from one change to another
as it pursues its lonely way
eventually toward its own destruction,
thus annihilating its own production.
Into its tempting web
we succumb in full seduction
very willingly because we love
Life. All other things it rises above.
We fit into it like a glove.
Our fingers begin, and the rest follows
till our whole body has been committed
to the cause of Life, with nothing omitted.
You don't even have to be previously fitted.
You've already been passionately in it,
daily, strenuously, up to the minute.

DOES LIFE HAVE TOO MUCH MEANING?

What's the meaning of life?
Who knows? Does it have any?
That's not the point. Maybe it has too many
to even bother with the surplus of many
by reducing it to "Does it have any?"
That eases my lot a lot
and leaves my mind a great big blot.

SPEAKING FOR JIMMY

During the course of our conversations,
many subjects had to be resumed later,
to be doubled down and reintroduced.
There were many ongoing threads
to be picked up during the many next times
we got together, so we had many topics
spinning on rather indefinitely
that we would of course get to.
Then he died. I lost my conversational partner.
The subjects reverberated in my head,
weighed down discontinued like lead.
I lacked his face to accompany them.
The words would begin in my head and then stop.
I was in continual mourning to him.
He transcended the words we didn't continue.
The sentence structures just broke off.
Death had become verbalized
in stops and starts.
We each had our separate parts.
I imagined what he was going to say
and took his role. It wasn't the same thing.
But I had entered his death
and distributed all our words in the same breath.

**LIFE CAN CURE YOUR ILLS,
WHEN YOU APPLY YOUR CO-OPERATIVE WILLS
AND ASK FOR INNUMERABLE REFILLS.**

Life is obviously your best bet
to resort to for whatever regret
and disappointment you have for it.
Apply to life always
to remedy your misery case
with its good old revival treatment
with its renewed benevolent greetment
at the very juncture where you need it.
Hungry for a better life? Go feed it.

EASE UP. DON'T TAKE THINGS HARD. LIVE A LITTLE.

Where does the world begin and the self end?
It's enough to send you around the bend
and confuse what meets what, how, and where.
But why is it my business anyway?
Well, it is, but do I have to attend to it?
I'll just assume the best for the best
and not take everything as a tense, dire test.
Preferable is relaxation and letting things go
and give my consciousness a plausible rest
and relax in philosophical idleness
to contemplate the length and wideness
in life's closely knit confinedness.
Oh, get me out of all this mess
so I can lounge on a hammock and fret less.
Leisure is a lovely pastime
where I can close my eyes and pass the unknown time.

DEATH SEEMED TO TRAIL LIFE AS ITS REVERSE MIRROR IMAGE, THE SHADOW IN WAITING

If you mention life, can death be far behind?
It shadows life, stands close to it,
imitating life's spontaneous movements
in vain and persistent blur
to mock life's dynamic stir,
reversing life prematurely
till it's time when death can open up
and show its own strut, original,
the reverse side of early life,
the minor image, now richly enlarged
to be its true self. Death's alive
to be the one to permanently thrive.
But don't forget. Life had its day
and put its complete potential into play
with only partial results
but at least it tried and now is done,
lost to death, the Number One.

THE LARGER PICTURE. BUT I'M A FIXTURE?

Without the world, where would you be?
In defense, I must proclaim:
Without me, where would the world be?
Its health would not be endangered by my loss,
so I guess I'm the inferior: the world the boss.
Does this upset my vanity?
Personally. But not my whole humanity.

WHAT'S IN STORE FOR YOU
BY INNOCENTLY BEING BORN,
TILL BY THE WORLD YOU'RE TORN

1.

Life is a co-operative endeavor
just to get born.
Necessary are a mother and father
to biologically fill their functions,
and there you are, you're alive
and thrown into the world at large
long before death issues your discharge.

2.

With all that time and space you're given,
what will you make of it all
before you fall in thrall
to entropy and dissolution
to undermine your former fruition
and your diploma at life's ignition
to learn the ropes and have a long life
and wrestle off your champion strife
so that for a while
survival and longevity will rule.
Then, for you, death's a-drool
and you're no longer in early school.

MONEY AS A FACTOR IN MARRIAGE CHOICE
LOUDER IN DEGREE THAN LOVE ALONE
IF YOU'RE LIVING ALREADY CLOSE TO THE BONE

Romance can lead to love
and love is valued above
quite anything else, with life's exception.
So when romance is available, your reception
is dramatically important for your future.
You may marry her. Who is she?
Pretty? Intelligent? Young enough?

For some young men, the real stuff
is how much money she has.
Does that sound too mercenary?
Not if it's really necessary,
depending on how poor the man is.
But he disguises this with polite manners
and pretends it's love alone
that hardens as a rock his penis bone.

ENERGY ON THE CHARGE
AND ENERGY RECEDING
BALANCE THE PURE EARTH'S BREEDING

Life is sometimes tiring.
Solution: take a rest.
But if life is actually expiring,
taking a rest is enforced
by genuinely earned fatigue
and other weariness in that league
of being worn out to the extreme
and thus losing life's invigorating dream
and also the entire living world
so abundantly boyed and girled
to let evolution swing away unfurled
by sheer mass reproduction
and other fertile energy suction.
Being born is the proper induction.
Then inveigle a dating introduction
and start a romance going,
leading to sex'es to-ing and fro-ing,
and hopefully a baby will be growing
if the favorable wind continues blowing.

WRITING'S VARIETIES

The flow of diction
can produce fiction
or else straight reporting
and sober recording.
Words can go anywhere
for all kinds of reasons,
limited by no seasons;
and seek their own adhesions
to all possible meanings,
and plunder the in-betweenings
of subtle discourse
and have recourse
even to deep philosophy
and abstruse ponderings
in the scribes' wanderings
over the map of what to write about
and what form to put it in:
Opportunity for stylists
to make clever lists
of verbal antics and assists
where imagination persists.
Even abstract surrealism
as opposed to realism
is within the writer's province.
Some writings make you wince,
starting long ago
and ever since,
on scraps of paper
in the mind's wild caper.
How eccentric writing can be,
leaving imagination to roam free
from dry land to unruly sea,
and advocate any old plea
that words can devise
in creation's verbal enterprise,
and create the privilege of surprise
for early learners

or the already shrewdly wise,
unbelieving of their own eyes.
Hail for the originality of surprise.

**AVOID UGLINESS IF YOU CAN,
OR IF YOU'RE STUCK WITH IT,
BE DOOMED TO A MISERABLE CHOICE OF MATES
DOWN IN YOUR LUCK AMONG THE UNRULY FATES.**

If you're too ugly, love is difficult to get
because you're a lesser choice by preferable mates
or any mates at all fortunate to have a better choice.
So the solution to this problem
is to try to make your ugliness less
if possibility is within your range
to improve your appearance with whatever minor change.
The beautiful glamour guys and gals
can fortunately choose from a better array of pals.

**GET IT RIGHT
OR REVERSE THE WRONG
AND SAIL ALONG
ON LIFE'S UNEVEN SONG.**

Life is full of hard choices
of who to marry and what job to have
and what you spend money on and where you live
and everything else that you have to puzzle through
and what to discard and what to make new.
Then if you make a mistake, change your course
and regain a better purchase on your life's force
that your inner wisdom decides to endorse.

WE'RE STUCK TO OUR OWN IDENTITY.
DON'T GO AFAR AFIELD.
REMAINING YOU IS ALL YOU CAN YIELD.
IDENTITY IS NOT PLASTIC.
IT FORCES YOU TO SIMPLY STICK.

The older I grow,
the more I regress
to the past unless
the Now gets ahold of me
with extreme fascination
and I'm lost in a new experience
never before imagined,
impossible to be fashioned
in reality's interesting guise.
So I learned something new
because I'm one of the guys.
I'm me, but I could be you
if circumstances were different.
But they're not, so I'm me
and you're free to keep on being you
in order to yourself to remain true,
since reality can't go otherwise
to stage you among a different set of guys.
So you're stuck with yourself
as far as you get
without the slightest tinge of regret.
To be someone else,
you've got to inhale a different set
of oxygen carbons in the air
and even beget from a different wife a new heir.
This kind of reality exchange
is confusing to the old identity.
It's a limit on how far you can feel free.
Identity confines you.
To that old self please be true.
The proven usual—

don't let it confusingly roam.
Stick snugly tight to your own home
close as ever to your familiar bone.

CONCERNING THAT MAJOR ISSUE: LIFE

Life is an opportunity to live it up.
But if something bad happens, you have to live it down.
If you're feeling weary and pepless
at a low-energy level,
then you have to put more life into what you do
and get out of your funk,
because life is more than just junk.
It enlivens you to have more spunk.
What to make of life is a philosophical recreation
debating on pro's and cons, here and there,
fording the metaphysical shallows
of how best to put your life
at the service of worthy causes.
But during your frequent pauses
and rhetorical clauses
examining what's worthy in life:
None's worthier than self-development
to give living a sophisticated edge
and make a dent in complacency, or a wedge.
What about your abandoned New Year's pledge?
For a sincere answer, don't hedge.
Life is always one to a customer.
Don't use it up in vain.
Put it to heavy duty,
or make it a slim beauty.
Don't die too soon
to cause your friends and pals to swoon
and slash the moon to half-mast
because your lovely life couldn't last.
It was so rich, but the decline too fast.

KEEPING ABOVEBOARD

Preferring pleasure to pain
always gives your morale a gain
when you convert discomfort to relief
and become of misery a thief.
Of your own body, are you chief?
Yes, get it into a zone
which guarantees happiness as your very own,
and denies suffering any access
to your private mood control.
And your vigilance will be constantly on patrol
to keep your comfortable well-being on a roll,
singing sweet madrigals to yourself
and hiding your despair on a hidden shelf.

A BUNCH OF NEGATIVES

When you die,
it's the same thing as if an insect or a horse dies.
You and they don't operate any more
and drop in an inanimate heap on the floor,
with no door leading anywhere
for the remotest afterlife chance,
with no savior to lead you.
You're simply dead. No more after that,
from a vague spiritual sunrise
that you had hoped for when alive.
Sorry, you can't pump life
in a poor corpse, whose skull
is more lifeless than dull.
No brain operates
to bewail such rotten fates
as losing your mates,
having no place to go,
and not even the flicker of a woe.
Your skeleton is useless
and the brain issues no thought.

This is what "destiny" has brought.
But what about religion?
As salvationless as a pigeon.
And as for god?
Go search in a pea pod.
And this is not even odd.
How about your soul?
It misses its own goal.
It has no part and no whole.

HOW SUPERSTITION GRANTS YOU UNQUESTIONABLE AFTERLIFE

People already mourn their own death
long before the event happens
and are unhappy about it.
But it's unavoidable.
What a great consolation is heaven!
Even though it doesn't exist, believe in it.
What relief that you'll have an afterlife
if only you believe in whatever savior
can escort you to those golden premises
if you prompt him with promises
to worship him as a kind of god
to deliver you if you kindly prod
him with his very good nature …
Nature?! He doesn't exist!
Still, you must persist
to get an enviable perch
in that wonderful afterlife promise
due to blind faith on what to believe
to guide you through your reprieve
and actually annihilate death
through permissive superstition
anointed in special dispensation
in this occult-prone nation.
From reason, take a permanent vacation.

CONVERT PLEASURE FROM PAIN FOR AN INSURMOUNTABLE GAIN

When displeasure comes,
correct it before it gets out of hand.
Try to compensate with something nice
compounded perhaps of sugar and spice.
Please take this frank, stern advice,
and you'll free your ugly body of loathsome lice
and never have to turn to the trade of vice
and other violations of law.
You will have been warned before
not to sweat pain from every pore.
Exude instead the wonders of pleasure
practiced always at work and leisure.

A BELIEVER PROCLAIMS HIS FAITH

People are afraid to die,
with good reason.
But are they not compensated
with some redemption for their trouble?
Heaven would fill the bill,
the soul could be well guaranteed
by paying worship to a savior
via the mental action of belief—
or "faith" is a stronger word
when venturing into the absurd.
As long as there's an afterlife,
my soul will be well cared for
as an honored underworld guest,
at majestic god's behest.
We know it's for the best.
So now that I've signed on,
the savior will guide me
across heaven's traverse
and I'll infinitely live
as a disembodied soul

and my faith will reward me whole.
Is there a hole or flaw in that reasoning?
As a church-goer, I'm not curious.
When god guides me, why complain?
Like trusting the pilot of an airplane
whose license is without flaw.
Place yourself in his paw
and give yourself to transparent awe,
and put yourself above reason's law.

**MORE THAN AN ADORNMENT,
THE BRAIN IS OUR PRIZED ORNAMENT
THAT CHANGES THE WHOLE EQUATION
WITH ITS INTELLECTUAL POWER STATION
THAT CONSTITUTES A RADICAL INNOVATION
FROM OUR MERE CRUDE BASIC ORIGINS
BARELY ABLE TO ISSUE A PRIMITIVE GRUNT
AND THE BELLIGERENCE OF A DEFENSIVE FRONT
NOT TOO SUBTLE BUT CRAZILY BLUNT.**

The brain is such an addition to life's
former bare bodily essentials.
It increases life's potentials
by creating the formidable intellect,
which garners knowledge wherever it can
and transforms mere fact into philosophy
and "where you are" into patriotism
accompanied by a whole horde of likely "isms,"
and of course national religions
that add piety and righteousness
to the brain's magical storehouse
that started humbly with a mere body
with its anatomical attendants
and basic raw amendments
that allowed us only some wretched crude grunts
and some necessarily belligerent fronts.
Oh, we're much better instead
with a brain operating from our proud firm head.
We've even transformed sex into getting properly wed.

THE PARTY-CRASHER'S RECOVERY WITH A BANG

Being alive with full consciousness
is how you discover yourself
when you wake up after fainting
and ask yourself if you're bruised.
Well-wishers ask what happened
as they gave way for you at the party.
You answer, "I drank a little too hearty.
Then I just about caved in.
I apologize for creating a scene
disruptive of a smooth-flowing party.
Now you all stay back and give me room
as I recover my senses after my swoon.
Give me a hand as I boost myself up."
How contradictory!—"stay back" and "give me a hand."
I ache awful where I managed to land.
Then I collapsed again
and found myself on the host's bed
sprawled out in complete comfort,
fussed over, but given another drink
to replenish my spilled one of before,
glad not to have been shown the door.
I feel a part of the general community
feeling fully pardoned and granted immunity
for a lapse of my equilibrium
that tended to knock me off my feet
and forced my dignity to pull up in retreat.
Now to find who the host is …?
and apologize for crashing his hospitality.
The host turned out to be a woman
who's now Mrs. Me. And that's my story.
From ignoniminity I found glory.
It ran the social gossip circuits.
I was a whizz as a celebrity circus.

HOW TO FAIL AT CRASHING A PARTY

To crash a party, first
don't be acquainted with the host.
Furtively wait outside,
not directly in front
of the conspicuous entrance.
And when the invited guests
start arriving in little clusters
or even pairs,
sidle in with them
as though belonging but invisible,
deftly maneuvering
as though you're a genuine invitee
knowing you haven't come for a cup of tea.
Others may bring bottles but it's not mandatory
under formal obligation
to make a casual contribution,
nor your identity have an attribution.
Dress like the others do
so you won't be ejected at the door
if someone confronts you with a list
of welcome guests without your name,
and you're exposed to your shame.
Protest that this isn't a police state
under stern dictatorship
of "in" people and you're out,
marginal, by the wayside,
lonely, unpartnered,
outside, longing for true love
and soaking in your self-pitying solitude.
The party is there but you can't intrude.
Just an isolated interlude
of feeling unbelonging.
You're barred, despite your lonely longing.
Your mouth is dry. You're not in the mood for songing.
"Poor myself!" you inwardly exclaim,
as a would-be party guest:
so deprived, you pretend it was all in jest.
Having failed, at least you tried your best.

NOT BEING A PROBLEM AS AN UNCOUTH PARTY-CRASHER

A collusion between host and guest
at a party requires you do your best
to be worth your place though you crashed the party
uninvited but you squirmed your way in
and now prove that you really fit,
and make your host's approval
so high as not to demand your removal.
Then you can eat all the food you want
and get drunk too at the liquor font,
but furtively by piece-by-piece
so as not to disturb the real guests' peace
and proficiently provide for their ease
so that your barrage of manners is bound to please
by not being a hog nor a free-loader
too conspicuously as to set you apart
to glare out that your host's party is not smart.
Then if you get drunk you have to stay
and not go home, to your host's dismay.
This farce is worthy of a Broadway play.

WHAT ROMANCE CAN EVENTUALLY LEAD TO ACCORDING TO CUSTOM IN THE HUMAN ZOO THAT'S QUITE SOCIALIZED FOR ME AND YOU

Want love? First pursue romance
that can lead to the erotic zone
where you can proclaim your cute mate your own
by the tightness of the close contact—
resulting in a marriage contract?
Maybe. If you both agree.
It takes two to tango, based on mutuality,
since marriage is approved by ethics and morality
and is a perfectly legal device
to nurture love for many years
though you still have mortality fears
not only yourself, but for your lovely mate.

Wouldn't living forever both together be great?
But get real. Learn reality before too late.

AN OBVIOUS CHOICE
IF YOU FOLLOW YOUR SANITY VOICE
AND ALLOW LIFE TO REJOICE

Pleasure being preferable to pain,
make your life an over-all gain
by pursuing the former and avoiding
the miserable latter choice.
Listen to your inner voice
to prefer the joys of pleasure
to pain's spoilage of your leisure
and corrupting the sanity of your measure.
Don't be perverse, you fool.
Go to where your delights drool.
Swim on the breathing side of the choking pool.

WHY I PREFER NOT TO BE LIKE A MOLE

Dealing with people is part of life.
I'd rather be popular than not.
Otherwise I'd be a lonely soul
and might as well live underground like a mole
who, influenced by rain, pops his head out
and, suspicious of society,
says, "Solitude is the art of propriety.
I'm virtuous when alone
but nasty when in a pack,
attuned to bite and attack
anyone who interferes with PRIVACY,
which renders me completely whole
and justifies my life as a mole.
Disciplined to non-eruption
when free of disruption,
I contemplate my solitary navel
so I can chew on my own flesh when able."

**CONFINED TO THE BATHROOM
TO DISPEL IRREGULAR GLOOM
AND FEEL YOUR COMFORT SPEEDILY ZOOM**

1.

To liberate my bowels
from the pains and howls
of constipation,
remind me to eat lots of prunes
to ease my digestion through
and convert those eager prunes
to plenty of bathroom poo,
a triumph performed at the loo.
The art of being regular
results in organic satisfaction
at the very seat of toilet action.
Comfort then is the automatic reaction.

2.

How can I put in words
the visual artistry of the turds
that once lived life as prunes
but switched nicely to other tones
accompanied by soft moans
within our cushy anus zones?

**A PLEA FOR BEING CHOOSY
EVEN IF SOMEONE HAS TO LOSE ME.
THIS IS IN REFERENCE
FOR THE RIGHT TO EXERCISE PREFERENCE.**

I like some people better than others.
Isn't that normal? I shouldn't be ashamed
not to like everybody equally
in the democratic method
of dis-applying any favoritism?
That's not a fault, right?—
to have different opinions about different people

with different scales of emotional balance
of who I like or dislike unequally?
Good. Now I can breathe better
choosing "him" for my best friend
and "that other one" to try to avoid.
They're human but so am I,
which I have the right to exercise
in my emotional attitudes
of giving some my gratitude
and others to make excuses for
my not reserving total affection for.
I'm a choosing human being,
so please allow me personal decisions
for my favorites and for my derisions,
depending on the gut reactions of my visions.

**THE WORLD GIVES ME A RIDE
TILL THE "ME" PART SLIPS TO SUBSIDE
AND LOSES MY MOMENTARY GRIP
WHILE THE WORLD CONTINUES ITS TRIP
WITH OTHERS FAR TO OUTSTRIP.**

The outside world and the inside me
meet inbetween, in neutral territory,
and are dual authors of our special story
that from chapter to chapter varies such,
steadily bringing the narrative to more and much,
disorderly but I grow older
with confidence to become somewhat bolder;
and cautious arrives the finish line
by accident, and oblivion is mine
shaken from the worldly grip
and I pull out from the world's next trip
minus its companion, me,
vastly stuck along the limbs of a tree
and the world slithers away, free.

MY WORLDLY VENTURE:
TO ME, AN ASTOUNDING ADVENTURE.
BUT THE WORLD IS PREOCCUPIED
IN OBSERVING ITS RATHER IMPERSONAL TIDE.

I'm me, but the worldly cosmos
prefers our companionship the most
as BRIEFLY I ride its company
till, alas, it must dump me
and fly laughingly away,
barely recalling my brief stay.

MY TENURE

The world gave me a friendly ride
on its own timetable of tide
till then it repulsed me off
and it continued hard, while I fell soft.

HOW TO END ALL DUE DELIBERATIONS
AND ACQUIRE YOUR FINAL LIBERATIONS

Some surprises are so quick
that they interfere with arithmetic
when you try to puzzle out
whom you owe to and what,
and who owes to you what
you need to get from him,
or your financial prospects are grim
and your outlook for the future
is so extremely problematic
as to provoke an automatic,
even instinctual, response
to quickly grapple with what
finally connects with the solutionary dot
as to put your problem to an end
when all the dangling threads knit into a blend
that dazzles you and you smile,

having overtaken the extra mile
needed to be taken
for your senses to thoroughly awaken.

SOMETHING VERY SERIOUS:
AIM AN ATOM BOMB, IT CAN'T MISS.

Sometimes life seems such a joy
that I dread if an atom bomb will destroy
the whole human race bit by bit,
so I bite, to blood, my lower lip
and complain to the United Nations
General Assembly please
don't let all people decease
by nuclear devastation
that plights each nation
in its area of map
to cause its local government to snap,
and other national tribes
to unresist the tempting bribes
that plague the earth to tremble with eruption
thanks to prevalent bureaucratic corruption,
and all "down" blows up to "up"-tion.
Can the globe survive this?
I already hear the ominous hiss.
If an atom bomb takes aim,
which dumb dictators are prominently to blame?
This is more than just a light-hearted game.
Will some hero rescue us and go to fame
provided history is still alive
and evolution's triumph helps us to survive
and we all have to crawl on bellies to strive
with remaining strength left
to lift the whole universe or just be bereft
and our organic unity is swept
away from sheer existence
despite the human spirit's insistence?

HOW TO WIN YOUR WIFE BACK AGAIN BY DOING IT MORE THAN JUST NOW AND THEN

To feel comfortable in your own skin,
you have to know where to begin.
Breathe so deeply it almost hurts
until your chest heaves the way out
and the breath bursts forth
in such gasps, your lungs ache
almost to the point of a belly ache,
but you remember you swallowed all your food
and have nothing to spit up.
But your wife says she wants to split up
with you whom she finds inadequate
as a husband and is ready to quit.
To prevent her, rely on your intellectual wit
and faint prominently to show you're not fit
to get divorced just yet and need
to win her back again, with due speed.
We argue. Will she concede?
She's vehement. I ask her why
and in what way I'm inadequate.
"When you screw me, you don't make me lit up
like a firecracker ready to burst,
so, dear, we must rehearse
to get back together again.
Increase our frequency rate
when we go through the ritual to mate;
but now try, for me, to make it great
till I sigh afterward with satisfaction
due to your increased action.
That's my forgiving reaction."
"Dear wife, I'll do what you say.
Undress now, that I may have my way.
I'll force us through to have a good day.
Let's vehemently couple
and I'll try to be more supple."

AN ODE TO PEOPLE NUMERICALLY.
ALL TOGETHER ACT SEMI-HEROICALLY
AND THEIR VOICES ALL SOUND PHONETICALLY.

Mothers gracefully lend their wombs
to launching the rides that fill the tombs.
There's big business in this: it booms.
Children successively leave their mothers
for a voyage ended in the tombs' smothers.
Later come the sisters and brothers
who flock and crowd in voluminously
for the same voyage that ends ruinously.
But that's the way we people are.
What others do is our guiding star.
Our bracket is conformity,
lending to big-time racket with enormity.
Undertakers and grave-diggers profit.
This was predictable by any prophet.
It's all in the public order of things.
People together: that's what it brings.
People in a group grow the public's fancy wings.

HURRY UP, CLOSE YOUR EYES
TO AVOID AN ABRUPT SURPRISE.

Life is really fun
sometimes. Otherwise it's not.
I arrived at this great insight
through the mechanism of thinking
as automatically as the eyes blinking
when a foreign object gets too close
and signifies possible danger
to the metabolistic mechanism
at a crucial instantism
that imposes on your visionism.

**FIRST THINGS FIRST.
THEN ALL IN A BURST
AND PLUNGE AHEAD, FOR BETTER OR WORST.
FOR DRENCHING DEATH, WE DIE WITH THIRST.**

Love, as a euphemism for sex,
is sometimes directly for its own sake,
and competes with money
for the honor of being praised
as what makes the world go round.
And by "world," I include "earth"
and all specimens subject to birth.
The world discharges its fertility
on whatever proves reproductive in its ability
to replicate from its original model
through male and female in a cuddle
after modest conversation in a huddle.
We all came from a pre-original puddle,
the formation of prolonged rain
that drenched us on an open plain
and made things grow—I can't explain.
The origin of the species,
like flowers fertilized by feces,
came from the muck of the mud
but sure proved itself no dud.
The world is too vast to wash with a sud.
The prodigious strength of our organic power
pounds its historical impact on the current hour.
Uplift your pride. Don't muddy yourself and cower.

**AIMING YOUR LIFE'S APPROACH
TO BE WELL OUT OF REACH
OF SOCIETY'S REPROACH.
TO THAT EXTENT, I'LL COACH.**

To live life well, go about it
to the point that you don't have to shout at it
that it's letting you down. It's your fault
that you don't do well to be worth your salt.

Be your own savior
so as to pave your
path to increased success
at whatever your attention will address.
If you gain, watch out that you don't regress.
So calm down your express to a local
and keep your eyes on the precise focal.
If people get in your way, poke all
so that they don't interfere
when you concentrate on the now and here,
which is your territory, within your sphere.
If they threaten you, give them a good lear
and let your sharp sneer
indicate what they yet have to fear.
Keep to your side of the fence
and increasingly fortify your defense.
But don't be paranoid.
Other people need not leave you always annoyed.

**HOW LIFE KEEPS GOING
LIKE A LAWN UNDERGOING
ITS PERIODICAL HEALTHY MOWING
UNTIL IT MUST BE SLOWING
DOWN FROM THE GROWING
AND THE LAWNMOWER STOPS
AND ITS MECHANISM POPS.**

Evolution being tenderly genderized
enables more babies to be periodically born
on the basis of the male horn
and the female vagina to be happily surprised.
What a great plan so ingeniously devised.

**ISABEL (THE HOSTESS)
VERSUS THE RAIN'S TIMING
JUST AS SHE WAS PRIMING
FOR A VERY PLANNED PICNIC
ON WHICH THE RAIN DECIDED TO PICK.
THAT DECISION WASN'T WORTH A LICK.**

The rained-on picnic is an obstacle
to good timing. Isn't it possible
for the rains to reserve an appropriate time
—but not a picnic—to come on strong?
By coincidence, the rain was wrong
to spray its deep wet song
on that planned and particular picnic
that it just happened, on the spot, to pick.
I would call this coincidence "sick."
Also the hostess: She was so miserable
that she (her name is Isabel)
wrote an apology letter to her guests
vindicating herself: she had tried her best
not to schedule that horrid rainfest
on a deplorable rainy day
with blankets spread on the grass.
And on the blankets, food and wine.
No wonder afterward she was heard to whine.
Couldn't the weather have decently turned out fine?
What bad luck it happened to be
that the timing upset the schedule with misery,
and what "could have been" wandered away, free
for the angry mind to contemplate.
A real social event! Well, that's fate.
Isabel (the hostess)
was just a rainstorm away from being the mostest.
Instead, she accused herself of being the grossest,
but decided to make the rain the scapegoat,
pinning the awful blame
on the arbitrary fluke of the game.
But still, isn't it lame

to cast any cowardly blame?
She may only cause her gut to inflame.

**SOME ADVICE FROM ME TO YOU
AS A PUBLIC SERVICE
TO REWARD THE READERS
OF WHAT I WRITE HERE DOWN
THOUGH IT MAY LACK RENOWN.**

Don't want what you can't get
if it's out of your reach.
Trying it, see if it fails,
and the tossed coin falls on "tails,"
to take wind far out of your sails
and you can't even receive your own mails.
Give up what you can't get
and see what other opportunities can beget,
before your downside begins to fret,
and all your past triumphs you only forget.
Trying hopefully somewhere is your best bet.
If you lose one thing, then try to get
an alternative compensatory to that.
If it succeeds, you can avoid falling flat
on your miserable aching behind
and give up the process of losing your mind.
Don't despair. Start trying to find
something congenial to your peace of mind,
though you may be in for an awful grind.
Hope that you're there for good luck to find
and pounce upon, greedily beset
to give your luck a new outlet
and exchange dry drought
for something else, but don't get wet.
Try to work everything out
and exchange a sneer for failure's pout.

A DESCRIPTION OF WHAT YOU CAN OR CAN'T DO.
HOW TO HOLD YOUR OWN IN MAYBE A VOLATILE WORLD

I'm so surprised! Look at me—I'm alive.
Well, this has been going on for years.
So the idea is to keep going. Health is important.
And whatever else comes up, deal with it.
Intervention in an emergency
requires bold steps—even drastic,
but don't overdo it and make a stupid mistake
that you could regret.
Steer or navigate your own life
or just sit tight. Don't fall down
and thump your own crown.
If you're foolish,
then the fool's identity could adhere to you
and you'd look bad.
Self-respect—take the lead
and the rest of the world will heed
and treat you with respect.
That's what you want. Even if you're behind,
keep up some legitimate front
so people will be nice to you
and boost your reputation
from fallen lapse.
Look good in this world.
Appearances count.

AN OPPORTUNE VERBAL COINCIDENCE
TO FULFILL UPON THE INCIDENCE

My arrival came from the womb,
my departure is due at the tomb.
What a life-spanning rhyme
is this convenience for the poet!
Easy to take advantage of—don't we know it!
Polish this felicity neatly,
using the womb-tomb opportunity
to melodically complete the unity.

Not to exploit it is a poetic lunacy.
If you fail, we grant you impunity
for the sake of a bridge-like span
from womb to tomb: the life-long plan.
Let philosophers riff on this when they can.

THE WOMB-TOMB DICHOTOMY
THAT GIVES POETS AN EASY RHYME
THAT SPANS OUR WHOLE LIVES UNDER TIME

My mother gave me a start in life
via her expressive womb
that launched my tomb-destined voyage
to end life's business with its usual destroyage.
But meanwhile new wombs are always born
to replenish the lives that are mercilessly torn.
Hence this facile rhyme so casually worn:
"Womb-to-tomb" sounds stale to the ear,
yet womb-to-tomb dates appear every year
on every sadly-etched tombstone far and near.

MEMORY, IN ITS PLUS AND MINUS,
FOR OLD FOLK OR MINORS

Life is sweet to live while you have it,
marred by many sour episodes
which memory records by the loads.
But memory has a positive side:
Inside you are lovely events
that you dearly re-live in your dear mind
and replay on the inner screen
of all the things you once had been or seen,
and sweetly recall.
You retain them—or nearly all.
That's why memory's loss is such a pall.

CRUELTY TO WIFE
ENDS OUR MARITAL LIFE.
A VERY TERMINAL STRIFE.

My wife served me a divorce
for abuse of physical force.
When brought to court, the court said, "Of course.
This man was undoubtedly coarse
in his brutish masculine response
to her refusal to obey his command.
Therefore the judge will demand
reparation to the wife,
and the husband's jail sentence
serving his duty of penitence."
Violence is cruel: what's the sense?
You POUND on your wife—
she gets recomPence,
thus combining pound and pence
by old British monetary system
that fit the world's financial rhythm.
As for wives, don't beat 'em, kiss 'em.

LARGELY FORGOTTEN
OR OVERLOOKED:
THAT'S YOUR FATE FOR BEING DEAD
WHICH ALREADY HAD ENOUGH DREAD.

A dead person soon is like a never-was,
unless he achieved fame and was written down
by scholars for history or memoir
that was read and became popular.
Otherwise a dead person is anonymous
except for a few dear friends
with whom his spirit still blends
in bonds that will prevail
far past his terminal ail.
Let the survivors wail.

**DEATH LOSES ITS BATTLE,
SUPPLANTED BY HEAVEN'S RATTLE.**

People believe what they want.
So they believe heaven's a permanent visit
to take the sting off death.
This divine compensation
is death's suitable elevation
into a flattering station.
People sure deserved it.
Heaven itself served it
to teach death a hard lesson
that death's assumed harm
turned into heaven's god-honored charm
on eternity's ever-productive farm,
that milks the pastures for infinity's worth
celebrating that majestic birth:
not solemn, but injecting carols of mirth
vastly beyond the dull ear of earth.

**GET YOURSELF DISILLUSIONED, YOU COWARD.
BEING DEAD, YOU'RE NOT THE LEAST EMPOWERED.**

If you die, you're mentally and emotionally nil.
The biggest bullshit is that you'll go to heaven or hell.
You have no eyes or lungs to see or yell.
Heaven and hell are no places at all.
They don't exist, no matter what you were made to believe.
If you die, okay, your loved ones may grieve.
There's nothing left of you, you have no "soul."
You have a material corpse and then bones.
But no consciousness, no awareness,
no organs for perception,
no means for cognitive conception.
Going to hell or heaven is bullshit.
The nullity of death proves that.
It's all in the head, don't you know?
But a skull needs the organs below
to even locate difference between skull-self and toe.

TO A FORMER BEAUTY WHO REJECTED ME

1.

The human body's anatomy
adheres to beauty standards.
The greater the beauty,
the more choices among marriage partners
that prospectively proclaim themselves,
infatuated with your beauty.
They gather round you like flies
and praise your beauty to the skies.
Quick, it's about time
to make a choice,
causing your parents to rejoice.

2.

But you choose a brute to wed,
who, though he's okay at bed,
beats you with ferocity that mars
your whole face, uglified with scars.
So beauty is a dangerous trap
that could wear down your beauty to a scrap
by making it a target
for an ugly temper of a horrible man
who destroys your young life as soon as he can
and imposes on you a lifelong ban
from all the beautified ranks
that you're never to join again
from the generalized company of men.

3.

Yours is an unusual case.
I loved you once but you rejected me.
What a different fortune if you had respected me
and my marriage proposal.
A perfect bond would have been at our disposal.
Now I won't renew my proposal

till you cosmetically reclaim yourself
and then I'll forgive your rejection;
though goodbye to our once-sought perfection.

**I CRASH A MEMORIAL PARTY
FOR SOME DEAD SUCKER I DON'T KNOW
AND PUT A STRANGER'S DISGRACE ON IT
AND CAN NEVER SHOW MY FACE THERE AGAIN
FOR WHATEVER NEXT DEAD PERSON
HER FAMILY PAYS TO MOURN THERE
AND WASTE A LOT OF EMPTY FUNERAL AIR.**

Someone died, and his friends made ceremony.
It was all based on what's phony.
There's nothing left of him, so why celebrate?
Exploit the ceremony, there's free food and drink.
Also you could meet someone for sex in the future
that could even lead to marriage,
and even yet, to a baby carriage.
Plus, you could gossip about the dead one,
get drunk, and have great conversations,
sprinkled with more humor than you know how to use.
If you feel mean, you can demean
the party's celebrant with foul abuse,
taking a risk with such insults
to make the real guests be mad at you
even to the point of asking you to leave,
since you haven't shown the decency to bereave.
So what? You drunkenly weave your way out,
having inflicted on the dead one dishonored flout,
and yourself a son-of-a-bitch reputation.
He's dead, so what's this bother anyway?
We're not stupid believers as to kneel and pray.
To hell with him—but there's no hell,
so what the hell? I feel nice and swell.
For what dead sucker is that funeral bell
that irrelevantly sounds with an empty knell?

**THE HEIGHT
OF SQUIRREL SPITE
AFTER A TREEWARD FLIGHT**

I was sitting on a park bench
when a squirrel slithered along the ground,
forcing my vision to look down.
He complained of instant starvation
and beggingly asked for a nut.
Annoyed for the intrusion,
I said I'm against squirrels in the first place
and would gladly contribute to their extinction,
the extermination of their total race,
which contributes no aesthetic distinction
to the New York party scene.
Then the squirrel scampered up a tree
and promptly dropped a found nut on me
as a form of retribution
for coming up with the Final Solution.

**EVOLUTION'S STUPENDOUS GIFT
TO THE HUMAN RACE.
IS THE HUMAN RACE THANKFUL?
NO, IT TAKES IT FOR GRANTED.
IT'S NOT EXHAUSTING ITS ENERGY
BY BEING TOO PANTED.**

What a great idea evolution came up with,
put immediately into practice,
though at a gradual time span!
It introduced an opposable thumb
on the right and left hand,
opposite the four other fingers,
so that grasping and clutching
could conveniently be done,
to allow little tasks to be won.
We've got to applaud that brilliant invention
which obeys much of our intention
and now has become an expected convention.

It helps architects and engineers
to overcome inconvenient fears
to put their blueprints into practice.
It allows us to perform exquisite actions.
Without evolution, where would we be?
Up the nearest convenient tree
swinging from branch to branch
like any circus acrobat.
At least that prevents us from being too fat.

THE PERMITTED EXCEPTION

Here I am, solitary in a room,
fleshly sitting on a chair
in my whole usual body.
Whose else would I be in?
It's the only body I've ever had
and no-one else could legally claim it,
not that it ever occurred to them.
The audacity! Stealing me!
And not even offering a borrowing fee.
And would I ever grant my consent?
Hardly. I would prevent
my body traveling without my permission
to somewhere else on some unknown mission
propelled and steered
on someone else's volition
foreign to my personal well-being
unsupervised under my own seeing.
I'm an autonomous human being,
bound to my own rigorous code,
and would certainly explode
with righteous indignation
if violated with my body taken over
unpermitted by my absolute consent.
Except for you, my darling,
my dear adored wife,
the sunshine of my life.

THE TRIUMPH OF BELIEF.
IT AFFORDS YOU BLESS-ED RELIEF.
IF YOU DISBELIEVE, YOU'RE A THIEF
LIKE A TREE TOO BARREN TO PRODUCE A LEAF.

His government caused suffering for the poor,
but nevertheless he was sound and sure
that his government, though despotic, was good,
because that's how rulership always stood.
Rationally he thought heaven and hell
scientifically sure didn't exist,
but was firm to believe that they did,
because his belief-system put in a winning bid.
Visually he could see that his wife was ugly,
but it flattered himself to believe in her beauty,
so belief won out over his eyes
and in a blink she was ravishing.
Doubt to the contrary he was savaging.
"Keep the faith" was his motto,
learned diligently at the game of lotto.
Whatever you want, be sure to get.
If you disbelieve in it, you're all wet.
Stupid intellectuals said there was no god.
He rightfully thought they were criminally odd
and continues believing in deity
as solid as when you look at a tree
where the image of "god" is on every leaf
to firmly affirm your sure-fire belief.
Don't be a nay-sayer and a faithless thief.
Twist your ideas to confirm your belief.
Otherwise suffer afterlife without relief:
Your "soul" is irretrievably lost in grief.

THE ORIGIN OF THE FAMILY.
LET THEM PROCEED ALONG AMBLY.

Women and men are quite a pair.
If you see them, move away to give them air.
If they're too close together,

they'd implode or explode, both,
if allowed to get too close:
with he the host & she the hostess
providing children for the mostest;
also their nephews and neices
to bring up the rear at the leastest.

AN UNRESOLVED DISPUTE

Two people argued about religion.
One said it shits on us like a pigeon.
The other defended religion as a custom
without which we don't know where we're from;
So he praised it up to Kingdom Come.

**A PLANETARY STATUS QUO OR MORE
TO KEEP UP THE BUSY STORE**

Give sex a great big hug
for its generous contribution
to the cause of evolution
which began long before history's fight
to keep reproduction normally upright
for the supply of babies
to breed and meet economic maybe's
so the planet will keep on spinning
and the birth rate maintains its standard of winning
to boast and gloat our proud breed
to keep up standards and even exceed
the already stupendous birth rate
to wonderfully keep our whole planet great
so destined to meet its prodigious fate
by maintaining sex between man and mate
and womanize the cause of motherhood
and whatever remains is as it should.

THE HARD JOB TO GET DONE
FOR A NEW BABY TO BE WON;
AND THE WIFE SIGHS, "THANK YOU, HON."

Erections have to be stiff
or else sex is a big "if"
and a baby might not be born
unless you deliver a prolonged horn
to the collision between the genders
that match perfectly their respective tenders
within the geography of tail enders
and a tornado of sperm spenders.

BETTER NOT PLAY WITH FIRE
UNLESS YOU THIRST TO EXPIRE.

1.

Life is neither one thing nor the other,
but lots of things all together
in a very mixed batch
from which nothing seems to hatch.
Go conflagrate it all with a match.
But that's self-arson,
so seek a pardon from a parson
who belongs to the fire department
as a volunteer serviceman.
But scared of religion, I'd be a nervous man.

2.

I won't touch any more matches
lest combustive material catastrophically catches
and reduces us all to bits and patches;
or if reaching bones, creates cracking fractures
performed on stage by a medley of actors
in agonized semblance of horror
from which nothing is apt to flower,
but only those flames that devour.

WORRYING ABOUT NOT ENOUGH FOOD TO ACCOMMODATE OUR WHOLE WORLDLY BROOD THAT KEEPS SENDING IN NEW BIRTHS: I CONTEMPLATE THE NEED FOR TWO EARTHS.

Birth keeps on arriving
by the bounty-ful
to refuel and fulfill
the roundly wide earth
to accommodate the plethora of rebirth
that swells up the population
of the earlier ones who are replenished
by new arrivals who will never end.
But will there be enough food for everyone
if the resource distribution will snap and bend?
And another planet perhaps
will be asked to collegiately lend
extra goodies and drinks too
to accommodate our worldly zoo
with enough supplementary nourishment
that religious gratitude will be fervently sent
by our globe to that one,
and our two globes will romance and merge
that are already on the verge
of interplanetary adulation
and wish to marry or at least elope
to enlarge our combined astronomical scope?
That at least is my abiding hope.
Let not overpopulation
endanger enough eating to starve
our dear men and women both.
Better instead we should sign a troth
to share our food-and-drink supplies
so no-one in the pitfall of death lies
pathetically before her time.
Premature starvation on a universal scale
makes my skin lose weight and my color pale.

**LIFE IS DERIVED FROM SEX
IN CIRCUMSTANCES OF VARIOUS SETS
FAMILIAR IN SOME CASES,
AND OTHERS, PROFOUNDLY PERPLEX.**

Bringing a little stranger into the world
who doesn't even exist yet
is engendered by a sexual act
between future father and mother
who may never be married yet
or who have yet to have even met.
The world may be populated illegitimately
in a great many of cases.
A world operated by strangers
is partly a matter of fact.
Sex is a strange and neutral act
not even preceded by an agreed-upon pact.
The world is a wide and straggly case
full of strangers who may get intimate
guided by that distant "theory," evolution,
that arrives at a bizarre solution
of new life to you or me
whose existence has been let free
by strangers' intimacy.
Go figure that one out.
If you make sense of it,
give, in language understood,
a report for the archives
of puzzling announcement of people's lives
controlled and erratic like bee hives.

**MY ORIGIN, BEFORE AND AFTER,
IN LIFE'S MANY RIDES
ALONG THE HILLS OF LAUGHTER
AND OTHER THINGS, BESIDES.**

Boys and girls together
on the sidewalks of New York.
Let's sing them a merry tune

that they DO get together
and the now-woman's stomach will balloon
after time has gone by
into the near-birth that becomes me.
That's a glimpse of my family tree.

**GETTING STARTED,
YOU WILL HAVE BEEN PARTED
FROM ACUTE NON-EXISTENCE
INTO THE ORDINARY PERSISTENCE
OF THE LIFE-SPARKLE
TILL THE LIGHTS TURN DARKLE.**

The key to the art of living
is first getting yourself born:
From non-existence to be torn
into the lively realm
of all your instincts at the helm.
How can you resist the overwhelm?

**THE VOYAGE FROM NON-EXISTENCE
WITH MOTHER'S HELP AND A LITTLE PERSISTENCE
INTO THE GREAT BEAM OF REAL LIFE
TO INTRODUCE A WORLD OF BOTHER AND STRIFE.**

Getting yourself born, resort to the mother
in whose deep old caverns you first suffer smother;
but then you're freed at last
to burst outright into life
with all the force of your vivacity
to your utmost organic capacity.
You learn speech, and thereby loquacity.

**DEAR EVOLUTION'S
HAPPY SOLUTION
TO REPLENISH POPULATION
TO OUR PLANET'S ELATION
BUT OUR BREEDING'S OVER-INFLATION**

Unless you sport the right genitalia,
reproduction is guaranteed a failure,
so embryos might not get fertilized
to get grandparents happily surprised
and big families get dynastized.
Have your genitalia all readied
for the birth rate to remain steadied
and infertility doubts get remedied
by giving evolution an extra feed
so our race shall happily exceed
the normal rate of our rapid breed.
Otherwise our planet shall famishly bleed
and babies somehow neglect to be born
despite from their mothers being about to be torn.
Entire future progeny will be forlorn.

**LIFE'S POLARITIES
AND ALSO DISPARITIES
AND TEMPORALITIES
AND OTHER EXTRALITIES**

Life is more than a business transaction
between inertia and lots of action.
Inertia quiets things down with boredom.
Action rives things up to restore them.
That's how we get our sleep and our doings,
depending on the moment's particular pursuings.
A balanced life is best to live,
saying what to take and what to give.
And in between, there's one big "if."
If you're too loose, get yourself stiff
and don't get your perplexes into a miff.

**DELAYING URINATION
TO MAXIMIZE RELIEF
WITH GROANING MOANS OF ECSTASY
TO POUR OUT YOUR WHOLE BREAKFASTY
IN DROP BY ECSTATIC DROP
TILL YOUR BLADDER HEAVES TO A STOP
AND YOUR MOMENTUM IS HEARD TO POP.**

Relief can be a terrific feeling,
the longer you wait.
If you moderately needed to urinate,
then no big deal to satisfy it,
it's hardly worth the thrill.
But the longer you wait,
the relief-charged result
will arrive with tumult
and the ecstasy to exult.
So the moral to this of course
is to delay as long as you can
the actual urination
as the culmination
of an ecstatically long wait
brought agonizing to a pitch
of sustained urge and itch.
There: I've made my pitch:
If you want relief's ecstasy,
take a long time till you almost split
your bladder in two halves
and you burst forth, with tittering laughs
and harsh orgasmic pants.
But watch out just in time
not to let your pee descend
on carefully groomed clothing
for a soiled though drip-worthy end.
What an adventure! Let's repeat it again.

THE VALUE OF SHEER RELIEF
AFTER WORRY AGONIZED TIME
LIKE SADISM'S SUPER THIEF

Here's how to feel wonderful
but it takes a long time.
It'll cost you suspenseful worry.
First locate somewhere along your skin
a possibly suspicious growth,
or rash for that matter.
You don't know how to interpret it.
The friends you show it to
have no clue.
Make a dermatologist appointment,
but he's booked up
for three long weeks.
That can afford you enough time
to start an obsessive campaign of worrying
that turns chronic and malign,
and you quiver with jitteryness
every time the horrible thought
of dermatoxic death
spoils your peace of mind
and invades your comfort zone
whose violated privacy upsets you,
and no friend of yours can help you
while you fret your misery
to an intolerable degree
amounting to private torture
and wrestling with self-loss.
No relief is available
for you to temptingly snatch.
Finally the three-weeks wait has arrived
with its fatally climactic climax.
Appointment time!
You arrive way too early,
with thoughts of funeral and death
corrupting your peace of mind
and spoiling your link with mankind.

The dermatologist takes one look
at that suspicious spot
and laughs you out of his office,
the word "nothing" trailing behind you.
Is that sweet relief?
Hasn't it all been worth it?
At the end, Shakespeare was right:
"All's well that ends well."
But at what cost! What a worry campaign!
We know the difference between pleasure and pain,
and don't forget that other duo: loss and gain.
Pure feeling is what you can't feign.

**GLOBE-CHASING RIVALS
RECYCLING TO RE-ARRIVALS**

Love makes the world go round?
But money is an arch competitor
to spin the world in its own sphere
and electrify people with fear.
Both are effective motivators—
the love business and that of the money.
"Oh why do you drive me so, honey?"

**DEATH AND LIFE, COMPARED.
THEIR DIFFERENCE IS SOLEMNLY AIRED.
CAN YOU EXPECT THEM TO BE PAIRED?**

Is death the foul reward for living
as a trophy or souvenir?
Sure. Long live death. You're not here.
Where are you? Gone.
Instead, death is here.
That would hardly raise from you a cheer.
You were great. But death is mere.
It doesn't even duplicate your fear.

QUIET. WE'RE SPEAKING OF LIFE

If your subject is life, talk about it
with a hushed tone, it's so venerable,
not to mention, of course, tentative.
So pay due attention to it,
with hushed reverie, but not religious.
Life in itself is prodigious.
But you have to think: Which is
this, and which is that,
in life's ongoing mystery
which converts itself, in due time, to history,
from some historians' point of view?
All together, since cavemen, we're in a mixed stew.
We're dealing with the old, but soon there's new,
promised to your neighborhood theater with a wide view.

**MULTIPLYING YOUR LIFE SOCIALLY,
INCREASING THEN THE SOUND VOCALLY**

In life, we have to consider others.
They're your sisters and brothers,
though not related in family.
So get on with people amiably.
Your social life is part of your life,
so try for a popularity prize
where people label you among the good guys.
If not, you'll be too lonely.
You're good looking, not too homely.
Go out and marry a wife.
Combine your friends with hers
to double your social life
as Mister and Missus Man and his Wife.
And get a few children too.
But not too much, or you marry a zoo
with too much going on at once,
to put extra gray hair on your head
and increase the death scene at your crowded bed.

Too many people—they go to your head.
They'll cause the death of you—or is it their fault?
No, your time was up with or without them.
But they filled up your life good
and built up your social neighborhood.
Altogether, you did what you would.

BELONGING TO HUMANITY IS A PROBLEM, MORE THAN ONE, SO LET'S GET TOGETHER AND SOLVE THEM.

Just being alive is a problem,
let along life itself.
What problems does living impose
on human beings who have to wear clothes
compared to all nature's other animals
and fish and birds too,
from the total evolutionary zoo?
We're stuck in the human mechanism,
but what makes us so complex?
Sometimes depression assaults us,
misery, panic, and upset.
A life filled with regret
for opportunities slipped away.
We're even annoyed by what we play.
We want, desire, and hope;
but earn the status, after all that grope,
of only a hopeless and defenseless dope.
No, not so bad as that,
perhaps I exaggerate.
We're all in somewhat of a funky state.
Greater minds than mine will thus debate
and grumble along to separate
those exciting polarities, love and hate.

**PUT YOUR POLARITIES BEHIND YOU
AND DON'T LET CONFUSION BLIND YOU.**

When you're polarized
between constipation and diarrhea,
with the latter you feel freer,
but too much would ease out
at intervals too frequent.
Your bowels were delinquent.
Constipation, however,
despite your endeavor,
takes too long forever
to get rid of your stuffed-up.
Better for diarrhea to errupt
and categorically interrupt
your frozen-hard bind
and up-tight behind.
These, my carefully chosen words,
empty me out, like obedient turds.

**I'M A WORLD WITHIN THE WORLD'S GALAXY.
FOR GALS I THANK FOR ALL THAT ECSTASY.
BUT BEING OLD, WHO HAS TO EXIT? ME.**

I need the world more than the world needs me.
So I grant the world precedence.
But I'm in residence,
so at least I count somewhat
and my existence has to make a mark.
But the world needn't acknowledge my spark.
But I must grant the world full respect
in respect of its being necessary
which is more than could be said for me.
I'm diminished by contrast,
or at least comparison
with my master, the world,
within which I'm luckily enfurled.
It even counts whether my birth was girled
or, as the case may be, boyed.

I'm buoyed up with the thrill
of gender's ongoing prominence
within my good old human race
that runs, I'd say, a frenzied pace.

THE SON ARRIVES.
THE MOTHER SIGHS
WITH WHISPERING CRIES.

Getting yourself born, make it easy for the mother
by narrowing yourself to get through the tube
extending from inside her pregnant body
to the outside world, where you jump out
and like a pugilist prepare for your bout.
Once outside you're free from squeezing
your stomach for easing
the organic passageway out,
so now you can be comfortably stout
while your mother mercifully breathes with a sigh,
whispering tenderly, "I have a son! Oh my!"

OUR CURRENT STATE
WHICH IMPLIES "TEMPORARILY,"
FROM DAY-TO-DAY STATUS
TILL FATE AT LAST WILL SPIT AT US.

Alas, I've grown so old,
my portfolio is about to fold,
and all my remains will have to be sold,
or rust of musty stale mold
like me myself, in skeletal disarray
with my decadent brain, in total decay.
Do I have a soul? If so, help me and pray.
Tomorrow is nowhere. How about one more day?

THE URINATION ACT
AS A MATTER OF FACT,
DROP BY DROP
WITH BATHROOM PROP.

Urination is such a relief
when enough time has passed
for new urine to build up
since the last time your urine passed
due to new signals of urgency
before an acute state of emergency.
Finally the flow when it starts going
gives an exquisite release,
and the continuity without surcease
creates sparkling relief
either whitish or yellowish in hue,
in a neat and lengthy arc
where your necessities are parked,
and it all comes out of you
within your perfect view,
when enough time goes by
and you build it up in other activity
and then what a prize you have
to prise the flow through
till dribbles ensue, the ending drops
which to save your laundry bill
you one by one control the spill
in parsimonious drops
with the bathroom as your props
and all in discrete privacy
directly in front of your eye-vacy.
Congratulations, you've done it.
The thrill was ordinary
and duly subsides
for normal activity resumption.
Zipper up, at your presumption.
The flow has passed, and droppage has stopped
and put your member back in the trouser box,
it's done its duty.

The whole process was a beauty.
The aftermath sigh
signals the when and the why
of self-congratulation
organized by sheer necessity
to control the liquid excessicity.
Ode to urination
at your humble bathroom station.

**HOW DARE THE READER
INTERRUPT OR DISRUPT
THE WRITER'S CREATIVITY
BY HIS AGGRESSIVE READING
INSTEAD OF PASSIVELY HEEDING
WHAT THE WRITER CLAIMS TO BE PLEADING.**

The reader needs to complete the writer's work,
but what if he reads in a different vein?
Then has the writer written in vain?
Maybe the reader improves the wobbling text
and out-creates the printed writer
with better technique, style, and imagination,
giving the writer a sullen vacation
from his craft when the reader takes over,
undergoing a whole different tome,
spinning other images that wildly roam
as strangely outside the original writer's
fierce but interrupted inspiration
now replaced in the reader's fevered brow
with a whole different text, don't ask me how.
It's not a transmission but a replacement
with the writer enraged at his effacement,
wishing to dump the reader in the script-splattered basement
for having totally a different case meant
despite an original honest intent.

HOW MY HONEY AND I OVERCAME AN AWKWARD START TO OUR WOOING. NOW WE CAN'T PART. WE TURNED ROMANCE INTO A FINE ART.

My honey and I just met. I tried to kiss her
directly on my honey's lipsticked kisser.
She acted like I committed nuclear fission.
"We just met. So I'm not your honey yet,"
she cautioned me, "Don't act so quick."
"Sorry that I was so premature.
Next time I'll moderate that impulse
till we know each other better."
She continued to scold: "Your kiss was wetter
than was appropriate for having just met."
I apologized with my keenest regret.
"Is it too late to woo you?" I asked.
"Not at all—" In our future marriage she basked,
and became my official honey,
kindly accommodating my lack of money,
for she had a trust fund, well trusted,
thus keeping our wedding vows from getting busted.

GOING TO A COMEDY MOVIE WITH MY HONEY. ISN'T THAT GROOVY?

Comedy is supposed to be funny
when you go to the movie with your honey.
To impress her that I understood the humor,
I roared out a huge guffaw.
She said that was too loud, under law,
in a decent middle-class theater.
So I moderated my laugh to be less weirder.
She still said it was the wrong reaction
to a scene in the movie with unfunny action.
So I moderated my laugh to a merely smile.
"Did you see me? I just modestly smiled,"
I timidly asked. "I did, but the hero died,
so your smile was inappropriate."
Apologetically, I vowed to keep alert

to time my reaction to the movie's action
and thus provide my honey with satisfaction.

**FEEL BAD? HURRY UP AND CHANGE IT.
PREFERABLY FOR THE BETTER, OF COURSE.
LENIENTLY APPLY YOUR FORCE.**

Is feeling awful part of human life?
Sure. How could you be alive otherwise?
The next step is to try to feel better.
There are various steps along the way
to describing yourself as having a good day.
What are you there for, except to adjust?
Form your plan of action—you must!
Then go ahead along your rigorous plan
(or flexible, as the case may be.)
Take action—don't be passive.
Change your state by homeostasis
to within the confines of your comfort zone
where you take claim: "To each his own."
Much better than chewing on a discarded bone
fraught with putrid disease
to cause death, or merely a sneeze.

**SOME PRACTICAL, COMMON-SENSE ADVICE.
APPLY IT IF YOU CAN, BUT NOT OTHERWISE.**

Play life to the right tune.
Don't go searching for the moon.
Leave it alone, it's too far away.
Look for something close with which to play,
conducive to convenience.
Apply thereby pragmatic genius.

**A FAIR WARNING:
DON'T VENTURE INTO THE ALARMING.
WATCH OUT. LIFE IS A TRAP.
DON'T GET CAUGHT, OR YOU'RE OFF THE MAP.**

Life could really be an awful drag
and you feel like a multi-used rag
discarded along a diseased path
used only by denizens of ghettos
who don't even try to peel their potatoes,
and as a result choke on them
and cough up a whole pot of phlegm.
Don't get caught up in that mentality.
Seize upon a more bourgeois reality
and conform to a better image,
or else succumb to an abysmal finish
to your pathetic life on the wrong track
who got stuck forever and never turned back.

**ON LIFE'S VICISSITUDES
AND OTHER PRECARIOUS INTERLUDES**

To live is not always easy.
Get out of your head that "life is breezy."
Rather, it's full of ups and downs
and erects its imbalance on whoozy grounds.
So don't take your life for granted.
It's not built on marble or granite.
If you're a bridge from your goal, then span it.
But here comes death. Can you overrun it
and be in the baby cradle again
before you ever become women and men?
Life is a cycle. It's a matter of now and then.

**THE VERBAL ART TO MAKE A SIGNIFICANT FRIEND
BY SHARING CONVERSATIONS ALL YOUR LIVES
AND NEVER RUN OUT OF WORDS
BY TAKING TURNS, GOOD AND FAIR,
FOR EACH TO HAVE HIS PROPER SHARE.**

The art of conversation
is to each take a fair turn
and not overspeak, even if at the peak
of your important communication.
Learn to condense, give the short version,
and watch him make a conversion
to your lifelong friend and pal
for allowing him to speak his piece
to his own fullest extent.
Give him space and time
to soundly communicate,
and watch him turn into your eternal mate.
Good for you, and good for him
to share each other's conversational whim.
At each other's shrine, share a mutual hymn.

**GETTING BORN IS NOT ENOUGH.
THERE'S MORE AHEAD, AND IT'S ROUGH.**

Getting born, all you have to do
to proceed in life is to be you.
"All?" Apparently that's not enough.
There are standards you have to be up against.
Otherwise life backs you up against a fence
and gives you a lesson on how not to be dense.
Otherwise your life is about worth two pence.
Increase their worth, if you have any sense.
Make money, and spend all you can
on practicality, not just fun.
Up to the challenge? There's a life to be won.
Don't just consider yourself already done.
Remember your father? Be his obedient son.

**WHAT TO LOOK FOR
AND WHAT TO AVOID.
KEEP YOURSELF UNDESTROYED.**

Between pleasure and pain
the choice need not be a strain,
but automatically you prefer
the emotionally comfortable feeling
and not the one that keeps you reeling
in the sorry plight of the doldrums.
Avoid melancholy if you can
and its uncomfortable satellites
that inflict on you unknown harm
to your nervous system and disarm
your ability to fight back
from the grips of a panic attack.
Make distressful feelings prominent in their lack.
Smooth sailing ahead, and no flack.
Adjust your emotional barometer
to the nearest available comforter
and set your sights for pleasure
and the serene joys of your leisure.
Store up your best treasure.

**LIFE MECHANICALLY IN ACTION
THROUGH AN APPARENT FREE WILL
TO TAKE OFF THE MECHANICAL CHILL.**

Life is a readjustment.
So if the weather is too cold
I wear extra clothes.
If the weather is too hot
I take off more clothes,
until my dilemma is at a close
and I've fought my "too-much" foes
down to their "not-enough" toes
by remedying whatever's woes;
so that comfort is my goal
to satisfy the body's temperature

at the right approximate measure:
since the body is the prime operator
and determines what's best or worse
after experimental rehearse
in our own private laboratory
for all this exploratory.
And it all tells a story,
efficiently to eliminate worry:
problem-solving in a hurry.
Efficiency we learn on the way
to free up more time to just play
and riddle our way through the day,
things being how they waywardly may.
Thus life goes on in a flow,
directionality to determine our go.

**LIFE, AND ITS WHOLE RETINUE
THAT GLADLY INCLUDES ME AND YOU.
AND DON'T FORGET THE WHOLE BAMBOOZLE, TOO.**

Life brings out our philosophy
but modernizes it with snaps of photography
that covers the land with its geography
and reinforces glamorized history
to populize it and erase its mystery.
Life does lots of other things besides.
Psychology explains lots of human beings.
Ocean roars with its renewing tides
like bombastic music with its vigorous rides.
Life puts me and my honey sides to sides.
We seize upon each other, the narrows and the wides
and also the soft and curvy parts.
We greedily accept what evolution imparts
and survey a museum full of fine arts.

**WHAT DEATH SEEMS TO BE LIKE,
FROM A MORBID PERSPECTIVE POINT OF VIEW.
I'M JUST TRYING TO BE TRUE.**

Life is so packed with substance,
and oppositely death has none.
You better adjust to life's side
and not be taken for a ride.
Death is not intriguingly seductive,
though it certainly is extremely reductive
and has hardly anything to say
after it's closed out your day
and put to sleep your silent dismay
no matter how fervently your relatives pray.
Now it's much too late.
There's nothing left on your plate.
Food is impossible to eat.
It goes to waste. You're complete.

**AN EXAMPLE NOT TO FOLLOW
UNLESS YOU REDUCE YOUR BODY
TO SKELETAL HOLLOW
AND HAVE YOUR WIDOW BELLOW.**

Don't do anything you may regret.
But how can you tell in advance?
Are you a mind-reader?
Can you foretell events
and narrate them by lengths?
If you knew which horse would win the race,
your bets would accumulate millions
in United States currency.
If the race occurred in Britain
you'd gain such a lot of pounds,
obesity would be your rap
with endangered health to go with it,
reducing your lifelong longevity
to a smaller estimate; and no levity
is polite for ridiculing you

with mocking fun at your expense.
Sometimes humor just isn't funny,
especially when it comes to overweight and money.
So be ready to take the tragic mode
to consecrate someone's soul
who can barely wobble on his feet
when sheer gravity drags him down
and reduces his physique to a clown
of sheer flab all along the waist
and ponderous poundage for his life to waste
and scrapbooks ready for obituary to paste.
If you follow his example, no need to haste.
The coffin's not ready for his corpse encased.

**LEARNING TO GIVE THE OTHER HIS TURN
BY SHUTTING UP YOURSELF
AND NOT LEAVE HIM HANGING ON THE SHELF.**

Conversation is a delicate art.
Don't hog the limelight or the floor
to monologue yourself into a bore.
Allow the other to reply
when you've used up your speaking part.
Be inquisitive what the other thinks,
giving him full vent to express himself
to his equal fair extent
and not repress anything for your sake.
Learn to give in to him, not just take.
Be a gentlemanly conversational mate.
Don't be condemned into his infernal hate—
Your social life would suffer: just wait.

**THE URGE
TO PURGE
WITH A SURGE.**

Materialize a fart
and make it solid.
Then your bowels
won't be horrid.
Don't just make an empty air
but complete its theoretical task
to give you real dung
on which your ease could be hung.
Finish what's flimsily sprung.
Give your push RESULTS,
not just airy insults:
solid religion, not preliminary cults.

TOTALING OUR LOSS

Dear life, I don't know what you are,
but you sure fit me
like a tailor-made suit.
Together we're a beaut.
I wish to keep you on, not to doff you,
even though the weather should get too hot.
I keep wearing you, so I sweat.
You're my inside and my outside.
To both your sides I must abide.
I'll not relinquish you
till death forces me to.
My reluctance is an oath to you.
We were both. Now we're half.
In gloom we part. Why not laugh?

**HOW POSTHUMOUSLY TO BOAST
TO YOUR MOURNING WIDOW
WHAT A GREAT MASCULINE GLOW
YOU SHED BEFORE YOU HAD TO GO.**

Loving life as I do,
losing it would be extra tragic,
unless I resorted to magic.
I'm not a fan of the occult,
not being of a religious bent.
But if my death would be an event,
here's the message I would have sent
to all my friends and sundry
on a church-bell-sounding Sunday:
"Dear friends and sundry:
Sorry to not be around,
because my body stopped being sound
and had to stop working.
Not even stop working, but stop playing too,
since death is not a leisure
nor permission to take pleasure.
On the contrary, death includes everything
you ever lived for.
I'd go on, but I don't want to be a bore.
So after receiving this message,
go to your local family store
and buy money to give my widow
who couldn't follow where I had to go.
With the extra money, she'll buy a new hubby
and find out how inferior to me
her new chosen husband is bound to be.
Then the last laugh will be mine,
and my deceased manhood on my very shrine
will illuminate the heavens with my shine."

**DEALING IN THE WORLD WITH OTHER PEOPLE,
YOU DON'T HAVE TO BE RIGID AS A METHODIST STEEPLE,
NOR BE VOYEURISTIC AS A PEEP-HOLE
TO SEE NUDITY AND SEE IT WHOLE.**

My life necessarily,
living in a city,
includes other people,
who interfere and intervene
and get inbetween
me and my humble purposes
like waiting in line for a ticket
or grocery shopping at the store.
Other people are hard to ignore.
But give them a break, they deserve to exist.
Being previously born, they must now persist
to make the most of the life they have.
They're entitled to it, right?
So why put up a bitter fight
that you deserve to breathe rarefied air
and they only a crude form of oxygen?
You'd like to box them out again
and prevent them from quality merchandise
like charming varieties of mid-eastern spice.
But if you start to eat something extra fancy,
give them a benevolent slice.
To make your way in the gregarious world,
it pays to build up a reputation:
You've got at least to pretend you're nice
and prove the pretense to be a real fact.
Emphasize the genuinity of your act
to show that your notions are not half cracked
but actually are realistically backed.

MAN, WOMAN, AND LOVE.
IS THERE ANY PROBLEM MORE ABOVE?
TO WHAT EQUATION DOES THIS ADD UP?
IS LOVE DRAINING OR RISING IN THE MUTUAL CUP?

Loving someone is a big gamble.
It has a contingent handle
that's twisting and devious.
Will she love you back
with equal reciprocity?
And durability through time?
Will our love dwindle and weaken?
Will her love rise to a peaken
commensurate with the rise of yours?
Will she love you with all her pores
till you cling to her with your paws
and your loves will intermingle
without the tremor of a pause,
so that you remove your defensive claws?
You and she may weary of each other
or you continue to love and she not.
Tie that into an insoluble knot.
Or she keep her love going for you,
and you want to drop out?
Leading to the parting of the ways
if your love or her love outweighs
the previous inequality division
that exacts mathematics with precision?
Oh, let's both handle this
and arrive serenely into marital bliss.
Let's not be subject to a further quiz
but keep going and get a few kids.
At least we avoided tripping on the skids,
and reserve for each other our precious ids.

A FLIRTATION IN THE TEETH OF DISMISSAL'S TIME BARRIER, WHICH IS THEORETICALLY IMPENETRABLE

(WOMAN) For some inexplicable reason, you attract me.

(MAN) Well, that's an insufficient reason, in view of my unassailable circumstances.

(W) Which are?

(M) Not only am I married, but I love her.

(W) Is your love permanent?

(M) Who can tell? It's only now.

(W) Does that give us time enough for you gradually to reverse your current officially marital love, to in turn first divorce her and then make me your number two wife to a permanent degree?

(M) Not the way I feel now. You could face a long wait.

(W) Well, my impetuous love for you is now getting the cold shoulder. I could feel the squeeze of its freeze.

(M) Your offer flattered me. When I go home to my wife, I'll describe it.

(W) Won't that make her jealous?

(M) No, I've already assured her that my steadfast marital love bears the extra security arrangement of permanence. My rejection of you is a lightweight gesture by me, but a heavyweight assurance for my wife of my permanent attachment, which your infatuation puts in no danger, placing itself in the teeth of my abrupt dismissal.

(W) Did my attempt place you in any temptation whatever toward infidelity toward your loving and beloved wife?

(M) Not yet. Time sometimes reverses previous decisions. Perhaps your obvious attractiveness, reinforced by persistence, can make a future dent, but I wouldn't bet on it.

(W) By then, I might already have put myself in the ranks of the irrefutable inaccessible, via an adored husband.

(M) Then it's my future loss. What a treasure you would have been! I'm already in a tinge of jealousy for him.

(W) No need to. He prospectively seems no match for you, in relative desirability.

(M) Are we in a time frame?

A SEXUAL CONFRONTATION, WITHIN SEPARATE COMPARTMENTS

(MAN) Love is supposed to be beyond time's reversal. Is that persuasive enough to allow my wooing to break through into your essential acceptance of me as your loving husband?

(WOMAN) Well, that's an impressive inducement for my reply of yes. But still, in realistic terms, I'm cautiously self-protective to the point of being tentative in the teeth of your rather strong-minded rhetoric. I'm a little shy, you see.

(M) Well, big strong me is all the more aroused to break through your flimsily flirtatious tentative abstaining of decision making.

(W) I can readily sympathize with your rather masculine quintessential aggression to undermine my barriers to your persuasive rhetoric. Within my vision, is your cock aroused?

(M) It's bulging with strain inside the secret compartment of my trousers, within the proverbial inch of staining the latter with my impetuous sperm in its overwhelmingly martial aggression versus your dainty maidenly ultra-seductive furtive reluctance to give in.

(W) Well, why not give vent to it, unless you match your shyness to mine in inter-gender contrast on the explosive verge of your forceful sperm overcoming puritanical inhibition?

(BRIEF INTERLUDE.)

(M) Oh! It's done.

(W) That was quick. Do you still fancy me despite having shot your load?

(M) Oh yes. But no longer so strenuously. In given time, I can renew my urge.

(W) Oh, what a man!

**IN LIFE, YOU'VE GOT TO WIN,
WHEREVER YOU ARE.
LET AMBITION SET THE BAR.**

My opinion of life varies.
If I were in the prairies,
I'd be in my cowboy guise,
like all the other guys
there in the same place.
But in the plains, I put on a different face.
Isn't that plain?
If I were a city dweller,
I'd be quite a different feller,
and be a ferocious yeller
to out-loudness the other guy,
roaring out ambition
in desperate search for fruition,
and if necessary, to use ammunition
to enforce my desire to win
in bloodthirsty competition
to run the other guy down,
and earn myself a juicy crown,
right at the top of my head,
and boast, indeed, that I'm well bred.
It consolidates my place ahead.
My food is always tastier
and my sword more of a rapier.
If I'm hunted, I'm more escape-ier.

**HE PURSUES. SHE RESISTS. HE PERSISTS. SHE CHANGES THE
RULES. HE OBEYS THE CHANGE. RECKON THE WINS AND
LOSSES FOR EACH AT THE OPEN END.**

(MAN) My honorable love implores you to relent to my heart-worn assault on your hoped-for reciprocal heart to unite with mine in the goal of marriage.

(WOMAN) It's not a mutual goal, lacking my equal aspiration for that joint status.

(M) You reject me?

(W) Out of hand.

(M) Well, should I stop persisting?

(W) Yes, don't be annoying. I've already proclaimed my emphatic reluctance to conform to your marital plans, since it takes two to tangle, so let's avoid a wrangle.

(M) But even in your defying me, you proceed in such a sweet voice that your very resistance inflames my insisting over your deliciously opposite wishes, that I get my way.

(W) My mind is unchanged. Unless you change your tune.

(M) I'll adjust to your reconsidering.

(W) Woo me unobtrusively. Give me a chance to initiate, not respond.

(M) Let you aggress?

(W) Yes, I'll take the traditional masculine role, and woo you off your feet.

(M) You won. I accept.

(W) Be my captive.

(M) Joyfully. I'm yours.

(W) Oh, you succumb so readily.

(M) Have I proven to be a pushover?

(W) All I had to do was initiate, and you fell down for me.

(M) Do you want a heartier resistance?

(W) Playing hard to get might win my heart over.

(M) By your perverse rule, I reject you.

(W) Oh, my love increases!

(M) Too late. You're finished.

DON'T LOSE YOUR HEAD, JUST FOR AN IDEA

When life gets too much for you,
feign death and take a rest.
But don't feign death too seriously
that you actually succumb to it,
like an actor who takes his role to his heart
and then from his whole career must part.
To do such extra hustle, was that smart?
Don't confuse the real thing with an art.
Watch out where you end, when you start.

SETTING: A YOUNG MAN AND WOMAN HAVE FRESHLY GRADUATED FROM THEIR RESPECTIVE SEMINARIES, AND MEET EACH OTHER TO GET ACQUAINTED AND TEST THE WATERS OF THE OUTSIDE WORLD.

(MAN) We're both fresh and pure graduates from virginal seminaries, so now we've got to explore the world, which means for example each other.

(WOMAN) But we're both timid and afraid of sex. Shouldn't we retain our modesty by refraining from making a crude, blunt beginning?

(M) In a word, no. Since we have genital apparatuses that differ from each other, we might as well explore to make use of their different functions.

(W) What are you suggesting?

(M) To put these genitalia opportunities into experimental action.

(W) But what about, above our genitalia, just you and me, plainly, as human personalities? Must the rest of us submit to being genitalia-driven, aside from other normal human traits?

(M) Oh, we'll get along, vis a vis each other, with our polite, agreeable social charms and amenities that we learned in our seminaries.

(W) But won't we be under the primary dictatorial auspices of our contrary genitalia, to the diminishment of our agreeable social charms?

(M) Your normal, usual body and brain qualities will work in unison, and so will mine. No need to worry. Our respective reproductive traits and mechanisms promise to behave and be only integral parts of us, joining in, not getting monopolized by obsessive sexual priority and going crazy to that extent.

(W) But I'd like to retain my amateur status by keeping my reticent feet clear and dry of the stormy, unruly waves of oceanic onslaught at the frontier of the dangerous beach.

(M) Oh come on! Get wet!

(W) The longer we modestly wait, the more romance gets a chance to take over, as opposed to brusk sex in its crude early fumbling sessions.

(M) Oh, let's get it over with.

(W) Is that an inducement? Stop seducing me.

(M) How did you fathom my intention? Well, your instincts seem soundly in place, setting the pace for our actions to follow suit.

(W) Follow SUIT!? I thought we'd be naked!

**TAKE ON THIS TONE
SO YOU WON'T YELP AND MOAN.
DON'T BITE YOUR OWN TELEPHONE.**

Don't let life get too much for you
that you scatter your brains and miss out.
Don't succumb to frantic panic
that sharply bites at your peace of mind.
Don't be the always jittery kind
that can't keep still for a calm minute.
When relaxation is available, get in it,
but don't squeeze it too tight.
Do the right thing, but keep it light.
For every aggravating opportunity, you don't have to bite.
Take life nice and easy
and cultivate the calm breezy
with a loose stomach, not queasy.
Moderately be either "he" or "she."
(Pardon the grammatical slip,
it fell out of my grip.)

YOU'RE LUCKY I'M TELLING YOU THIS

Life is something we all have to deal with,
and in some cases it's a big deal.
What I'm speaking about, it's real.
How you approach life—handle it delicately,
but don't get unnerved and up-tight.
On you, let life train its strongest light
and don't get tangled up into a complex blight.
Are you taking this wisdom in the right way?
From my learn-ed precepts please don't stray.
My considered advice is not a frivolous matter of play.
You're lucky I'm dispensing my wisdom to you
from my high, almighty, haughty point of view.
Consider yourself among the extremely privileged few.

ANNA RECOLLECTS A PICNIC-SPOILING STORM FROM WHICH EVERYONE SCATTERED, ESPECIALLY HER FRIEND BERTHA WHOSE DISLOYALTY SHE FINALLY FORGIVES, SHEDDING THE SUDDEN SHOWER OF A BLESSING.

(ANNA) Bertha, you betrayed me.

(BERTHA) What an accusation! I automatically refute it. But just for the record, what was it? Before you answer, may I add that I'm indignant?

(ANNA) No, that's MY role. I'm the rightfully indignant one.

(BERTHA) All right, what am I accused of?

(ANNA) Last week I invited "everyone" to a picnic. Helped by my boyfriend Bob, I brought food and bottles of wine to the announced park scene spot.

(BERTHA) Sure, it was beginning to be fun, till the skies thunderously spoiled it all with a heavy deluge.

(ANNA) You ran away, bolted, absented.

(BERTHA) Everyone did, including even your boyfriend Bob, the great sprinter. Didn't also you, for self-survival's sake? Due to scrambling away from that chaotic storm to seek desperate shelter with frantic desperation, I lost track of you who were lost to my situational indifference. "Were you soaked?" I'm asking you sympathetically.

(ANNA) Thanks for your belated noticing. I was.

(BERTHA) Well, why didn't you alertly take the necessary panic of haste, self-defensively, as the circumstances came unexpectedly to demand?

(ANNA) I tried to, but tripped and fell in the new-sprouted mud. My boyfriend Bob had disloyally given up on me and fled, and I felt betrayed by mainly him, and you yourself, supposedly my good friend, you forsaker!

(BERTHA) I apologize. What happened both to the opened and the unopened wine?

(ANNA) Abandoned, and the food too drenched to save, even mashed, beyond recipe instructions in the lost chaos of missing a picnic meal.

(BERTHA) Well, some of us had need to lose weight, so all wasn't lost in the force of nature that the storm was. Not everything is undiluted "bad." There had been, unpunctually, a silver lining.

(ANNA) You're dreaming like a mystic. But I forgive you, and therefore feel divine. All is well. The past has now so receded that all my dryness shows no aftermath effects from my dear storm that's now exorcised.

(BERTHA) Do you feel fully survived from that wet trauma?

(ANNA) I bask in the blessing of relief.

(BERTHA) But a week has slipped by.

(ANNA) Week it was. Strong am I.

THE ONLY BIG DIFFERENCE

To die is the worst event
in your life, occurs at the end
and there's no recourse otherwise
to answer that final blow.
Avoiding or delaying it
is your desperation measure.
Preserving life's treasure
is a humble and selfish goal
if you can dearly manage it.
Vigilance and luck you need
to prolong life's daily deed.

YOU CALL THAT A LIFE?

The hard life of a stone
doesn't have the subtlety of a bone.
It's a lumpen piece of bulk,
lacking brains, but it's a hulk.
Solitary, it doesn't converse with folk.
Sexually, it can't give a poke.
It keeps to itself, of course.
Lacking refinement, it's somewhat coarse.
With total continuity, it goes the course.
What it lacks is drive and force—
meaning, in human terms, ambition.
It's only what it is. Isn't that enough?
But by durability's standards, it's tough.
When rain comes, it can face the rough.
Its life, however, lacks love.
It doesn't have the lightness to rise above.

A MAN INNOCENTLY EVADES AN UNFAIR CASE OF BEING ARRESTED ON UNJUSTIFIABLE GROUNDS

(MAN 1) I have an internal conflict.

(MAN 2) Sorry if you're burdened. What is it?

(1) Any time a policeman passes by, even if he notices nothing but his own idle daydream, I automatically become plunged in innocent guilt.

(2) Boy, you're a nut case. What guilt are you trying to hide from that nevertheless oblivious policeman?

(1) The guilt of imagining doing a crime even if I never pulled it off.

(2) Are you a fool? Or a nitwit?

(1) I can do with more sympathy and less mockery.

(2) How can I sympathize with someone who declares war on himself?

(1) When that policeman finally walks away from my path with his back turned to me, I'm able to escape from the furtive act of concealing my imaginary crime from a would-be belligerent cop loaded with potential

suspicion that threatens jail sentence to an unwarranted degree, according to court analysis.

(2) Have you tried a psychiatrist?

(1) No. I already know what's going on inside that complex anti-brain of mine. But the second a cop is walking toward within my obliquely confrontational path in any forward or sidelong direction, I start to freeze and exude fear, like a dame confronting molestation by a seemingly harmless guy on a trial first date.

(COP STROLLS INTO THE SCENE.)

(1) Look! A cop is coming in my direction. I'm starting to freeze within a torrent of sweat.

(2) Try not to stumble on him conspicuously, like a self-defeating oaf.

(1) (SPUTTERING:) Hello, officer. I didn't do nothing. (APOLOGETICALLY:) I'm innocent.

(COP) What are you innocent of, wise guy?

(1) Of almost bumping into you.

(COP) Yeah? You smell with guilty sweat. I oughta turn you in.

(1) What for, dear officer. I'm law-abiding.

(COP) Yeah? Tell that to the judge. (HORSE-COLLARING MAN1.)

(COP) Ugh! You stink of sweat. I'm turning you loose because I have a hot date tonight and don't want to minimize my cause by stinking of your second-hand sweat. Just consider yourself lucky. (COP LEAVES, SQUEEZING HIS NOSTRILS BETWEEN FINGERS.)

(1) Lucky me! What a sweet parole I inveigled! The lord is on my side, and I'll reward Him with a hot-shot prayer tonight as I kneel before bed in a holy sanctum of light.

(2) Yeah, but you're still stuck with the same old complex. Stink THAT one out, you bum! (GOES OFF PINCHING HIS NOSTRILS.)

A SWIFT ROMANCE DEFLATED BY A LESS IMMEDIATE REJECTION

(MAN) I really love you. Seriously. I can't help it.

(WOMAN) That's too bad. You're so sudden, on impact.

(M) True, we only met an hour ago, so my courtship seems premature. Perhaps I'm impetuous. I should have taken preliminary stages, before this rash, abrupt proposal, which defies the conventional time scale that gives romance a chance to mature on both sides from my solo budding.

(W) Give me a chance to consider. Who are you? I don't know you.

(M) Won't you give me priority access, the better to find out if my worthiness clicks with your (as yet to me) unknown standards?

(W) There's a problem.

(M) Is it tantamount to an obstacle?

(W) Yes, an insurmountable one. I'm already married.

(M) Oh. How intensely do you love him? If it's lukewarm or tepid, then my chance is still bright and eager for a swift replacement that puts me in line to be number two husband for you.

(W) It's number three. My obvious beauty had already exercised its attractiveness before you belatedly advertised yourself as a willing number three before even knowing you had predecessors.

(M) Can you excuse my understandable ignorance, which gets confused with bliss?

(W) Anyway, you're too late. I'm hopelessly smitten with number two.

(M) Is that the end of my wooing, by way of undeniable rejection on your part of me, in decisive terms?

(W) Yes. Is your sudden love for me collapsing, in view of my circumstances?

(M) Well, the air has been taken out of it.

(W) You're taking my discouraging in good part. Nice meeting you. I'm homeward bound now to cook dinner not only for husband number two but for our little baby, the fruit of number two's loins.

(M) Well, I crash into my doom. Goodbye.

(W) Sorry. No, I'm not sorry. I'm permanently in love with number two.

A FRESH GRADUATE FROM PSYCHIATRIC COLLEGE IS AMBITIOUSLY LOOKING TO RECRUIT HIS VERY FIRST CLIENT ON A CUT-RATE BASIS.

(GRADUATE) Hello. I just graduated from Psychiatric College and have gone into business from a rented office in a prestigious part of town where the posh residents can afford me. Can you be my first client, at reduced fee because of my relative inexperience?

(MAN) Sorry. I don't need you.

(GRADUATE) Well, if you don't bring your own neurosis along, could I please induce a neurosis on a trial basis, because I'm desperate for clients?

(MAN) Your offer would be tempting, if I knew what's in it for me.

(GRADUATE) If I could instill a complex in you, it might make you a more nuanced character for a movie or television play which you could be the author of, on an autobiographical basis of inventing a complex character for the audience or reader to be intrigued by, with so much fascination that you'll have a great money-making career and get popularity and women that way, even celebrity if you hit it right.

(MAN) No, you talk like a charlatan. Is that what they taught you in Psychiatric College? A course in "Charlatanism 101"?

(GRADUATE) Only in my senior year. Stop maligning my new profession. I declare you neurotic on the basis of excessive suspiciousness and caution. In fact, your case seems too complex for me. Either I'm underqualified or overqualified to take on your slippery case. Though I might give you a complex by rejecting you, so that your expectation of rejection amounts to an obsessive phobia to the point almost of insanity itself, giving me requisite professional practice at a high-class level.

(MAN) If you do, I won't take my business to you as a patient. It would be self-defeating.

(GRADUATE) Can you blame me for trying?

(MAN) No, not with your future career at stake.

(GRADUATE) What about YOUR career as a patient?

(MAN) I'm not in a hurry. I'll be so cautious as to be SUPER patient.

(THEY PART, UNFRIENDILY.)

A PRETTY "CREATIVE WRITING" STUDENT EXCITES HER OLDER INSTRUCTOR'S LUST. HE OFFERS AN IMMORAL SOP TO OFFSET HER SEXUAL REFUSAL.

(INSTRUCTOR) Since you're my pretty "Creative Writing" student, and I'm not only your instructor but, in my own right, a successfully published author, can we come to an agreement that in return for my special favoritism in being your mentor in out-of-class sessions, you'll be my secret mistress?

(STUDENT) No. It sounds like prostitution, which puts me in a dishonorable position. You're too old for me anyway.

(INSTRUCTOR) But I offer you terrific inducements for accepting my somewhat immoral offer. I'll put at your disposal my sure-fire contacts and connections in the literary and publishing worlds, virtually guaranteeing you early publications to jump-start your career at a young age, causing your fellow "Creative Writing" students to envy you to the point even of hatred, if it should go that far.

(STUDENT) I may be too mediocre a talent for even you to transform me into a published author just because of the influence you wield in the literary and publishing industries, with their cut-throat competitiveness.

(INSTRUCTOR) But I could bribe my publishing and editing colleagues from out of my own munificent pocket, since my successful career has earned me extra money to spend on your behalf. A beauty such as you shouldn't be a career publishing wash-out, which would be in disharmony with my exciting lust for you as a young woman, irrespective of your mere relative writing talent.

(STUDENT) Am I that lovely?

(INSTRUCTOR) Enough for me to make this unique offer. To cut the suspense, I await your response.

(STUDENT) To increase the suspense, may I ask you what's your opinion of my writing so far?

(INSTRUCTOR) I'm frankly compelled, in due self-defeating honesty, to say it stinks. You have no chance, even if publishers succumb to my bribe. With this confession, I've ruined my own chances to enjoy sessions of lust with you.

(STUDENT) What a sacrifice! My pity goes to you. Also to myself, for being a no-talent writer. Sorry we both lose out. Failure is so frequent in many aspects, in this world we share.

(INSTRUCTOR) Well, if it's any consolation, we come to some kind of subsidiary agreement in our double mutual failures. Should we shake hands in conciliation? (OFFERS HIS HAND, WHICH SHE DROPS.)

(STUDENT) No. It may excite your lust, which seems rippling on the surface, like an explosive that may spontaneously go off with sudden immensity.

(INSTRUCTOR) That's not too bad. Let's go on with this fragile handshake. Let's quiver on it together.

THE CLOUD, THE CLOCK, AND OTHER CONTRARIES THAT DISCUSSION SOON BURIES BY EXHAUSTING THEM AND OTHER WORRIES

(MAN 1) What's the difference between a cloud and a clock?

(MAN 2) The cloud has no urgent duty, either to give or prevent rain. It just floats on aimlessly, sometimes joining other clouds socially.

(MAN 1) Is it responsibilityless?

(MAN 2) Not a worry in the world. Its life is ambitionlessly empty, like a puff of vapor.

(M 1) Is the clock its opposite?

(M 2) Frantically. It's got to be on time.

(M 1) How urgent is that?

(M 2) Depends on who's using it. If it needs correction, being fixed is at hand.

(M 1) Good. Why worry? (PAUSE) When is worry necessary?

(M 2) It depends on what's going on.

(M1) Situationally? Circumstantially? Practically?

(M2) All those contingency factors. But look. Let me level with you. Why are we being so fussy about things?

(M1) You mean these inquiries to each other? Like the cloud, the clock, and the relative importance of things? Us people have "dialogue minds."

(M2) That's how we use each other?

(M1) Yes, it fills up the needy time and the aimless cloud. We can't ALWAYS work and play.

DON'T MAKE THIS INTO A GLOBAL CONFLICT

(CHARACTERS: TWO MEN WHO STARTLINGLY LOOK AND DRESS LIKE EACH OTHER)

(MAN 1) My will has an urgent need to prevail over anyone else's contrary will, due to my former inferiority complex as a helpless child. I compensate by getting my way. So do your duty and submit.

(MAN 2) But that's not fair. Shouldn't we be equal?

(M 1) Not if your will is crushed by mine.

(M 2) But what's the bone of contention?

(M 1) Anything I say it is.

(M 2) Your need to predominate, no matter what the stakes, puts me down in a cruel way. It undermines the democratic ideal of fair play.

(M1) Not in this dog-eat-dog world I elaborately create to smash any opposition you put up.

(M2) But envy and anger compel me to oppose you.

(M1) Your stupid display of courage in the face of my predominance is doomed to be overwhelmed and put in its place.

(M2) What have you determined to be my place?

(M1) Lowliness, in relation to mine.

(M2) In all walks of life? Wholesale, complete annihilation?

(M1) You're speaking my language. Now put action in the place of those submissive words.

(M2) But that implies, or even necessitates, comparison.

(M1) Inevitably. I'm beyond compare.

(M2) That's what YOU say, you bully.

(M1) Are you bringing our opposition, or your resistance, to the decisive test?

(M2) Assertively.

(M1) I weasel out. I'm afraid.

(M2) Good. I upset the original odds in your favor, and come up with a surprise underdog reversal, due to your submissive fear.

(M1) I got too big for my britches, then shrunk back to my normal size.

(M2) Your bully boasting of supremacy got itself annihilated by my surprise victory. It's beyond analysis. Let's not explain it, whose elaboration might undo the victory I narrowly seized by your sudden capitulation.

(M1) Pulling victory out of the snatches of defeat?

M2) Stop your retrograde words. History has declared itself, and decisive action must prevail and we close the chapter.

(M1) But isn't history an ongoing process?

(M2) I snapped it shut, with my foot on your prone body, like a snapshot of photography.

(M1) But can't I wrench myself up to reverse your reversal, as the comeback kid?

(M2) Our stakes were arbitrarily phantom. I declare the books closed.

(M1) Then what are these blank pages suddenly mushrooming (much-rooming) themselves?

HOW EVOLUTION IS AMORAL, IT JUST WANTS US TO BE. SO HERE WE ARE, THRILLINGLY.

The diversity between boys and girls:
Thus the human race unfurls.
From birth to death we fly along
on high evolution's lowly song.
Everyone's alive is welcome to belong,
scorning the difference between right and wrong.
What does evolution care? It just wants to bear
all of us on the planetary ride
to pleasure and pain and more beside.
If you have humanity, just come along
on this thrilling ride between life and death
utilizing every ounce of your precious breath.

**HOW EVOLUTION UTILIZES THE SEX MAGIC
TO GIVE US EVERYTHING COMIC AND TRAGIC
VIA THE BIOLOGICAL SPECIFIC
ORGANICALLY RELATED TO OUR RACE TERRIFIC**

Evolution got me started,
the parental way to birth,
I owe it to them,
he looked at the hem
of her tall-legged dress
and began to bless
sexuality's part
in creating a baby,
turned out to be you,
and then you grew up,
a fully complete member
of our very human race
creating families by the series
of our high-flying species
that rode the road to evolution
or was it the reverse?
Evolution's here to stay
by way of our double gender
that mechanically is the true blender.

**TAKE CARE OF YOURSELF—
IT'S YOUR OWN AND ONLY LIFE.
PROTECT IT FROM HARMFUL HURT.
AVOID INFECTION FROM UGLY DIRT.
BE CAREFUL WITH WHOM YOU FLIRT.**

For your own sake, keep life alive
by preserving it at all cost.
Exercise at all times such caution
that you take no chance of an accident
that on your delicately fragile skin might make a dent.
Keep track of where you are at all times
with vigilant care that you keep intact.
Stay out of the way where crime is manifest

and don't get too near a homicidal pest.
Don't trip down the stairs and break a bone.
Don't go in dark streets precariously all alone.
Keep your heart spinning at the right rate
and lock the door to your house and to your gate.
Don't forget you bear along your precious freight
and keep yourself from harmful injury prone,
and be sure to put iodine on your next earthly moan.
Keep infection from yourself far away
and don't live TOO robustly, come what may.
Keep yourself securely under wraps
and wherever you go, bring along your maps
that inform you completely where you are.
If you're accidentally hurt, soon get a scar
to solidify your sanitary healing.
For your health's sake I urge this appealing
to protect your vital life
in its constant bouts with strife.
But don't go lax on exercise,
and your surveying brain should always be wise.
Swallow your food but don't choke.
From carelessness be soon awoke.
Don't mess life by something getting broke.
Insert health in your skin after a good soak.

**MAKE THE RIGHT CHOICE
AND WELL MAY YOU REJOICE.
HEAR A HEARTENING VOICE.**

To live life well,
avoid misery's hell
and ring the happiness bell
till the sound gongs in your head
to entertain in your bed
an orgasmic partner instead
of someone who's misery bred
and is already half dead.
Life needs life to liven things up
like a dog who gives birth to a sweet little pup.

EVOLUTION'S LIFE CYCLE WITH EARLY AND LATE CHARACTERS ALONG TIME'S RIDDLED CHAPTERS

Life's exciting ride through evolution
gradually produced you and me.
But by what arrangement was
finally our romance to be?
Through luck that we met
to capitalize on the bet
that chemistry between us
made combustion at its best,
thus our little baby behest.
May our family always be blessed,
and little baby too, our recent guest.
Join, little one, in rich life's fest:
Your parents dead one day,
and you have to work, beyond your play.

TWO FRIENDS LAUNCH INTO A HUMOR-ANALYZING DIALOGUE, DEADENING HUMOR'S SPIRIT.

(A SELF-DIALOGUE REPRESENTED BY TWO MEN WHO ARE REALLY TWO SELVES OF THE SAME MAN.)

(1) Where does humor come from?

(2) As an unexpected surprise.

(1) That's redundant. How can you expect a surprise?

(2) Get in the mood for it. Encourage it to happen. Prepare your smile.

(1) Give an example?

(2) No. I'm not in a jokey mood. My anticipation doesn't include the unexpected.

(1) What a lot of fun you're shutting out!

(2) For good reason. I don't want to be a set-up target, like a laboratory rat test by near-sighted scientists.

(1) You've lost your sense of fun and daring. Daring is the ground-work for fun to happen. Open up your head.

(2) We're too analytically self-conscious to be spontaneous. I feel self-manipulated.

(1) Can you be the paranoid target of your own self?

(2) Yes. I'm distrustful of me.

(1) You're the source of your own enmity? That's self-defeating.

(2) Go on. Make humor of this—in the guise of self-mockery. Our assault on humor has declined to bitterness.

(1) Are we still friends?

(2) Sure, protected by the constant temporariness of all our little fits and assertions.

(1) Can analyzing be paralyzing, stifling us from letting go?

(2) But I feel a mood change coming on.

(1) Yes. Do lighten up.

THE LOVELY INVENTION OF NOSTALGIA REVIVES THE PAST AND PREVENTS NEURALGIA.

Remembering old friends who died,
your nostalgia will hardly subside
till the tears spill out of your eyes
and you beg for the hearty surprise
that reversed death lets your friends arise
to greet you with a bellow of hello's.
You weep so much, you must wipe your nose.
Forgotten are old life's remedial woes.
Welcome to the land where nostalgia grows,
when life enjoyed infinitudes of praise
before my friends fell below old radium's rays.
But my stubborn head won't let them fade.
And in my eyes' drench, my slippers wade
till I join pals ranked in skeletal parade
with provided canes hoisted to give aid.
Thus, the remade return from the unmade.
So in essence those broken pals have stayed,
the same that would have been had I prayed.

SOME REFERENCES TO LIFE, ON A LOOSE BASIS, ASKING JUST WHAT THE HUMAN RACE IS

Life is so precious,
you gotta be gracious,
its land is so space-ish,
broad and wide both.
Fit into it neatly
and let go completely
to absorb its quintessence
by your very special presence.

After all that, any question?
Lots. Make a selection.

AN UNCELEBRATED LIFE OF ANONYMOUS POSTERITY CLOSES OUT, LACKING PUBLIC FAME AS PUNISHMENT FOR NEVER HAVING ENTERED THE RANKS OF CELEBRITY. ACHIEVEMENT: CITIZEN.

I'm pathetically old. Is death the next step?

(BIOGRAPHER) Realistically, yes, to be logical about it.

Can't I go back to my baby-hood, and start all over again?

That feeble scenario is in your bewildered head, but your lonely body has outlived that likelihood and has no chance to hold out. Resign yourself as doomed.

But what an enchanted life I lived! Worthy of a biography. Will you be writing it?

I couldn't get a contract. The publishers turned me down due to your failure to claim fame as a life's achievement. You arrived at the finishing line far short of even a tiny flicker of the celebrityhood that would justify the hard line of a successful publication. By monetary standards, the publishers refuse to risk financial stupidity. Your feeble, unattended, and disregarded memoirs mean you'll die anonymous without the consolation of print.

The public be damned. Life is more important.

You fail in both counts. Without a contract, I won't waste any more time on you. (LEAVES THE DEATH ROOM.)

Well, as I die in these gloomy remnants of a failed hospital, having outlived friends and relatives, with no family members attending, barren of potential mourners such as widows, and having refused the dubious consolation of outmoded clergy in obsolete church service semblance, my last flickering sights are of anonymous hospital personnel, the sub doctors and sub nurses and sub attendants wandering aimlessly around with maybe duties to pursue. That potential young but seedy biographer has fled, because publishers wouldn't give him a contract to write futile pages on my life, which physically is ending short of literary demarcation. No compassion from this sub-medical personnel consoles me. Here's a non-celebrity ending, bleak, unattended. My life flashes goodbye. I don't exist. (DIES, WITH A LURCH FROM HIS THROAT THAT POPS A VESSEL.)

Hello. I'm an apparition representing posterity, in rags, to cover the dead face with ending sheets, wrinkled and ragged, long in the duration of service, scruffily unlaundered, having seen perhaps better days in the dear ranks of Linen's ideal yesteryear, stiff and sparkling with white starch.

PROFESSOR CARLE'S SELF-FULFILLING STATEMENT ON TIME'S ESSENTIAL NATURE, WHICH BEARS REPEATING, BUT THE CONSTANT REPETITION OF WHICH COST HIM HIS JOB, BUT HE GOT ANOTHER APPOINTMENT IN A DIFFERENT UNIVERSITY, WHICH SALVAGED HIS TEACHING CAREER.

"Time is what prevents everything from happening at once, so we need it," said Professor Carle, and he was given a timely applause for his efforts. But time has meanwhile arrived to end this class session, so the room emptied of students while Professor Carle whiled away the time preparing for his next class. When the students took their seats, Professor Carle greeted them with "Time is what prevents everything from happening at once," which was a cautionary warning against simultaneity. In a timely fashion, the collective class applauded, and time drew his last class to a close, separating today's two classes from yesterday's two classes, proving his theorem that ritually opened every class with that same opening statement, which let him breathe easily, knowing that all tomorrow had to do was to be waited for, with its usual two successive classes to be confirmed in their neat, orderly schedule sequence. Time had proven him to be always right. So his classes never deviated from a continuously proven formula. But in the lapse of time he was eventually fired by the faculty head for excessive repetition. So it did him in. It was a monotonous way to lose his university tenure, but in time he was hired by another university, so his career escaped calamity, ending well with a pension to serve out his old age of free time.

A FRIEND TRIES TO HELP A MAN SUFFERING FROM A NERVOUS BREAKDOWN IF DIAGNOSTICALLY THAT'S WHAT IT IS, INCLUDING HYSTERIA AND ITS URGENT PRELUDE SYMPTOMS.

Melancholy is getting me down.

Get up and fight it.

Depression is reinforcing it.

Take them both on.

Panic is adding in.

Just part of the same thing, inflating the package. Reverse what's ailing you, by main will.

It doesn't work that way. I'm not an automaton with switches to turn on and off. I can't even manipulate myself.

As your friend, I'll help you.

But we just had a falling out.

We'll erase that, and proceed in this emergency.

"A friend in need is a help indeed."

That's a bromide. But here are more health aids I proffer. One is to locate your comfort zone and snuggle in there.

It sounds like a geographic entity, and smells too much of the abstract and the mystical, those minions of pop psychology.

All right. I'll give you a rallying pep talk.

Yeah, but will it work? I'm desperate and can't hold out: "on the ropes," as they say in boxing terminology.

We keep on borrowing metaphors to help us out in this predicament.

What do you recommend? Should I turn myself in to the emergency room of the psychological ward of a "drop in" hospital?

What's your desperation index?

Acute.

As low as it gets, to a suicidal point or even past it?

I'm at the end of my metaphorical rope.

They say that when you reach extreme darkness at the end of a tunnel, that's the point where flickering light will start its squeaky dawning, however minutely.

Is that meant to cheer me up? Or just drive despair deeper into the giving-way burial ground that oozily seduces helpless me?

I don't know how to tackle your question. But maybe continued dialogue will escape you out from that triangulation symptom comprising melancholy, depression, and panic.

But they're only words.

But aren't they distracting you?

Yes, but that means we should never stop.

I'm prepared to go all out on a marathon push. First I'll take a bathroom break, because I'm bursting. Then I'll grab some eating from the icebox and offer you some and even open a wine bottle. Then I'm ready to recommence the continuation of our so far endless dialogue, in a mutually all-out effort to fillibuster your acute emotional agony.

I'm ready to resume once I duplicate your bathroom break and then reduplicate or mooch on your raiding the icebox for sustenance to carry our marathon to however a non-fruitless end or else a less terminal outcome, whichever comes first.

(HURRIEDLY:) Oh, I forgot. We overlooked—How about emergency ward at a drop-in hospital's psychiatric department?

Let's just keep talking. Don't drop the ball.

Boy, isn't language wonderful? Without it, where would we be?

Up on a tree, somewhere.

A PRESENTABLE MAN TRIES TO "PICK UP" A PRESENTABLE WOMAN IN A MUNICIPAL ART MUSEUM, IN FRONT OF A REMBRANDT.

Trying to "pick me up" in front of a Rembrandt which you interrupted from my admiring, is risky. Who are you anyway?

Just a guy visually attracted to you, taking a whimsical chance as a total stranger.

I'm not intrigued. This is a vast and sprawling museum, so go away to some other gallery to cover the embarrassment I assume you're decent enough to be experiencing, now that I've decisively rejected your bold advance that gave me no warning, but just plunged in like a headless horseman.

I'm unprotectedly helpless in the sudden onslaught of your abrupt rejection. My wading in to pick you up was a friendly and sexually hopeful gesture of surrendering myself to potential embarrassment, which you've heavy-handedly administered with prompt and un- thinking dispatch. Can you atone for that merciless reaction?

(INDIGNANT) I reversed your audacity by being at fault for saying "no"? That's an unfair accusation! Your presumption occasioned my natural code of defense: a stranger wishing publicly to remain such. Legally and morally, I'm beyond reproach, with unassailable prerogative to put you in your place as a public chance-taker faced with empty reward.

You stripped me of dignity and plunged me to embarrassment. My "pick-up" line was not an assault. It was a friendly public gesture, with hopeful sexual rewards, which you failed to pick up on.

Was I required to?

(NO ANSWER.)

No. Just walk away. I want to stay staring at my Rembrandt. Don't start analyzing my involvement with Rembrandt as a futile gesture to extend your audacity into a successful encounter. Accept rejection like a man, not like a spoiled, jilted baby of clueless naivete who wails in his mother's apron like a snotty, defeated brat repudiated by the innocent adult that I am, within my perfect rights.

You sound like a lawyer.

I won't encourage you further, by honoring your clever ruse to trick me into prolonged conversation via question and civil answer in the accepted conventions of civil strangerhood according to the protocol of courtesy.

(WHILE IN THE PROCESS OF SAYING THAT, SHE SNAPS OUT OF IT TO NOTICE SHE'S SUCCEEDED IN "LOSING" HIM, AS HE'S NOWHERE PRESENT. HOW DOES SHE REACT?)

(WITH SURPRISE, BUT HARDLY DISAPPOINTMENT: MORE LIKE RELIEF AND SELF-CONGRATULATION FOR A SELF- JUSTIFIED DEFENSE WELL CARRIED OUT DESPITE CIRCUM- STANTIAL NON-PREPARATION. SHE RE-ATTENDS REMBRANDT, VISIBLY SHAKEN.)

DIALOGUE-ING BIG SUBJECTS

Is life divided into genders?

That's how life gets created. The woman's genitalia is hers distinctively. She exults in it, substantiating her difference from the male's, who exults in his difference-making unique sexual characteristics that identify him as distinctively male.

(Let's hope they get along.) So that's how evolution got ifself started and to this day maintains itself?

It's a formula for reproduction that's provenly tried and true. There's only one problem, though.

And what might that be?

That though evolution endures in its massive thoroughness, the individual loses itself commonly to death, quaffing his flame. It's burn-out.

Are we helpless to not do anything about that?

In the long run, yes. There are methods of delaying it, like nutrition and gym-work.

Then the big "but"?

In the individual case, even bigger than that.

A spoiler.

Only at the end.

Well, at least we're given the "till-then," as a sop or consolation.

It works for a while.

A PRESENTABLE WOMAN TRIES TO "PICK UP" A PRESENTABLE MAN IN A MUNICIPAL ART MUSEUM, IN FRONT OF A VAN GOGH. SHE GETS INCREASINGLY DESPERATE.

(WOMAN) Excuse me and pardon my boldness in interrupting your staring, with obvious admiration, at that van Gogh.

(MAN) (SURPRISED:) Hello. What's your point?

(W) I'm compelled to take a chance on making your acquaintance, because you strike me as making an impression of a charasmatically handsome man of astonishing beauty. I'm not bad-looking myself: some admirers say I'm a "catch." Should we go for a coffee or a drink?

(M) I don't mean to discourage your admiration of my appearance, but it's misguided because I'm one hundred percent gay, with an adorable lived-in lover who's famously faithful to me in circles of gay social community.

(W) Really?

(M) Plus, so far as people of your gender are concerned, I'm a complete heterosexual virgin with a perfect record of abstinence with women, despite a few stray and harmless friendships under the title of "Platonic."

(W) Oh. So?

(M) Have I clued you in that I'm a non-candidate for the pick-up intimate affair that you've boldly attempted?

(W) Must we remain strangers? Can this go no further? I'm so irresistibly sexy that I can convert you from man-loving to me-loving by my practiced wiles of seduction.

(M) I reject you outright, as well as up-tight. May this awkward and star-crossed introduction never proceed into the dangerous territory of abrupt and unprecedented infidelity to my sweet and innocent Leonard.

(W) Is that his name? At least I've pulled THAT out of you. It's a start, toward instigation of a break-up tragedy of my pulling off the startling event of your having—due to me—to betray Leonard's hitherto dominance of your holy and unimpeachable love life.

(M) Intruder! I'll call a museum guard to protect me from your raid on my most precious values.

(MUSEUM GUARD, APPROACHING) You two are too loud. Tone it

down. Treat this here like a library with readers pouring over their volumes in the sanctity of publicly ordained silence.

(W, AGITATED:) We must settle this now. Let's decisively get out of here together. Leonard need never know. (THEY HURRIEDLY LEAVE TOGETHER, AS SHE PULLS HIM AWAY, SEEMING TO WRESTLE HIM.)

(M) Stop! Rape!

(W) (PANTING IN DESPERATE HURRY:) Leonard need never know. We'll enforce the old proverb on him, "Ignorance is bliss."

(M EVADES HER, TWISTING AROUND CORNERS, MANEUVERING HIMSELF OUTSIDE TO A QUICK TAXI ESCAPE. SHE'S STUNNED AND LOST, ALREADY MOURNING HER LOSS, STARING AHEAD AS THE FOYER CROWD SURROUNDS HER INTO PATHETIC ANONYMITY, INSTEAD OF HER PULLING OFF A ROARING SUCCESS AGAINST STUBBORN ODDS OF HER NOW LOST INTENDED'S LIVED-IN LOYALTY TO THE INNOCENTLY UNSUSPECTING LEONARD, DOZING OFF AT HOME, AWAY FROM ALL THAT MANIC MUSEUM AGITATION IN THE SANCTITY OF HONORED ART.)

**PREPARING TO GO IT ON YOUR OWN,
SEVERED FROM MOTHER,
WHO WANTS TO OWN
YOU, BUT YOU RESIST.
BUT MOTHER MUST INSIST.**

That bond is severed
umbilically between you and mother,
the cord is broken,
the separation is open.
You and mother are split.
Now she'll give you a piece of her lip
when as a baby you misbehave.
In the meantime be brave
from newborn to grown older
and, defying her, become bolder.
Slip that in your "to do" folder.

DIALOGUE ON LIFE FRIENDSHIP (STARTING OR RESUMING FROM ANYWHERE DOWN THE UN-TWINNED ROADS)

We're of different life experiences including backgrounds. But a common language may reconcile, through communication and understanding, our different "takes" on the world including our lives.

Language is the great equalizer, but also the great separator.

Are we more part? Or apart?

A mixture.

Well, we get along.

That's the minimum to expect.

Let's enforce the expectation and drive the minimum forward into the category of the maximum.

Through gradual stages and other phases.

In that case, we'll arrive at decent friendship level.

That's a bond we can both carry equally.

Sharing. You narrate to impart from what you know to tell me what's new to me or re-establish the familiar; and I do likewise through the same process to you.

There's a song called "Getting to know you." So let's follow that song till it culminates, to the point that "We're mates," as they say in Britain, "We're pals," as they say here.

What do the French say? "Ami."

That's where "amiable" comes from. Let's carry it from there.

To points unknown. We'll share our paths to "wheres."

Till they wear down?

(TRANSITION TO RHYME:)

But variety and rebounds are renew-abilities.
However we're disrupted, we'll resume full of ease.
Thus our friendship owns a life ticket, if you please.
If we get too old, we'll combine our nasal wheeze
to unfurl our friendship to forever's sweet ripe breeze.

THE ARGUMENT THAT EVENTUALLY GOT TEMPORARILY NOWHERE, AS FAR AS IT WENT. THEN THE DISPUTANTS ROARED TO A STOP.

The hard life of a stone.

Yeah? What about it?

What about it!? It's what you make of it.

Are you referring to its hardness? Or to its life? Or to the otherwise mineral nature of the stone itself?

Everything you mention.

Well, let me set you straight. Here's where you started off wrong. The stone HAS NO LIFE.

Not as such?

Such? What is "such"?

Oh, stop being pedantic.

Who's going to stop me? You?

Halt your pugnacity. This is not a debate.

Are you setting the rules?

No, it's only a suggestion. If you want to converse, let's be kind and co-operative. Don't you like me?

Of course. A lot. I need you, let's keep going.

Where were we at?

I said the stone has no life, per se. It's not organically biological enough, by nature's rules. I'm trying to be scientific.

Okay, I grant you that. The stone has no life, for the literal-minded who don't want to be metaphorical.

Are we at an impasse? Are we arguing?

Right now, we should both shut up, while we're behind.

That's an opportunity. Quickly embrace it, and we both storm ahead.

A MAN HAS A CONVERSATION WITH HIS OWN INSOMNIA, AS THEY GET TO KNOW EACH OTHER DURING THE LONG NIGHTS THEY'RE FORCED TO SPEND IN EACH OTHER'S WEARY COMPANY.

(INSOMNIA) You're my special assignment.

(VICTIM) Should I be flattered? Who are you?

Insomnia. (LOOKS AT WATCH.) It's time, after a long day. Are you tired enough to go to sleep?

Sure, especially because you were at me last night, which exhausted me.

Let's repeat it. One good turn deserves another. (ROLLS UP HIS SLEEVES, EAGER TO GET TO WORK.)

You have a sadistic streak?

It's virtually my middle name. Tormenting you is my specialty. Start rolling over in your bed, now that you're prepared with your pajamas on and your pillow all puffed up.

How long will it last?

All night long. The longer the merrier. And I have a special assistant.

Indeed, who?

His lengthy name is "Frequent Nocturnal Bladder Syndrome." His work is to encourage more urination on your part, to make my job easier.

He's your torture assistant?

I siphon off part of my salary to give him his cut.

This seems so methodical. Being your victim is so exhausting.

That's my job.

Who pays you?

YOU pay me, really. Through the teeth. Through your nose. I drain you.

I pay you through my agony? Can't you ease up?

Sure, I'm able to relent some nights. It's arduous to keep exhausting you. You wear me out.

I can say the same thing about you. But I have to get up and work in the morning, while you, free of me, can afford to rest.

I need it, to build up my strength. Who are your DAYTIME enemies? I'd like to get to know my sunny-weather colleagues.

Not always sunny. But they're indebted to you.

(TITLE FOLLOWS DIALOGUE)

The cloud floats around aimlessly, seemingly without an object.

On the contrary, the clock is rigidly fixed in its determination.

What determination?

To be on time. That's what it's for.

That sounds mechanically precise, which is a clock's nature.

Nature? The cloud belongs to nature more than the artificially manufactured clock, built from social necessity to help society's business.

Yes, the cloud doesn't seem busy at all. It's too aimless to bother with responsibility.

Where do WE fit in?

Us? We have both in us, the clock and the cloud.

(GLOATING) A tribute to a well-balanced life.

BELATED TITLE: HAVING A WELL-BALANCED LIFE, THAT HAS CONTRARY BUT NECESSARY INGREDIENTS WHICH COOPERATIVELY, POSSIBLY ANTAGONISTICALLY, CONTRIBUTE TO A TORN BUT MIXED CENTER OF CONTINUAL READJUSTMENT.

**TO MY FAVORITE COUPLE:
SWEETLY SOFT AND SUPPLE.**

I love Colin and Maggie
and carry my sandwich in a baggie
and munch from it occasionally
while wandering unstationary
with a lack of complacency
to day's end and back again
with reverse thoroughfare now and then.

TWO NEW FRIENDS TOY WITH DIALOGUE COMPLICATIONS

Speech between us is more a trial than mere talk between you and yourself. With another person you have to reconcile points of view and patterns of speech. But dealing with yourself is along familiar grounds, except when you surprise yourself with unprecedented ideas, for which rise necessity for newly appropriate terms. Anyway, you're speaking to me. What's your issue?

The hard life of a stone.

It's not so hard. It just sits there.

How can it sit, without a precise backside to set forth dimensions?

I'm not referring to human anatomy, but just to the nature of "resting."

Soft or hard, our stone's life is also no life at all, in life's organically anatomical meaning broken down to species.

It belongs to mineral species, which have to supply their own virtual means of vitality.

A stone doesn't go anywhere unless someone picks it up and throws it.

(DUCKS) Stop getting belligerent. Compose your mind and put your subject to rest. Just let a stone be.

You annoy me. What's your point?

Though hard, a stone's life is hardly arduous.

Speech is as hard as a stone when burdened with metaphors and inferences that complicate rather than facilitate communication.

The lazy way is to talk to yourself, like an idiot. Dealing with me, you're forced to have to please me, by coming to terms with another head.

Cut the stress. It's easier if we know each other already instead of starting off being strangers to forge new territory of difficult compatibility.

Well, I know you, so we're on easy grounds that needn't bear complications. Just relax into friendship, which has already set our path from which easily to proceed. Isn't our future assured?

It inspires my complacency, but you're a piece of marble I won't take for granite.

UNEQUAL LUCK DISTRIBUTION, BAD FOR HER AND GOOD FOR ME IN EQUALITY'S ASYMMETRY. WHAT MORTAL IS ACCIDENT FREE?

(Women's contrasting dialogue)

I've had a run of misfortune
ruinous to my well being.

I've had better luck
and wish you soon recovery
to give your life needed improvement.

Do you mind if I envy you?

Yes. Envy and resentment go together
and breed the poison of hatred
directed at innocent me
just because I'm happy and free.

I'll guard you from being my scapegoat
for all the things that go wrong
in my dirge-like misery of a song.
To blame you is utterly wrong.

Thanks for protecting my cheerful lot
from the curse of guilt toward you
for my better luck in the world
whose results are unequally unfurled,
with distribution good for me
but bad for poor burdensome you
who drank too much from an ill-cooked brew
and got herself in an insupportable stew.

**AN INFERIOR MAN CONFESSES
IN ONE OF HIS SELF-ACCUSING ADDRESSES
HOW HIS LIFE IS A SERIES OF MESSES.**

The woman I had hopes for
turned me down. "You're not for me,"
she firmly and decidedly declared.
Thus my only choice was to despair.
This gave me a melancholy air
appealing to a different woman
who sweetly forced herself on me
to the happy tune of marriage
and its "inevitable" baby carriage.
But secretly I preferred the rejecting woman
who saw through me perfectly
and understood i'm an inferior man.
That accurate opinion went to my head.
It loomed with truth. What could I think instead?

**OPEN TO SUPPOSITIONS,
THE HARD LIFE OF A STONE
CONFRONTS ME, ALONE.**

The hard life of a stone
is lumpenly no life at all,
lacking the necessaries
of organic parts
in fits and starts
in the open marts.
At least it has bulk.
Quicksilver it's not.
It's its own whole lot
as far as it got,
and not a whit left
other than its own heft.
Beyond substance, it's bereft.
It can't move around
except by others.
Life has passed it by

and it's too stuck to go high.
Life as such is not much.
It's not "realized," save by touch.
Who's going to do it? Not by me.
The moss it's gathered is too countrified
and maybe poisonous, if I tried.
It has no equal force to be defied.

ADVICE FOR AN AMBITIOUS CAREERIST: BUT FIRST TREMBLEY WRITE DOWN YOUR FEAR LIST.

Getting born is your admission ticket
from your mother's narrow, pressured canal
to the larger, outer world
where you struggle to compete
for the best academic seat
or thorough professionalism
for university and career,
trying to out-distance your peer,
but they're all so talented, you fear.
Set your sights on making a living
in some prestigious field.
May most competitors yield
to your chosen supremacy
without harsh and ugly enmity.
Get a lovely wife, and exercise
to be fit for longevity ahead.
Let by ambition you be wisely led.
If you're in a mess, consult your other head
for a fresh look at what's been wrong,
to tune up your tonsils for a better song.

**AN OPEN INVITATION TO TAKE CARE
THAT YOU DON'T TRIP AND UNDERGO DESPAIR
IF DAMAGE MANGLES YOUR BODY FAIR
WITH ACCIDENT BEYOND PHYSICAL REPAIR.**

Life being your most valuable asset, guard it.
Safety as you cross at the red light—
I mean green—is so fundamental,
that habit guides you as an automaton
but requires your alertness as extra
for obsessive alive-keeping
and damage prevention
to stop quick the horrors of regret
if your wager loses your safety bet,
and with misfortune you're miserably met.
One slip in the open gutter
as you cross the city street
causes your oath to mutter,
"I'm the enemy I hate to meet."

**IF THINGS TURN WRONG,
YOU'RE IN THE WRONG SONG,
SO FIND THE RIGHT MELODY
TO KEEP A FELLOW FREE.**

Life is a self-correcting machine.
If you're too fat, you turn lean.
If you're too melancholy, you stop
and sheer happiness will pop
into your alleviating brain,
leaving not a whit of melancholy's stain.
All you have to do is the wrong thing,
to induce the right one to take its stead.
An example: If drowsiness envelops you,
stern sleep applies the remedy
and unfatigues itself of the yawning enemy.
So leave life to its own devices.
If the meal is too bland, apply the spices.
If the bread is too uncuttably thick,

slice it into many compartments
to create a feast of thin divisions
to correct sameness with many incisions.
Commit a crime? Then outlaw all the prisons.
If death breathes too heavily
over your whole body
with its foul and merciless breath,
perfume it immediately away,
turning grim evil night into lovely day,
and immortality beckons you to play.
Happiness reigns, and is planning to stay.
Dear life, thanks for protecting me.
Your sheer resilience is salvation's key.

**A LOVELY EVENT
BLESSING TWO ADULTS AND BABY.
THEY HAD DIFFERENT TIME SLOTS
BUT UNITED TO THE BEST PLOTS.**

Loving your girlfriend, or even your wife,
is quite permissible, if you please.
If your body and heart ache for her,
don't keep them imprisoned in a vague blur,
but out with your benevolent weapon
with which to leap upon
your pliable prey, and do away
with puritanical reluctance
and ply your id with all your will
until ounces of semen will surely spill
till a baby is bawling in the future,
"Please, can I come out and play?
My time is ripe. We all have a good day."
That, I'd call a divine incident.
When evolution beamed on us, it was no accident.
Ask your body, then, to make a dent.
Surely weren't our time and sperm well spent?

Photo by Maggie Beale

Marvin Cohen is an American essayist, novelist, playwright, poet, humorist, and surrealist. He is the author of nine published books and several plays. His short fiction and essays have appeared in more than 80 publications, including *The New York Times, The Village Voice, The Nation, Harper's Bazaar, Vogue, Fiction, The Hudson Review, Quarterly Review of Literature, Transatlantic Review,* and *New Directions* annuals. His 1980 play *The Don Juan and the Non-Don Juan* was first performed at the New York Shakespeare Festival as part of the Poets at the Public Series. Staged readings of the play have featured actors Richard Dreyfuss, Keith Carradine, Wallace Shawn, Jill Eikenberry, Larry Pine, and Mimi Kennedy. Born in Brooklyn in 1931, Cohen has described himself as one who has "risen from lower-class background to lower-class foreground." He studied art at Cooper Union but left college to focus on writing, supporting himself with a series of odd jobs including mink farmer and merchant seaman. He also taught creative writing at The New School, the City College of New York, C.W. Post of Long Island University, and Adelphi University. Cohen currently lives in New York City with his wife, a retired paperback editor.

www.ingramcontent.com/pod-product-compliance
Lightning Source LLC
Chambersburg PA
CBHW030851170426
43193CB00009BA/572